DATE DUE

NOV 2 0 2011

Pragmatics of Human Communication

Pragmatics of Human Communication

A Study of Interactional Patterns, Pathologies, and Paradoxes

Paul Watzlawick, Ph.D.
Janet Helmick Beavin, A. B.
Don D. Jackson, M. D.

MENTAL RESEARCH INSTITUTE,
PALO ALTO, CALIFORNIA

NEW YORK

W · W · NORTON & COMPANY · INC ·

Our special thanks go to the many authors and publishers who gave their permission to quote excerpts from their works.

Attention must be drawn to the following specific copyrights:
For material from *Who's Afraid of Virginia Woolf?* by Edward Albee: "Copyright © 1962 by Edward Albee. Reprinted by permission of the author and Atheneum Publishers. CAUTION: Professionals and amateurs are hereby warned that *Who's Afraid of Virginia Woolf?*, being fully protected under the copyright laws of the United States of America, the British Empire, including the Dominion of Canada, and all other countries of the Berne and Universal Copyright Conventions, is subject to royalty. All rights, including professional, amateur, motion picture, recitation, lecturing, public reading, radio and television broadcasting, and the right of translation into foreign languages, are strictly reserved. Particular emphasis is laid on the question of readings, permission for which must be secured from the author's agent in writing. All inquiries should be addressed to the William Morris Agency, 1740 Broadway, New York, N.Y. 10019."

Copyright for all materials from the journal *Psychiatry* is held by the William Alanson White Psychiatric Foundation.

Excerpts from *Marriage Lines* by Ogden Nash, by permission of Little, Brown and Co., copyright 1940 by The Curtis Publishing Company.

The material from *Nineteen Eighty-Four* by George Orwell, Harcourt, Brace & World, Inc. Copyright, 1949 by Harcourt, Brace and Company, Inc. Reprinted by permission of Brandt & Brandt.

The story *"Subjugation of a Ghost"* is originally from *Zen Flesh, Zen Bones* by Paul Reps. Copyright 1957 Charles E. Tuttle Co. Rutland, Vt. & Tokyo, Japan.

For quotation from a review by Howard Taubman © 1962 by The New York Times Company. Reprinted by permission.

To Gregory Bateson,
Friend and Mentor

Table of Contents

7

CONTENTS

Introduction

This book deals with the pragmatic (behavioral) effects of human communication, with special attention to behavior disorders. At a time when not even the grammatical and syntactic codes of verbal communication have been formalized and there is increasing skepticism about the possibility of casting the semantics of human communication into a comprehensive framework, any attempt at systematizing its pragmatics must seem to be evidence of ignorance or of presumption. If, at the present state of knowledge, there does not even exist an adequate explanation for the acquisition of natural language, how much more remote is the hope of abstracting the formal relations between communication and behavior?

On the other hand, it is obvious that communication is a *conditio sine qua non* of human life and social order. It is equally obvious that from the beginning of his existence a human being is involved in the complex process of acquiring the rules of communication, with only minimal awareness of what this body of rules, this *calculus* of human communication, consists of.

This book will not go much beyond that minimal awareness. It does not claim to be more than an attempt at model building and a presentation of some facts that appear to support such a model. The pragmatics of human communication is a science in its infancy, barely able to read and write its own name, and is far from having evolved a consistent language of its own. Particularly, its integration with many other fields of scientific endeavor is a thing of the future. However, with hope of such future integration, this book addresses itself to workers in all those fields where problems of systemic interaction in the widest sense are encountered.

It may be argued that this book ignores important studies that are directly related to its subject matter. The paucity of explicit

13

references to nonverbal communication may be one such criticism, the lack of reference to general semantics another. But this book cannot be more than an introduction to the pragmatics of human communication (an area that so far has received conspicuously little attention) and cannot, therefore, point to all the existing affinities to other fields of research without becoming encyclopedic in the bad sense of the term. For the same reason a limitation had to be imposed on references to numerous other works on the theory of human communication, especially when such works limit themselves to the study of communication as a one-way phenomenon (from speaker to listener) and stop short of looking at communication as an *interaction* process.

The interdisciplinary implications of the subject matter are reflected in the manner of its presentation. Examples and analogies were chosen from as wide a range of subjects as seemed applicable, although predominance remained in the field of psychopathology. Especially where *mathematics* was invoked for analogy, it should be clearly understood that it was used only as a *language* which is eminently suited for the expression of intricate relationships, and that its use was not meant to imply that we felt our data are ready for quantification. Conversely, the rather liberal use of examples taken from literature may seem scientifically objectionable to many readers, for to prove something by reference to the figments of artistic imagination may seem poor proof indeed. However, not proof but illustration and elucidation of a theoretical point by presentation in a more readily understandable language is intended by these quotations from literature; it is not implied that they prove anything in and by themselves. In short, these examples and analogies, then, are *definition* models and not predictive (assertive) models.

At various points in this book basic concepts from a variety of other fields require definitions which to any expert in that particular field will be unnecessary. To forewarn him, but also for the convenience of the general reader, a brief outline of the chapters and their sections is given.

Chapter 1 attempts to draw the frame of reference. It introduces basic notions such as function (s. 1.2 [1]), information and feedback (s. 1.3), and redundancy (s. 1.4), and postulates the existence of an as yet unformalized code, a *calculus* (s. 1.5) of human communication whose rules are observed in successful communication but which are broken when communication is disturbed.

Chapter 2 defines some of the axioms of this hypothetical calculus, while the potential pathologies implied by these axioms are examined in *Chapter 3*.

Chapter 4 extends this theory of communication to the organizational or structural level, based on a model of human relationships as *systems*; thus most of the chapter is devoted to discussion and application of General Systems principles.

Chapter 5 is pure exemplification of the systems material, intended to give some life and specificity to this theory, which is, after all, concerned with the immediate effects of human beings on each other.

Chapter 6 deals with the behavioral effects of paradox. This requires a definition of the concept (s. 6.1, 6.2, and 6.3), which can be omitted by the reader acquainted with the literature on antinomies and especially the Russellian paradox. Section 6.4 introduces the less well known concept of pragmatic paradoxes, especially the Double Bind theory and its contribution to the understanding of schizophrenic communication.

Chapter 7 is devoted to the therapeutic effects of paradox. Except for the theoretical considerations in s. 7.1 and 7.2, this chapter was written especially with a view toward the clinical application of paradoxical patterns of communication. The chapter concludes with a brief excursion into the role of paradox in play, humor, and creativity (s. 7.6).

An *Epilogue* dealing with man's communication with reality in the wider sense does not claim to be more than an outlook. It postulates that an order, analogous to the level structure of Logical Types, pervades human awareness of existence and determines the

[1] The decimal subdivision of chapters was introduced not to confuse or impress the reader, but to indicate clearly the organizational structure of a chapter and to facilitate cross references within the book.

ultimate knowability of his universe.

As the manuscript was being critically evaluated by a variety of experts from psychiatrists and biologists to electrical engineers, it became apparent that any given section might be considered primitive by one and too specialized by another. Similarly, the inclusion of definitions—either in the text or as footnotes—might be considered offensively patronizing to someone for whom the term is part of his everyday professional language, while to a general reader the lack of definitions often seemed to have the annoying implication that "If you don't know what that means, we cannot be bothered to tell you." It was therefore decided to include, at the end of the book, a *glossary* that contains only those terms not available in ordinary dictionaries and not defined in the text. (The location of definitions given in the text can be found in the index, where the page numbers are set in bold type.)

The authors want to express their thanks to the many persons who read all or parts of the manuscript and provided help, encouragement, and advice, especially to Paul S. Achilles, Ph.D., John H. Weakland, M.A., Carlos E. Sluzki, M.D., A. Russell Lee, M.D., Richard Fisch, M.D., and Arthur Bodin, Ph.D., all colleagues of ours at the Mental Research Institute; Albert E. Scheflen, M.D., Eastern Pennsylvania Psychiatric Institute and Temple University School of Medicine; Karl H. Pribram, M.D., Ralph I. Jacobs, M.D., and William C. Dement, M.D., of the Stanford University School of Medicine; Henry Longley, B.S.E.E., Project Engineer, Western Development Laboratories (Philco); Noël P. Thompson, M.D., M.S.E.E., Chief of the Division of Medical Electronics, Palo Alto Medical Research Foundation; and John P. Spiegel, M.D., Center for Research in Personality, Harvard University. Responsibility for positions taken and errors which may have been made rests, of course, exclusively with the authors.

This work was supported by the National Institute of Mental Health (Grant MH 07459–01), the Robert C. Wheeler Foundation, the James McKeen Cattell Fund, and the National Association for Mental Health, whose aid is gratefully acknowledged.

Palo Alto, March 1966

Pragmatics of Human Communication

Chapter 1

The Frame of Reference

1.1

Consider the following diverse situations:

The fox population of a certain area of northern Canada shows a remarkable periodicity in the increase and decrease of its numbers. In a cycle of four years it reaches a peak, declines to near extinction, and finally starts rising again. If the attention of the biologist were limited to the foxes, these cycles would remain unexplainable, for there is nothing in the nature of the fox or of the whole species that would account for these changes. However, once it is realized that the foxes prey almost exclusively on wild rabbits, and that these rabbits have almost no other natural enemy, this *relation between* the two species provides a satisfactory explanation for an otherwise mysterious phenomenon. For it can then be seen that the rabbits exhibit an identical cycle, but with increase and decrease reversed: the more foxes there are, the more rabbits are killed by them, so that eventually food becomes very scarce for the foxes. Their number decreases, giving the surviving rabbits a chance to multiply and thrive again in the virtual absence of their enemies, the foxes. The fresh abundance of rabbits favors the survival and increase of foxes, etc.

A man collapses and is rushed to hospital. The examining physician observes unconsciousness, extremely low blood pressure, and, generally, the clinical picture of acute alcoholic or drug intoxication. However, tests reveal no trace of such substances. The patient's condition remains unexplainable until he regains consciousness and reveals that he is a mining engineer who has just returned from two years years' work at a copper mine located at an altitude of 15,000 feet in the Andes. It is now clear that the patient's condition is not an illness in the customary sense of an organ or tissue deficiency, but the problem of adaptation of a clinically healthy organism to a drastically changed environment. If medical attention remained focused on the patient only, and if only the ecology of the physician's customary environment was taken into account, his state would remain mysterious.

In the garden of a country house, in plain view of passers-by on the sidewalk outside, a bearded man can be observed dragging himself, crouching, round the meadow, in figures of eight, glancing constantly over his shoulder and quacking without interruption. This is how the ethologist Konrad Lorenz describes his necessary behavior during one of his imprinting experiments with ducklings, after he had substituted himself for their mother. "I was congratulating myself," he writes, "on the obedience and exactitude with which my ducklings came waddling after me, when I suddenly looked up and saw the garden fence framed by a row of dead-white faces: a group of tourists was standing at the fence and staring horrified in my direction." The ducklings were hidden in the tall grass, and all the tourists saw was totally unexplainable, indeed insane, behavior. (96, p. 43)

These seemingly unrelated examples have one common denominator: a phenomenon remains unexplainable as long as the range of observation is not wide enough to include the context in which the phenomenon occurs. Failure to realize the intricacies of the relationships between an event and the matrix in which it takes place, between an organism and its environment, either confronts the observer with something "mysterious" or induces him to attribute to his object of study certain properties the object may not possess. Compared with the wide acceptance of this fact in biology, the behavioral sciences seem still to base themselves to a large extent on a monadic view of the individual and on the time-honored method of isolating variables. This becomes particularly obvious when the object of study is disturbed behavior. If a person exhibiting disturbed behavior (psychopathology) is studied in isolation, then the inquiry must be concerned with the *nature* of the condition and, in a wider sense, with the *nature* of the human mind. If the limits of the inquiry are extended to include the effects of this behavior on others, their reactions to it, and the context in which all of this takes place, the focus shifts from the artificially isolated monad to the *relationship* between the parts of a wider system. The observer of human behavior then turns from an inferential study of the mind to the study of the observable manifestations of relationship.

The vehicle of these manifestations is communication.

We want to suggest that the study of human communication can be subdivided into the same three areas of syntactics, semantics, and pragmatics established by Morris (*106*), and followed by Carnap (*33*, p. 9) for the study of semiotic (the general theory of signs and languages). Applied to the framework of human communication, then, the first of these three areas can be said to cover the problems of transmitting information and is, therefore, the primary domain of the information theorist. His concern lies with the problems of coding, channels, capacity, noise, redundancy, and other statistical properties of language. These problems are primarily *syntactical* ones, and he is not interested in the meaning of message symbols. Meaning is the main concern of *semantics*. While it is perfectly possible to transmit strings of symbols with syntactical accuracy, they would remain meaningless unless sender and receiver had agreed beforehand on their significance. In this sense, all shared information presupposes semantic convention.

Finally, communication affects behavior, and this is its *pragmatic* aspect. While a clear conceptual separation is thus possible of the three areas, they are nevertheless interdependent. As George (55, p. 41) points out, "in many ways it is true to say that syntax is mathematical logic, semantics is philosophy or philosophy of science, and pragmatics is psychology, but these fields are not really all distinct."

This book will touch upon all three areas, but will deal mainly with the pragmatics, that is, the behavioral effects, of communication. In this connection it should be made clear from the outset that the two terms communication and behavior are used virtually synonymously. For the data of pragmatics are not only words, their configurations, and meanings, which are the data of syntactics and semantics, but their nonverbal concomitants and body language as well. Even more, we would add to personal behavioral actions the communicational clues inherent in the *context* in which communication occurs. Thus, from this perspective of pragmatics, all behavior, not only speech, is communication, and all communication—even the communicational clues in an impersonal context —affects behavior.

Further, we are not only concerned, as pragmatics generally is, with the effect of a piece of communication on the receiver but, inseparably linked with this, also with the effect the receiver's reaction has upon the sender. Thus we would prefer to focus less on the sender-sign or receiver-sign relations and more on *the sender-receiver relation, as mediated by communication.*

Since this communicational approach to the phenomena of human behavior, both normal and abnormal, is based on the observable manifestations of *relationship* in the widest sense, it is, therefore, conceptually closer to mathematics than to traditional psychology, for mathematics is the discipline most immediately concerned with the relations between, not the nature of, entities. Psytoward a monadic view of man and, consequently, toward a reification of what now reveal themselves more and more as complex chology, on the other hand, has traditionally shown a strong trend patterns of relationship and interaction.

The affinity of our hypotheses with mathematics will be noted whenever possible. This should not deter the reader who has no special knowledge in the field, for he will not be confronted with formulae or other specific symbolism. While human behavior may one day find its adequate expression in mathematical symbolism, it definitely is not our intention to attempt such a quantification. Rather, we will refer to the enormous body of work done in certain branches of mathematics whenever these results promise to provide a useful language for the description of the phenomena of human communication.

1.2

The Notion of Function and Relationship

The main reason why mathematics should be invoked for analogy or explanatory principle lies in the usefulness of the mathematical concept of *function*. To explain this, a brief excursion into number theory is required.

The philosophers of science seem to agree that the most significant step in the development of modern mathematical thinking was the gradual emergence of a new number concept from Descartes to the present day. For the Greek mathematicians, numbers were concrete, real, perceivable magnitudes understood as the properties of equally real objects. Thus geometry was concerned with measuring and arithmetic with counting. Oswald Spengler, in his lucid chapter "On the Meaning of Numbers" (*146*), shows not only how the notion of zero as a number was unthinkable, but also that negative magnitudes had no place in the reality of the classical world: "Negative magnitudes have no existence. The expression $(-2) \times (-3) = +6$ is neither something perceivable nor a representation of magnitude" (p. 66). The idea that numbers were the expression of magnitudes remained dominant for two thousand years and, as Spengler elaborates:

> In all history, so far, there is no second example of
> one Culture paying to another Culture long extin-

guished such reverence and such submission in matters of science as ours has paid to the Classical. It was
very long before we found courage to think our proper
thought. But though the wish to emulate the Classic
was constantly present, every step of the attempt took
us in reality further away from the imagined ideal.
The history of Western knowledge is thus one of *progressive emancipation* from Classical thought, an
emancipation never willed but enforced in the depths
of the unconscious. *And so the development of the
new mathematics consists of a long, secret, and finally
victorious battle against the notion of magnitude.*
(p. 76)

There is no need to go into the details of how this victory was
won. Suffice it to say that the decisive event occurred in 1591, when
Vieta introduced letter-notations instead of numbers. With this,
the idea of numbers as discrete magnitudes was relegated to a secondary place, and the powerful concept of *variable* was born, a
concept which to the classical Greek mathematician would have
been as unreal as a hallucination. For, in contrast to a number
signifying a perceivable magnitude, variables do not have a meaning of their own; they are meaningful only in relation to one another. A new dimension of information was realized with the introduction of variables, and thus was the new mathematics formed.
The relation between variables (usually, but not necessarily, expressed as an equation) constitutes the concept of *function*. Functions, to quote Spengler once more,

> are not numbers at all in the plastic sense but signs
> representing a connection that is destitute of the hall-
> marks of magnitude, shape and unique meaning, an
> infinity of possible positions of like character, an en-
> semble unified and so attaining existence as a *num-
> ber*. The whole equation, though written in our un-
> fortunate notation as a plurality of terms, is actually

one single number, *x*, *y*, *z* being no more numbers than + and = are. (p. 77)

Thus, for instance, the equation $y^2 = 4ax$, in establishing a specific relation between x and y, comprises all the properties of a curve.*

There exists a suggestive parallelism between the emergence of the mathematical concept of function and the awakening of psychology to the concept of relationship. For a long time—in a certain sense since Aristotle—the mind was conceived of as an array of properties or characteristics with which an individual was endowed to a greater or lesser degree, very much as he might have a slender or heavy body, red or fair hair, etc. The end of the last century saw the beginning of the experimental era in psychology and with it the introduction of a far more sophisticated vocabulary that, however, was not essentially different in one sense: it was still made up of single and more or less unrelated concepts. These concepts were referred to as psychic functions—unfortunately, because they bear no relation to the mathematical concept of function, and no such relation was, indeed, intended. As we know, sensations, perceptions, apperceptions, attention, memory, and several other concepts were defined as such functions, and an enormous amount of work was and still is being done to study them in artificial isolation. But, for instance, Ashby has shown how the assumption of *memory* is directly related to the observability of a given system. He points out that for an observer who is in possession of all the necessary information any reference to the past (and, therefore, to the existence of a memory in the system) is un-

---

* How deceptive the meaning of numbers as magnitudes can be even when they are primarily *intended* to signify concrete magnitudes, e.g., in economics, is illustrated in a recent article by J. David Stern (*149*). Writing about the national debt, he shows that, examined in isolation, and, therefore, in terms of absolute magnitude, the national debt of the United States has undergone a staggering increase from $257 billion in 1947 to $304 billion in 1962. However, if placed in its proper context, i.e., expressed in relation to the net disposable personal income, a drop from 151 per cent to 80 per cent during this period becomes evident. Laymen and politicians are especially inclined to this particular economic fallacy, though economic theorists have long appreciated only systems of economic variables and not isolated or absolute units.

necessary. He can account for the system's behavior by its state *now*. He gives the following practical example:

> . . . suppose I am in a friend's house and, as a car goes past outside, his dog rushes to a corner of the room and cringes. To me the behaviour is causeless and inexplicable. Then my friend says, "He was run over by a car six months ago." The behaviour is now accounted for by reference to an event of six months ago. If we say that the dog shows "memory" we refer to much the same fact—that his behaviour can be explained, not by reference to his state now but to what his state was six months ago. If one is not careful one says that the dog "has" memory, and then thinks of the dog as *having* some*thing,* as he might have a patch of black hair. One may then be tempted to start looking for the thing; and one may discover that this "thing" has some very curious properties.
>
> Clearly, "memory" is not an objective something that a system either does or does not possess; it is a concept that the *observer* invokes to fill in the gap caused when part of the system is unobservable. The fewer the observable variables, the more will the observer be forced to regard events of the past as playing a part in the system's behaviour. Thus "memory" in the brain is only partly objective. No wonder its properties have sometimes been found to be unusual or even paradoxical. Clearly the subject requires thorough re-examination from first principles. (5, p. 117)

As we interpret it, this statement in no way denies the impressive advances of neurophysiological research on information storage in the brain. Obviously, the state of the animal is different since the accident; there must be some molecular change, some newly established circuit, in short, "something" which the dog "has" now. But Ashby clearly takes issue with the construct and its reification.

Another analogy, supplied by Bateson (*17*), is that of a chess game in progress. At any given point, the state of the game can be understood solely from the present configuration of pieces on the board (chess being a game with complete information), without any record or "memory" of the past moves. Even if this configuration is construed to *be* the memory of the game, it is a purely present, observable interpretation of the term.

When eventually the vocabulary of experimental psychology was extended to interpersonal contexts, the language of psychology still remained a monadic one. Concepts such as leadership, dependency, extroversion and introversion, nurturance, and many others became the object of detailed study. The danger, of course, is that all these terms, if only thought and repeated long enough, assume a pseudoreality of their own, and eventually "leadership," the construct, becomes Leadership, a measureable quantity in the human mind which is itself conceived as a phenomenon in isolation. Once this reification has taken place, it is no longer recognized that the term is but a shorthand expression for a particular form of ongoing relationship.

Every child learns at school that movement is something relative, which can only be perceived in relation to a point of reference. What is not realized by everyone is that this same principle holds for virtually every perception and, therefore, for man's experience of reality. Sensory and brain research have proved conclusively that only relationships and patterns of relationships can be perceived, and these are the essence of experience. Thus when, by an ingenious device, eye movement is made impossible so that the same image continues to be perceived by the same areas of the retina, clear visual perception is no longer possible. Likewise, a steady, unchanging sound is difficult to perceive and may even become unnoticeable. And if one wants to explore the hardness and texture of a surface, he will not only place his finger on the surface but move it back and forth, for if the finger remained motionless, no useful information could be gained, except perhaps a sensation of temperature, which again would be due to the relative difference between the temperatures of object and finger. These examples could easily be multiplied and would all point to the fact that in one way or another a process of change, motion, or scanning is involved in all perception (*132*, p. 173). In other words, a relationship is established, tested over as wide a range as a given contingency allows, and an abstraction is eventually gained that, we hold, is identical with the mathematical concept of function. Thus, not "things" but functions are the essence of our perceptions; and functions, as we have seen, are not isolated magnitudes, but "signs representing a connection . . . an infinity of possible positions of like character. . . ." But if this be so, then it should no longer be found surprising that even man's awareness of himself is essentially an awareness of functions, of relationships in which he is involved, no matter how much he may subsequently reify this awareness. All these facts, incidentally, from the disturbances of the sensorium to the problems of self-awareness, are borne out by the now extensive literature on sensory deprivation.

1.3

Information and Feedback

Freud broke with many of the reifications of traditional psychology when he introduced his psychodynamic theory of human behavior. His achievements require no emphasis here. One aspect, however, is of particular relevance to our topic.

Psychoanalytic theory is based on a conceptual model in keeping with the epistemology that was prevalent at the time of its formulation. It postulates that behavior is primarily the outcome of a hypothesized interplay of intrapsychic forces considered to follow closely the laws of conservation and transformation of energy in physics, where, to quote Norbert Wiener speaking of that era, "Materialism had apparently put its own grammar in order, and this grammar was dominated by the concept of energy" (*166*, p. 199). On the whole, classical psychoanalysis remained primarily a theory of intrapsychic processes, so even where interaction with outside forces was evident, it was considered secondary, as for instance in

the concept of "secondary gain." [1] On the whole, the interdependence between the individual and his environment remained a
neglected field of psychoanalytic pursuit, and it is precisely here
that the concept of *information exchange,* i.e., of communication,
becomes indispensable. There is a crucial difference between the
psychodynamic (psychoanalytic) model on the one hand and any
conceptualization of organism-environment interaction on the other,
and this difference may become clearer in the light of the following analogy (*12*). If the foot of a walking man hits a pebble, energy
is transferred from the foot to the stone; the latter will be dis-
placed and will eventually come to rest again in a position which
is fully determined by such factors as the amount of energy transferred, the shape and weight of the pebble, and the nature of the
surface on which it rolls. If, on the other hand, the man kicks a
dog instead of the pebble, the dog may jump up and bite him.
In this case the relation between the kick and the bite is of a
very different order. It is obvious that the dog takes the energy
for his reaction from his own metabolism and not from the kick.
What is transferred, therefore, is no longer energy, but rather information. In other words, the kick is a piece of behavior that communicates something to the dog, and to this communication the
dog reacts with another piece of communication-behavior. This is
essentially the difference between Freudian psychodynamics and
the theory of communication as explanatory principles of human
behavior. As can be seen, they belong to different orders of complexity; the former cannot be expanded into the latter nor can
the latter be derived from the former: they stand in a relation
of conceptual discontinuity.

This conceptual shift from energy to information is essential
to an almost vertiginous development in the philosophy of science
since the end of World War II, and it has had a particular impact
on our knowledge of man. The realization that information about
an effect, if properly fed back to the effector, will ensure the latter's

---

[1] The so-called "Neo-Freudians" have, of course, placed much more emphasis
on individual-environment interaction.

stability and its adaptation to environmental change, not only opened the door for the construction of higher-order (i.e., error-controlled, goal-directed) machines and led to the postulation of cybernetics as a new epistemology, but also provided completely new insights into the functioning of the very complex interacting systems found in biology, psychology, sociology, economics, and other fields. While, at least for the time being, the significance of cybernetics cannot be even tentatively assessed, the fundamental principles involved are surprisingly simple and shall be reviewed here briefly.

As long as science was concerned with the study of linear, unidirectional, and progressive cause-effect relations, a number of highly important phenomena remained outside the immense territory conquered by science during the last four centuries. It may be a useful oversimplification to state that these phenomena have their common denominator in the related concepts of *growth* and *change*. To include these phenomena in a unified view of the world, science since the days of the ancient Greeks has had to resort to variously defined but always nebulous and uneasy concepts resting on the notion that there is purpose in the course of events and that the eventual outcome "somehow" determines the steps which lead up to it; or, these phenomena were characterized by some form of "vitalism" and so excluded from science. Thus some 2,500 years ago the stage was set for one of the great epistemological controversies, which has continued to rage until our time: the quarrel between determinism and teleology. To return once again to the study of man, psychoanalysis clearly belongs to the deterministic school while, for instance, Jung's analytical psychology relies to a considerable extent on the assumption of an "entelechy" immanent in man.

The advent of cybernetics changed all this by showing that the two principles could be brought together in a more comprehensive framework. This view became possible through the discovery of *feedback*. A chain in which event *a* effects event *b*, and *b* then effects *c*, *c* in turn brings about *d*, etc., would have the properties of a deterministic linear system. If, however, *d* leads back to *a*, the system is circular and functions in an entirely different way. It exhibits behavior that is essentially analogous to that of those phenomena which had defied analysis in terms of strict linear determinism.

Feedback is known to be either positive or negative; the latter will be mentioned more frequently in this book since it characterize homeostasis (steady state) and therefore plays an important role in achieving and maintaining the stability of relationships. Positive feedback, on the other hand, leads to change, i.e., the loss of stability or equilibrium. In both cases, part of a system's output is reintroduced into the system as information about the output. The difference is that in the case of negative feedback this information is used to decrease the output deviation from a set norm or bias—hence the adjective "negative"—while in the case of positive feedback the same information acts as a measure for amplification of the output deviation, and is thus positive in relation to the already existing trend toward a standstill or disruption.

While the concept of homeostasis in human relations will be taken up in greater detail in s. 4.4, it must be made clear now that it would be premature and inaccurate to conclude simply that negative feedback is desirable and positive feedback disruptive. Our main point is that interpersonal systems—stranger groups, marital couples, families, psychotherapeutic, or even international relationships, etc.—may be viewed as feedback loops, since the behavior of each person affects and is affected by the behavior of each other person. Input into such a system may be amplified into change or may be counteracted to maintain stability, depending on whether the feedback mechanisms are positive or negative. From studies of families containing a schizophrenic member there can be little doubt that the existence of the patient is essential for the stability of the family system and that the system will react quickly and effectively to any internal or external attempts to change its organization. Clearly, this is an undesirable type of stability. Since the manifestations of life are evidently distinguished by both stability and change, negative and positive feedback mechanisms must occur in them in specific forms of interdependence or complementarity.

Pribram (*117*) has recently shown that the achievement of stability makes for new sensitivities and that new mechanisms differentiate to cope with these. Thus stability is not a sterile end-point even in a relatively constant environment but rather, in the familiar words of Claude Bernard, "the stability of the internal medium is the condition for the existence of free life."

Feedback has been accurately referred to as the secret of natural activity. Systems with feedback distinguish themselves not only by a quantitatively higher degree of complexity; they are also qualitatively different from anything that falls into the domain of classical mechanics. Their study requires new conceptual frames; their logic and epistemology are discontinuous from some traditional tenets of scientific analysis, such as the "isolate one variable" approach or the Laplacean belief that the complete knowledge of all facts at a given point in time will enable one to predict all future states. Self-regulating systems—systems with feedback—require a philosophy of their own in which the concepts of *pattern* and *information* are as essential as those of matter and energy were at the beginning of this century. Research with these systems is, at least for the time being, greatly hampered by the fact that there exists no scientific language sophisticated enough to be the vehicle for their explanation, and it has been suggested, for instance by Wieser (*167*, p. 33), that the systems themselves are their own simplest explanation.

1.4

Redundancy

Our emphasis on the discontinuity of systems theory and traditional monadic or linear theories is not to be construed as a statement of despair. If the conceptual difficulties are stressed here, it is to point out that *new* avenues of approach have to be found, simply because the traditional frames of reference are clearly inadequate. In this search we are finding that advances have been made in other fields which are of immediate relevance to the study of human communication, and these isomorphies are the main focus

THE FRAME OF REFERENCE

of examination in this chapter. Ashby's homeostat (*4*, pp. 93 ff) is an excellent case in point and will, therefore, be mentioned here at least briefly. This device consists of four identical self-regulating subsystems that are fully interconnected so that a disturbance caused in any one of them affects, and is in turn reacted to, by the others. This means that no subsystem can attain its own equilibrium in isolation from the others, and Ashby has been able to prove a number of most remarkable "behavioral" characteristics of this machine. Although the circuitry of the homeostat is very simple when compared with the human brain or even with other manmade devices, it is capable of 390,625 combinations of parameter values, or, to make the same statement in more anthropomorphic terms, it has that number of possible adaptive attitudes to any changes in its internal or external medium. The homeostat achieves its stability by going through a random search of its combinations, continuing until the appropriate internal configuration is reached. This is identical with the trial-and-error behavior of many organisms under stress. In the case of the homeostat the time required for this search may range from seconds to hours. It is easy to see that for living organisms this time lag would almost invariably be excessive and would be a serious handicap for survival. Ashby carries this thought to its logical extreme when he writes:

> If we were like homeostats, waiting till one field gave us, at a stroke, all our adult adaptation, we would wait forever. But the infant does not wait forever; on the contrary, the probability that he will develop a full adult adaptation within twenty years is near to unity. (*4*, p. 136)

He then goes on to show that in natural systems some conservation of adaptation is achieved. This means that old adaptations are not destroyed when new ones are found, and that the search need not be initiated all over again as if a solution had never been achieved before.

What all this has to do with the pragmatics of human communication will become clearer after the following consideration. In the homeostat, any one of the 390,625 internal configurations has at any time an equal probability of being brought about by the interplay of the four subsystems. Thus the occurrence of a given configuration has absolutely no effect on the occurrence of the next configuration or sequence of configurations. A chain of events in which every element has at all times an equal chance of occurrence is said to show randomness. No conclusions can be drawn from it and no predictions can be made about its future sequence. This is another way of saying that it carries no information. However, if a system like the homeostat is provided with the ability to store previous adaptations for future use, the probability inherent in the sequences of internal configurations will undergo drastic change in the sense that certain groupings of configurations will become repetitive and, therefore, more probable than others. It should be noted at this juncture that there is no need to attribute any meaning to these groupings; their existence is their own best explanation. A chain of the type just described is one of the most basic concepts in information theory and is called a *stochastic process*. Thus, stochastic process refers to the lawfulness inherent in a sequence of symbols or events, whether the sequence is as simple as the results of drawing white and black marbles from an urn, or as complex as the specific patterns of tonal and orchestral elements employed by a certain composer, the idiosyncratic use of language elements in the style of a given author, or the diagnostically highly important patterning contained in the tracings of an electroencephalogram. According to information theory, stochastic processes show *redundancy* or *constraint,* two terms which can be used interchangeably with the concept of *pattern* which has been used freely in the foregoing. At the risk of excessive redundancy, we shall stress again that these patterns do not, and need not, have any explanatory or symbolic meaning. This does not exclude, of course, the possibility that they may be correlated with other occurrences, as, for instance, is the case with the electroencephalogram and some medical conditions.

Redundancy has been extensively studied in two of the three

areas of human communication, syntactics and semantics; the pioneer work of Shannon, Carnap, and Bar-Hillel should be mentioned in this connection. One of the conclusions that can be drawn from these studies is that each of us possesses an enormous amount of knowledge about the lawfulness and the statistical probability inherent in both the syntactics and the semantics of human communications. Psychologically this knowledge is of a very interesting kind, for it is almost totally outside of human awareness. Nobody, except perhaps an information expert, can state the sequential probabilities or the ranking orders of letters and words in a given language, yet all of us can spot and correct a misprint, replace a missing word, and exasperate a stammerer by finishing his sentences for him. But to know a language and to know something *about* a language are two very different orders of knowledge. Thus, a person may be able to use his mother tongue correctly and fluently and yet not possess a knowledge of grammar and syntax, i.e., of the *rules* he observes in speaking it. If this man were to learn another language—except by the same empirical acquisition as his mother tongue—he would also have to learn explicitly *about* languages.[2]

Turning now to the problems of redundancy or constraint in the pragmatics of human communication, a review of the literature shows that very little has been published so far on this subject, especially as far as pragmatics as *interactional* phenomena is concerned. By this we mean that most of the existing studies appear to limit themselves mainly to the effects of person *A* on person *B*, without taking equally into account that whatever *B* does influences *A*'s next move, and that they are both largely influenced by, and in

---

[2] Benjamin Whorf, the great linguist, has pointed again and again to this phenomenon, e.g., in the chapter "Science and Linguistics":

> Scientific linguists have long understood that ability to speak a language fluently does not necessarily confer a linguistic knowledge of it, i.e., understanding of its background phenomena and its systematic process and structure, any more than ability to play a good game of billiards confers or requires any knowledge of the laws of mechanics that operate upon the billiard table. (*165*, p. 213)

turn influence, the context in which their interaction takes place.

It is not too difficult to see that pragmatic redundancy is essentially similar to syntactic and semantic redundancy. Here, too, we possess an immense amount of knowledge that enables us to evaluate, to influence, and to predict behavior. In fact, in this area we are particularly susceptible to inconsistencies: behavior that is out of context, or that shows certain other kinds of randomness or lack of constraint, immediately strikes us as much more inappropriate than merely syntactical or semantic errors in communication. And yet it is in this area that we are particularly unaware of the rules being followed in successful, and broken in disturbed, communication. We are constantly being affected by communication; as suggested earlier, even our self-awareness depends on communication. This has been cogently stated by Hora: "To understand himself man needs to be understood by another. To be understood by another he needs to understand the other" (65, p. 237). But if linguistic understanding is based on the rules of grammar, syntax, semantics, etc., what then are the rules for the kind of understanding meant by Hora? Again it appears that we know them without knowing that we know them. We are in constant communication, and yet we are almost completely unable to *communicate about communication*. This problem will be a major theme of this book.

The search for pattern is the basis of all scientific investigation. Where there is pattern there is significance—this epistemological maxim also holds for the study of human interaction. This study would be relatively easy if it consisted merely in interrogating those engaged in the interaction and in thus learning from them what patterns they habitually follow, or, in other words, what rules of behavior they have established between themselves. A customary application of this idea is the questionnaire technique. However, once it is realized that statements cannot always be taken at face value, least of all in the presence of psychopathology—that people can very well *say* something and *mean* something else—and, as we have just seen, that there are questions the answers to which may be totally outside their awareness, then the need for different approaches becomes obvious. Roughly speaking, one's rules of behavior and interaction may show the same degrees of consciousness that Freud postulated for slips and errors: (1) they may be clearly within a person's awareness, in which case questionnaire and other simple question-answer techniques can be used; (2) a person may be unaware of them, but able to recognize them when they are pointed out to him; or (3) they may be so far from a person's awareness that even if they were defined correctly and brought to his attention, he would still be unable to see them. Bateson has sharpened this analogy with levels of consciousness and stated the problem in terms of our present conceptual framework:

> . . . as we go up the scale of orders of learning, we come into regions of more and more abstract pattern- ing, which are less and less subject to conscious in- spection. The more abstract—the more general and formal the premises upon which we put our patterns together—the more deeply sunk these are in the neu- rological or psychological levels and the less accessible they are to conscious control.
>
> The *habit* of dependency is much less perceptible to the individual than the fact that on a given occa- sion he obtained help. This he may be able to recog- nize, but to recognize the next more complex pattern, that having looked for help, he commonly bites the hand that feeds him, this may be excessively difficult for him to scan in consciousness. (*16*)

Fortunately for our understanding of human interaction, the picture is a different one to an outside observer. He is like someone who understands neither the rules nor the objective of chess watch- ing a game being played. Let the unawareness of the "players" in real life be represented in this conceptual model by the simplified assumption that the observer does not speak or understand the players' language and is, therefore, unable to ask for explanations. It will soon become clear to the observer that the behavior of the players shows varying degrees of repetitiveness, of redundancy, from which tentative conclusions can be drawn. He will, for example, notice that almost invariably a move of one player is followed by a move of the other. It will thus be easy to deduce from this behavior that the players are following a rule of alternation of moves. The rules governing the moves of the individual pieces cannot be so easily inferred, partly on account of the complexity of the moves and partly on account of the greatly different frequencies with which the single pieces are moved. It will, for instance, be easier to infer the rule underlying the moves of the bishops than that of such an unusual and infrequent move as castling, which may not occur at all in the course of one particular game. Notice also that castling involves two consecutive moves by the same player and thereby seems to invalidate the rule of alternation of moves. Yet, the much greater redundancy of alternation of moves will prevail in the observer's theory-building over the lesser redundancy of castling, and even if the apparent contradiction remains unresolved, the hypotheses formulated so far need not necessarily be abandoned by the observer. From the foregoing it can be seen that after watching a series of games, the observer would in all probability be able to formulate with a high degree of accuracy the rules of chess, including the end point of the game, the checkmate. It must be stressed that he could arrive at this result without the possibility of asking for information.

Does all this mean that the observer has "explained" the behavior of the players? We would prefer to say that he has identified a complex pattern of redundancies.[3] Of course, if he were so inclined, he could attribute a *meaning* to every single piece and to every rule of the game. In fact, he could create an elaborate mythology about the game and its "deeper" or "real" meaning, including fanciful tales about the origin of the game, as has in fact been done. But all this is unnecessary for the study of the game itself, and such an explanation or mythology would have the same relation to chess as

[3] Such complex patterns, and patterns within patterns, on the interpersonal level (in a series of psychotherapeutic interviews) have been extensively studied by Scheflen (*139*). His pioneer work demonstrates not only that these patterns exist but that they are of an unbelievably repetitive and structured nature.

astrology has to astronomy.[4]

One final illustration may unify our discussion of redundancy in the pragmatics of human communication. As the reader may know, computer programming consists of setting a relatively small number of specific rules in order (the program); these rules then guide the computer into a large number of quite flexible, patterned operations. Precisely the opposite happens if, as suggested above, one watches human interaction for redundancy. From observing the particular system in operation one then tries to postulate rules underlying its functioning, its "program," in our computer analogy.

1.5

Metacommunication and the Concept of Calculus

The body of knowledge gained by our hypothetical observer studying the pragmatic redundancy of the behavioral phenomenon "chess playing" reveals a suggestive analogy with the mathematical concept of *calculus*. A calculus, according to Boole (*31*, p. 4), is "a method resting upon the employment of symbols, whose laws of combination are known and general, and whose results admit of a consistent interpretation." We have already implied that such a formal representation is conceivable in human communication, but some of the difficulties of discourse *about* this calculus have also been made apparent. When mathematicians no longer use mathematics as a tool to compute, but make this tool itself the object of

---

[4] That there is no necessary relation between fact and explanation was illustrated in a recent experiment by Bavelas (*20*): Each subject was told he was participating in an experimental investigation of "concept formation" and was given the same gray, pebbly card about which he was to "formulate concepts." Of every pair of subjects (seen separately but concurrently) one was told eight out of ten times at random that what he said about the card was correct; the other was told five out of ten times at random that what he said about the card was correct. The ideas of the subject who was "rewarded" with a frequency of 80 per cent remained on a simple level, while the subject who was "rewarded" only at a frequency of 50 per cent evolved complex, subtle, and abstruse theories about the card, taking into consideration the tiniest detail of the card's composition. When the two subjects were brought together and asked to discuss their findings, the subject with the simpler ideas immediately succumbed to the "brilliance" of the other's concepts and agreed that the latter had analyzed the card accurately.

their study—as they do, for instance, when they question the consistency of arithmetic as a system—they use a language that is not part of but about mathematics. Following David Hilbert (*64*), this language is called metamathematics. The formal structure of mathematics is a calculus; metamathematics is this calculus expressed. Nagel and Newman have defined the difference between the two concepts with admirable clarity:

> The importance to our subject of recognizing the distinction between mathematics and meta-mathematics cannot be over-emphasized. *Failure to respect it has produced paradoxes and confusion.* Recognition of its significance has made it possible to exhibit in a clear light the logical structure of mathematical reasoning. The merit of the distinction is that it entails a careful codification of the various signs that go into the making of a formal calculus, free of concealed assumptions and *irrelevant associations of meaning.* Furthermore, it requires exact definitions of the operations and logical rules of mathematical construction and deduction, many of which mathematicians *had applied without being explicitly aware of what they were using.* (*108*, p. 32; italics ours)

When we no longer use communication to communicate but to communicate *about* communication, as we inevitably must in communication research, then we use conceptualizations that are not part of but *about* communication. In analogy to metamathematics this is called metacommunication. Compared with metamathematics, research in metacommunication is at two significant disadvantages. The first is that in the field of human communication there exists as yet nothing comparable to the formal system of a calculus. As shall be shown presently, this difficulty does not rule out the usefulness of the concept. The second difficulty is closely related to the first: while mathematicians possess two languages (numbers and algebraic symbols to express mathematics, and natural language for the expressions of metamathematics), we are mainly restricted to natural language as a vehicle for both communications and meta-communications. This problem will arise again and again in the course of our considerations.

What, then, is the usefulness of the notion of a calculus of human communication, if the specifics of such a calculus are admittedly a thing of the distant future? In our opinion its immediate usefulness lies in the fact that the notion itself supplies a powerful model of the nature and the degree of abstraction of the phenomena we want to identify. Let us recapitulate: we are looking for pragmatic re-dundancies; we know that they will not be simple, static magnitudes or qualities, but patterns of interaction analogous to the mathe-matical concept of function; and, finally, we anticipate that these patterns will have the characteristics generally found in error-controlled, goal-directed systems. Thus, if with these premises in mind we scrutinize chains of communications between two or more communicants, we shall arrive at certain results which certainly cannot yet claim to be a formal system, but which are in the nature of axioms and theorems of a calculus.

In their above-quoted work, Nagel and Newman describe the analogy between a game like chess and a formalized mathematical calculus. They explain how

> The pieces and the squares of the board correspond to the elementary signs of the calculus; the legal posi-tions of pieces on the board, to the formulas of the calculus; the initial positions of pieces on the board, to the axioms or initial formulas of the calculus; the subsequent positions of pieces on the board, to formu-las derived from the axioms (i.e., to the theorems); and the rules of the game, to the rules of inference (or derivation) for the calculus. (*108*, p. 35)

They go on to show how the configurations of the pieces on the board are "meaningless" as such, while statements *about* these configurations are quite meaningful. Statements of this order of abstraction are described by the above-mentioned authors:

> . . . general "meta-chess" theorems can be established whose proof involves only a finite number of permissible configurations on the board. The "meta-chess" theorem about the number of possible opening moves for White can be established in this way; and so can the "meta-chess" theorem that if White has only two Knights and the King, and Black only his King, it is impossible for White to force a mate against Black. (*108*, p. 35)

We have quoted this analogy at length because it illustrates the concept of calculus not only in metamathematics but also in metacommunication. For if we expand the analogy to include the two players we are no longer studying an abstract game but, rather, sequences of human interaction that are strictly governed by a complex body of rules. The only difference is that we would prefer to use the term "formally undecidable" rather than "meaningless" when referring to a single piece of behavior (a "move" in the game analogy). Such a piece of behavior, *a,* may be due to a pay raise, the Oedipus conflict, alcohol, or a hail storm, and any arguments as to which reason "really" applies will tend to have the qualities of a scholastic disputation on the sex of the angels. Unless and until the human mind is open for outside inspection, inferences and self-reports are all we have, and both are notoriously unreliable. However, if we notice that behavior *a*—whatever its "reasons"—by one communicant elicits behavior *b, c, d,* or *e* in the other, while it evidently excludes behaviors *x, y,* and *z,* then a metacommunicational theorem can be postulated. What is suggested here, then, is that all interaction may be definable in terms of the game analogy, that is, as sequences of "moves" strictly governed by rules of which it is immaterial whether they are within or outside the awareness of the communicants, but about which meaningful *metacommunicational* statements can be made. This would mean that, as suggested in s. 1.4, there exists an as yet uninterpreted calculus of the pragmatics of human communication whose rules are observed in successful, and broken in disturbed, communication. The existence of such a calculus can, in the present state of our knowledge, be compared to that of a star whose existence and position is postulated by theoretical astronomy but has not yet been discovered by the observatories.

1.6

Conclusions

If one approaches human communication with the above criteria in mind, several conceptual changes impose themselves. These will now be reviewed briefly within the context of psychopathology. This reference to psychopathology does not mean that these points are only valid there, but simply that we consider them particularly relevant and evident in this area.

1.61—THE BLACK BOX CONCEPT

While the existence of the human mind is only denied by particularly radical thinkers, research into the phenomena of the mind, as is painfully known to all workers in the field, is tremendously difficult because of the absence of an Archimedean point outside the mind. Much more than any other disciplines, psychology and psychiatry are ultimately self-reflexive: subject and object are identical, the mind studies itself, and any assumptions have an inevitable tendency toward self-validation. The impossibility of seeing the mind "at work" has in recent years led to the adoption of the Black Box concept from the field of telecommunication. Applied originally to certain types of captured enemy electronic equipment that could not be opened for study because of the possibility of destruction charges inside, the concept is more generally applied to the fact that electronic hardware is by now so complex that it is sometimes more expedient to disregard the internal structure of a device and concentrate on the study of its specific input-output relations. While it is true that these relations may permit inferences into what "really" goes on inside the box, this knowledge is not essential for the study of *the function of the device in the greater system of which it is a part.* This concept, if applied to psychological and psychiatric problems, has the heuristic advantage that no ultimately unverifiable intrapsychic hypotheses need to be invoked, and that one can limit oneself to observable input-output relations, that is, to *communication.* Such an approach, we believe, characterizes an important recent trend in psychiatry toward viewing symptoms as one kind of input into the family system rather than as an expression of intrapsychic conflict.

1.62—CONSCIOUSNESS AND UNCONSCIOUSNESS

If one is interested in observing human behavior in terms of the Black Box assumption, he sees the output of one Black Box as the input of another. The question whether such an exchange of information is conscious or unconscious loses the paramount importance it has in the psychodynamic framework. This is not to be construed as meaning that, as far as the reactions to a specific piece of behavior are concerned, it makes no difference whether this behavior is taken to be conscious or unconscious, voluntary, involuntary, or symptomatic. If someone has his toes stepped on by another, it makes a great deal of difference to him whether the other's behavior was deliberate or unintentional. This view, however, is based on *his* evaluation of the other person's motives and, therefore, on assumptions about what goes on inside the other's head. And, of course, if he were to ask the other about his motives, he could still not be certain, for the other individual might claim his behavior was unconscious when he had meant it to be deliberate, or even claim it was deliberate when in fact it was accidental. All this brings us back to the attribution of "meaning," a notion that is essential for the subjective experience of communicating with others, but which we have found to be objectively undecidable for the purposes of research in human communication.

1.63—PRESENT VERSUS PAST

While there can be no doubt that behavior is at least partly determined by previous experience, the search for causes in the past is notoriously unreliable. Ashby's comments on the peculiarities of "memory" as a construct were noted earlier (s. 1.2). Not only is it based mainly on subjective evidence and, therefore, liable to suffer from the same distortion the exploration is supposed to eliminate, but whatever person *A* reports about his past to person *B* is inseparably linked to and determined by the ongoing relationship between these two persons. If, on the other hand, the communication between the individual and the significant others in his life are observed directly—as was suggested in the chess analogy and as is done in conjoint psychotherapy of couples or entire families—patterns of communication can eventually be identified that are diagnostically important and permit the planning of the most appropriate strategy of therapeutic intervention. This approach, then, is a search for pattern in the here and now rather than for symbolic meaning, past causes, or motivation.

1.64—EFFECT VERSUS CAUSE

If seen in this light, the possible or hypothetical causes of behavior assume a secondary importance, but the effect of the behavior emerges as a criterion of prime significance in the interaction of closely related individuals. For instance, it can be seen time and again that a symptom that has remained refractory to psychotherapy in spite of intensive analysis of its genesis suddenly reveals its significance when seen in the context of the ongoing marital interaction of the individual and his or her spouse. The symptom may then show itself as a constraint, as a rule of their particular interactional "game," [5] rather than the outcome of an unresolved conflict between hypothesized intrapsychic forces. In general, we feel that a symptom is a piece of behavior that has profound effects in influencing the surroundings of the patient. A rule of thumb can be stated in this connection: where the *why?* of a piece of behavior remains obscure, the question *what for?* can still supply a valid answer.

[5] It cannot be emphasized too strongly that in this book the term "game" should not be taken to have any playful connotation, but derives from the mathematical Theory of Games and refers to sequences of behavior which are governed by rules.

1.65—THE CIRCULARITY OF COMMUNICATION PATTERNS

> All parts of the organism form a
> circle. Therefore, every part is both
> beginning and end.—Hippocrates

While in linear, progressive chains of causality it is meaningful to speak about the beginning and end of a chain, these terms are meaningless in systems with feedback loops. There is no beginning and no end to a circle. Thinking in terms of such systems forces one to abandon the notion that, say, event *a* comes first and event *b* is determined by *a*'s occurrence, for by the same faulty logic it could be claimed that event *b* precedes *a*, depending on where one arbitrarily chooses to break the continuity of the circle. But, as will be shown in the next chapter, this faulty logic is constantly used by the individual participants in human interaction when both person *A* and person *B* claim only to be reacting to the partner's behavior without realizing that they in turn influence the partner by their reaction. The same kind of reasoning is applied to this hopeless controversy: is a given family's communication pathological because one of their members is psychotic, or is one member psychotic because the communication is pathological?

1.66—THE RELATIVITY OF "NORMAL" AND "ABNORMAL"

The earliest psychiatric research was done in mental hospitals and was aimed at the classification of patients. This approach had several practical values, not the least of which was the discovery of certain organic conditions, such as general paresis. The next practical step was the incorporation of this conceptual differentiation of normality and abnormality into legal language, thus the terms "sanity" and "insanity." However, once it is accepted that from a communicational point of view a piece of behavior can only be studied in the context in which it occurs, the terms "sanity" and "insanity" practically lose their meanings as attributes of individuals. Similarly does the whole notion of "abnormality" become questionable. For it is now generally agreed that the patient's condition is not static but varies with his interpersonal situation as well as with the bias of the observer. When, further, psychiatric symptoms are viewed as behavior appropriate to an ongoing interaction, a frame of reference emerges that is diametric to the classical psychiatric view. The importance of this shift in emphasis can hardly be overrated. Thus, "schizophrenia" viewed as the incurable and progressive disease of an individual mind and "schizophrenia" viewed as the *only* possible reaction to an absurd or untenable communicational context (a reaction that follows, and therefore perpetuates, the rules of such a context) are two entirely different things—and yet the difference lies in the incompatibility of the two conceptual frameworks, while the clinical picture to which they are applied is the same in both cases. The implications for etiology and therapy that follow from these differing viewpoints are also highly discrepant; hence our interest in examining and stressing the communication point of view is not mere armchair exercise.

Chapter 2

Some Tentative Axioms

of Communication

2.1

Introduction

The conclusions reached in the first chapter generally emphasized the inapplicability of many traditional psychiatric notions to our proposed framework and so may seem to leave very little on which the study of the pragmatics of human communication could be based. We want to show next that this is not so. However, to do this, we have to start with some simple properties of communication that have fundamental interpersonal implications. It will be seen that these properties are in the nature of axioms within our hypothetical calculus of human communication. When these have been defined we will be in a position to consider some of their possible pathologies in Chapter 3.

2.2

The Impossibility of Not Communicating

2.21

First of all, there is a property of behavior that could hardly be more basic and is, therefore, often overlooked: behavior has no opposite. In other words, there is no such thing as nonbehavior or, to put it even more simply: one cannot *not* behave. Now, if it is accepted that all behavior in an interactional situation [1] has message

---

[1] It might be added that, even alone, it is possible to have dialogues in fantasy, with one's hallucinations (*15*), or with life (s. 8.3). Perhaps such internal "communication" follows some of the same rules which govern interpersonal com-

value, i.e., is communication, it follows that no matter how one may try, one cannot *not* communicate. Activity or inactivity, words or silence all have message value: they influence others and these others, in turn, cannot *not* respond to these communications and are thus themselves communicating. It should be clearly understood that the mere absence of talking or of taking notice of each other is no exception to what has just been asserted. The man at a crowded lunch counter who looks straight ahead, or the airplane passenger who sits with his eyes closed, are both communicating that they do not want .to speak to anybody or be spoken to, and their neighbors usually "get the message" and respond appropriately by leaving them alone. This, obviously, is just as much an interchange of communication as an animated discussion.[2]

Neither can we say that "communication" only takes place when it is intentional, conscious, or successful, that is, when mutual understanding occurs. Whether message sent equals message received is an important but different order of analysis, as it must rest ultimately on evaluations of specific, introspective, subject-reported data, which we choose to neglect for the exposition of a behavioral theory of communication. On the question of misunderstanding, our concern, given certain formal properties of communication, is

---

munication; such unobservable phenomena, however, are outside the scope of our meaning of the term.

[2] Very interesting research in this field has been carried out by Luft (*98*), who studied what he calls "social stimulus deprivation." He brought two strangers togehter in a room, made them sit across from each other and instructed them "not to talk or communicate in any way." Subsequent interviews revealed the highly stressful nature of this situation. To quote the author:

> . . . he has before him the other unique individual with his ongoing, though muted, behavior. At this point, it is postulated, that true interpersonal testing takes place, and only part of this testing may be done consciously. For example, how does the other subject respond to him and to the small non-verbal cues which he sends out? Is there an attempt at understanding his enquiring glance, or is it coldly ignored? Does the other subject display postural cues of tension, indicating some distress at confronting him? Does he grow increasingly comfortable, indicating some kind of acceptance, or will the other treat him as if he were a thing, which did not exist? These and many other kinds of readily discernable behavior appear to take place. . . .

with the development of related pathologies, aside from, indeed in spite of, the motivations or intentions of the communicants.

2.22

In the foregoing, the term "communication" has been used in two ways: as the generic title of our study, and as a loosely defined unit of behavior. Let us now be more precise. We will, of course, continue to refer to the pragmatic aspect of the theory of human communication simply as "communication." For the various units of communication (behavior), we have sought to select terms which are already generally understood. A single communicational unit will be called a *message* or, where there is no possibility of confusion, *a* communication. A series of messages exchanged between persons will be called *interaction*. (For those who crave more precise quantification, we can only say that the sequence we refer to by the term "interaction" is greater than one message but not infinite.) Finally, in Chapters 4–7, we will add *patterns of interaction,* which is a still higher-level unit of human communication.

Further, in regard to even the simplest possible unit, it will be obvious that once we accept all behavior as communication, we will not be dealing with a monophonic message unit, but rather with a fluid and multifaceted compound of many behavioral modes— verbal, tonal, postural, contextual, etc.—all of which qualify the meaning of all the others. The various elements of this compound (considered as a whole) are capable of highly varied and complex permutations, ranging from the congruent to the incongruent and paradoxical. The pragmatic effect of these combinations in inter-personal situations will be our interest herein.

2.23

The impossibility of not communicating is a phenomenon of more than theoretical interest. It is, for instance, part and parcel of the schizophrenic "dilemma." If schizophrenic behavior is ob-served with etiological considerations in abeyance, it appears that the schizophrenic tries *not to communicate.* But since even non-sense, silence, withdrawal, immobility (postural silence), or any other form of denial is itself a communication, the schizophrenic is faced with the impossible task of denying that he is communicating and at the same time denying that his denial is a communication. The realization of this basic dilemma in schizophrenia is a key to a good many aspects of schizophrenic communication that would otherwise remain obscure. Since any communication, as we shall see, implies commitment and thereby defines the sender's view of his relationship with the receiver, it can be hypothesized that the schizophrenic behaves as if he would avoid commitment by not communicating. Whether this is his purpose, in the causal sense, is of course impossible of proof; that this is the effect of schizophrenic behavior will be taken up in greater detail in s. 3.2.

2.24

To summarize, a metacommunicational axiom of the pragmatics of communication can be postulated: *one cannot not communicate.*

2.3

The Content and Relationship Levels of Communication

2.31

Another axiom was hinted at in the foregoing when it was suggested that any communication implies a commitment and thereby defines the relationship. This is another way of saying that a communication not only conveys information, but that at the same time it imposes behavior. Following Bateson (*132,* pp. 179–81), these two operations have come to be known as the "report" and the "command" aspects, respectively, of any communication. Bateson exemplifies these two aspects by means of a physiological analogy: let *A, B,* and *C* be a linear chain of neurons. Then the firing of neuron *B* is both a "report" that neuron *A* has fired and a "command" for neuron *C* to fire.

The report aspect of a message conveys information and is, therefore, synonymous in human communication with the *content* of the message. It may be about anything that is communicable regardless of whether the particular information is true or false, valid, invalid,

51

or undecidable. The command aspect, on the other hand, refers to what sort of a message it is to be taken as, and, therefore, ultimately to the *relationship* between the communicants. All such relationship statements are about one or several of the following assertions: "This is how I see myself . . . this is how I see you . . . this is how I see you seeing me . . ." and so forth in theoretically infinite regress. Thus, for instance, the messages "It is important to release the clutch gradually and smoothly" and "Just let the clutch go, it'll ruin the transmission in no time" have approximately the same information content (report aspect), but they obviously define very different relationships. To avoid any misunderstanding about the foregoing, we want to make it clear that relationships are only rarely defined deliberately or with full awareness. In fact, it seems that the more spontaneous and "healthy" a relationship, the more the relationship aspect of communication recedes into the background. Conversely, "sick" relationships are characterized by a constant struggle about the nature of the relationship, with the content aspect of communication becoming less and less important.

2.32

It is quite interesting that before behavioral scientists began to wonder about these aspects of human communication, computer engineers had come across the same problem in their work. It became clear to them that when communicating with an artificial organism, their communications had to have both report and command aspects. For instance, if a computer is to multiply two figures, it must be fed this information (the two figures) *and* information about this information: the command "multiply them."

Now, what is important for our consideration is the relation existing between the content (report) and the relationship (command) aspects of communication. In essence it has already been defined in the preceding paragraph when it was mentioned that a computer needs *information* (data) and *information about this information* (instructions). Clearly, then, the instructions are of a higher logical type than the data; they are *metainformation* since

they are information *about* information, and any confusion between the two would lead to a meaningless result.

2.33

If we now return to human communication, we see that the same
relation exists between the report and the command aspects: the
former conveys the "data" of the communication, the latter how
this communication is to be taken. "This is an order" or "I am only
joking" are verbal examples of such communications about communication. The relationship can also be expressed nonverbally by
shouting or smiling or in a number of other ways. And the relationship may be clearly understood from the context in which the
communication takes place, e.g., between uniformed soldiers, or in
a circus ring.

The reader will have noticed that the relationship aspect of a
communication, being a communication about a communication, is,
of course, identical with the concept of metacommunication elaborated in the first chapter, where it was limited to the conceptual
framework and to the language the communication analyst must
employ when communicating about communication. Now it can be
seen that not only he but everyone is faced with this problem. The
ability to metacommunicate appropriately is not only the *conditio
sine qua non* of successful communication, but is intimately linked
with the enormous problem of awareness of self and others. This
point will be explained in greater detail in s. 3.3. For the moment,
and by way of illustration, we merely want to show that messages
can be constructed, especially in written communication, which offer highly ambiguous metacommunicational clues. As Cherry (*34,*
p. 120) points out, the sentence "Do you think that one will do?"
can have a variety of meanings, according to which word is to be
stressed—an indication that written language usually does not supply. Another example would be a sign in a restaurant reading "Cus-
tomers who think our waiters are rude should see the manager,"
which, at least in theory, can be understood in two entirely different
ways. Ambiguities of this kind are not the only possible complica-

tions arising out of the level structure of all communication; consider, for instance, a notice that reads "Disregard This Sign." As we shall see in the chapter on paradoxical communication, confusions or contaminations between these levels—communication and metacommunication—may lead to impasses identical in structure to those of the famous paradoxes in logic.

2.34

For the time being let us merely summarize the foregoing into another axiom of our tentative calculus: *Every communication has a content and a relationship aspect such that the latter classifies the former and is therefore a metacommunication.*[3]

2.4

The Punctuation of the Sequence of Events

2.41

The next basic characteristic of communication we wish to explore regards interaction—exchanges of messages—between communicants. To an outside observer, *a series of communications can be viewed as an uninterrupted sequence of interchanges.* However, the participants in the interaction always introduce what, following Whorf (*165*), Bateson and Jackson have termed the "punctuation of the sequence of events." They state:

> The stimulus-response psychologist typically confines his attention to sequences of interchange so short that it is possible to label one item of input as "stimulus" and another item as "reinforcement" while labelling what the subject does between these two events as "response." Within the short sequence so excised, it is

---

[3] We have chosen, somewhat arbitrarily, to say that the relationship classifies, or subsumes, the content aspect, although it is equally accurate in logical analysis to say that the class is defined by its members and therefore the content aspect can be said to define the relationship aspect. Since our primary interest is not information exchange but the pragmatics of communication, we will use the former approach.

possible to talk about the "psychology" of the subject. In contrast, the sequences of interchange which we are here discussing are very much longer and therefore have the characteristic that every item in the sequence is simultaneously stimulus, response and reinforcement. A given item of A's behavior is a stimulus insofar as it is followed by an item contributed by B and that by another item contributed by A. But insofar as A's item is sandwiched between two items contributed by B, it is a response. Similarly A's item is a reinforcement insofar as it follows an item contributed by B. The ongoing interchanges, then, which we are here discussing, constitute a chain of overlapping triadic links, each of which is comparable to a stimulus-response-reinforcement sequence. We can take any triad of our interchange and see it as a single trial in a stimulus-response learning experiment.

If we look at the conventional learning experiments from this point of view, we observe at once that repeated trials amount to a differentiation of relationship between the two organisms concerned—the experimenter and his subject. The sequence of trials is so punctuated that it is always the experimenter who seems to provide the "stimuli" and the "reinforcements," while the subject provides the "responses." These words are here deliberately put in quotation marks because the role definitions are in fact only created by the willingness of the organisms to accept the system of punctuation. The "reality" of the role definitions is only of the same order as the reality of a bat on a Rorschach card—a more or less over-determined creation of the perceptive process. The rat who said "I have got my experimenter trained. Each time I press the lever he gives me food" was declining to accept the punctuation of the sequence which the experimenter was seeking to impose.

> It is still true, however, that in a long sequence of interchange, the organisms concerned—especially if these be people—will in fact punctuate the sequence so that it will appear that one or the other has initiative, dominance, dependency or the like. That is, they will set up between them patterns of interchange (about which they may or may not be in agreement) and these patterns will in fact be rules of contingency regarding the exchange of reinforcement. While rats are too nice to re-label, some psychiatric patients are not, and provide psychological trauma for the therapist! (*19*, pp. 273–74)

It is not the issue here whether punctuation of communicational sequence is, in general, good or bad, as it should be immediately obvious that punctuation *organizes* behavioral events and is therefore vital to ongoing interactions. Culturally, we share many conventions of punctuation which, while no more or less accurate than other views of the same events, serve to organize common and important interactional sequences. For example, we call a person in a group behaving in one way the "leader" and another the "follower," although on reflection it is difficult to say which comes first or where one would be without the other.

2.42

Disagreement about how to punctuate the sequence of events is at the root of countless relationship struggles. Suppose a couple have a marital problem to which he contributes passive withdrawal, while her 50 per cent is nagging criticism. In explaining their frustrations, the husband will state that withdrawal is his only *defense against* her nagging, while she will label this explanation a gross and willful distortion of what "really" happens in their marriage: namely, that she is critical of him *because of* his passivity. Stripped of all ephemeral and fortuitous elements, their fights consist in a monotonous exchange of the messages "I withdraw because you nag" and "I nag because you withdraw." This type of interaction has already been mentioned briefly in s. 1.65. Represented graphically, with an arbitrary beginning point, their interaction looks somewhat like this:

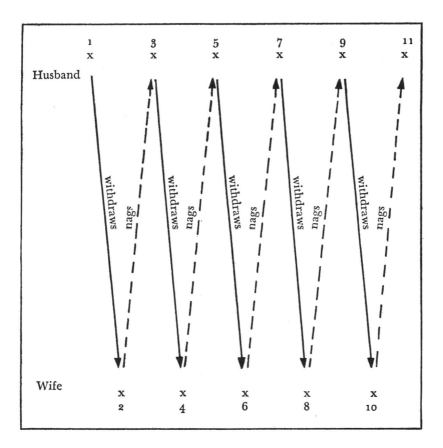

It can be seen that the husband only perceives triads 2–3–4, 4–5–6, 6–7–8, etc., where his behavior (solid arrows) is "merely" a response to her behavior (the broken arrows). With her it is exactly the other way around; she punctuates the sequence of events into the triads 1–2–3, 3–4–5, 5–6–7, etc., and sees herself as only reacting to, but not determining, her husband's behavior. In conjoint psychotherapy with couples one is frequently struck by the intensity of what in traditional psychotherapy would be referred to as "reality distortion" on the part of both parties. It is often hard to believe that two individuals could have such divergent views on many elements of joint experience. And yet the problem lies primarily in an area already frequently mentioned: their inability to metacommunicate about their respective patterning of their interaction. This interaction is of an oscillatory yes-no-yes-no-yes nature which theoretically can go on ad infinitum and almost invariably is accompanied, as we shall see later, by the typical charges of badness or madness.

International relations, too, are rife with analogous patterns of interaction; take for instance C. E. M. Joad's analysis of arms races:

> . . . if, as they maintain, the best way to preserve peace is to prepare war, it is not altogether clear why all nations should regard the armaments of other nations as a menace to peace. However, they do so regard them, and are accordingly stimulated to increase their armaments to overtop the armaments by which they conceive themselves to be threatened. . . . These increased arms being in their turn regarded as a menace by nation A whose allegedly defensive armaments have provoked them, are used by nation A as a pretext for accumulating yet greater armaments wherewith to defend itself against the menace. Yet these greater armaments are in turn interpreted by neighbouring nations as constituting a menace to themselves and so on. . . . (79, p. 69)

2.43

Again, mathematics supplies a descriptive analogy: the concept of "infinite, oscillating series." While the term itself was introduced much later, series of this kind were studied in a logical, consistent manner for the first time by the Austrian priest Bernard Bolzano shortly before his death in 1848, when, it would appear, he was deeply involved with the meaning of infinity. His thoughts appeared posthumously in the form of a small book entitled *The Paradoxes of the Infinite* (*30*), which became a classic of mathematical literature. In it Bolzano studied various kinds of series (S), of which perhaps the simplest is the following:

$$S = a - a + a - a + a - a + a - a + a - a + a - \ldots$$

For our purposes this series may be taken to stand for a communicational sequence of assertions and denials of message *a*. Now, as Bolzano showed, this sequence can be grouped—or, as we would say, punctuated—in several different, but arithmetically correct, ways.[4] The result is a different limit for the series depending on how one chooses to punctuate the sequence of its elements, a result which consternated many mathematicians, including Leibnitz. Unfortunately, as far as we can see, the solution of the paradox offered eventually by Bolzano is of no help in the analogous communicational dilemma. There, as Bateson (*17*) suggests, the dilemma arises out of the spurious punctuation of the series, namely, the pretense that it has a beginning, and this is precisely the error of the partners in such a situation.

2.44

Thus we add a third metacommunicational axiom: *The nature of a relationship is contingent upon the punctuation of the communicational sequences between the communicants.*

[4] The three possible groupings ("punctuations") are:
$$S = (a - a) + (a - a) + (a - a) + (a - a) + \ldots$$
$$= O + O + O + \ldots$$
$$= O$$
Another way of grouping the elements of the sequence would be:
$$S = a - (a - a) - (a - a) - (a - a) - (a - a) - \ldots$$
$$= a - O - O - O \ldots$$
$$= a$$
Still another way would be:
$$S = a - (a - a + a - a + a - a + a - \ldots)$$
and since the elements contained in the brackets are nothing but the series itself, it follows that:
$$S = a - S$$
Therefore $2S = a$, and $S = \dfrac{a}{2}$. (*30*, pp. 49–50)

2.5

Digital and Analogic Communication

2.51

In the central nervous system the functional units (neurons) receive so-called quantal packages of information through connecting elements (synapses). Upon arrival at the synapses these "packages" produce excitatory or inhibitory postsynaptic potentials that are summed up by the neuron and either cause or inhibit its firing. This specific part of neural activity, consisting in the occurrence or nonoccurrence of its firing, therefore conveys binary digital information. The humoral system, on the other hand, is not based on digitalization of information. This system communicates by releasing discrete quantities of specific substances into the bloodstream. It is further known that the neural and the humoral modes of intraorganismic communication exist not only side by side, but that they complement and are contingent upon each other, often in highly complex ways.

The same two basic modes of communication can be found at work in the field of man-made organisms: [5] there are computers which utilize the all-or-none principle of vacuum tubes or transistors and are called *digital,* because they are basically calculators working with digits; and there is another class of machines that manipulate discrete, positive magnitudes—the analogues of the data—and hence are called *analogic.* In digital computers both

---

[5] Interestingly enough, there is reason to believe that computer engineers arrived at this result quite independently from what the physiologists already knew at the time, a fact which in itself provides a beautiful illustration of von Bertalanffy's (25) postulate that complex systems have their own inherent lawfulness that can be followed throughout the various systemic levels, i.e., the atomic, molecular, cellular, organismic, individual, societal, etc. The story goes that during an interdisciplinary gathering of scientists interested in feedback phenomena (probably one of the Josiah Macy Foundation meetings), the great histologist von Bonin was shown the wiring diagram of a selective reading device and immediately said: "But this is just a diagram of the third layer of the visual cortex. . . ." We cannot vouch for the authenticity of this story, but would hold it with the Italian proverb "se non è vero, è ben trovato" (even if it is not true, it still makes a good story).

data and instructions are processed in the form of numbers so that often, especially in the case of the instructions, there is only an arbitrary correspondence between the particular piece of information and its digital expression. In other words, these numbers are arbitrarily assigned code names which have as little resemblance to actual magnitudes as do the telephone numbers assigned to the subscribers. On the other hand, as we have already seen, the analogy principle is the essence of all analogic computation. Just as in the humoral system of natural organisms the carriers of information are certain substances and their concentration in the bloodstream, in analogue computers data take the form of discrete and, therefore, always positive quantities, e.g., the intensity of electrical currents, the number of revolutions of a wheel, the degree of displacement of components, and the like. A so-called tide machine (an instrument composed of scales, cogs, and levers formerly used to compute the tides for any given time) can be considered a simple analogue computer, and, of course, Ashby's homeostat, mentioned in Chapter 1, is a paradigm of an analogue machine, even though it does not compute anything.

2.52

In human communication, objects—in the widest sense—can be referred to in two entirely different ways. They can either be represented by a likeness, such as a drawing, or they can be referred to by a name. Thus, in the written sentence "The cat has caught a mouse" the nouns could be replaced by pictures; if the sentence were spoken, the actual cat and the mouse could be pointed to. Needless to say, this would be an unusual way of communicating, and normally the written or spoken "name," that is, the word, is used. These two types of communication—the one by a self-explanatory likeness, the other by a word—are, of course, also equivalent to the concepts of the analogic and the digital respectively. Whenever a word is used to *name* something it is obvious that the relation between the name and the thing named is an arbitrarily established one. Words are arbitrary signs that are manipulated according to the logical syntax of language. There is no particular reason why the three letters "c-a-t" should denote a particular animal. In ultimate analysis it is only a semantic convention of the English language, and outside this convention there exists no other correlation between any word and the thing it stands for, with the possible but insignificant exception of onomatopoeic words. As Bateson and Jackson point out: "There is nothing particularly five-like in the number five; there is nothing particularly table-like in the word 'table' " (*19*, p. 271).

In analogic communication, on the other hand, there *is* something particularly "thing-like" in what is used to express the thing. Analogic communication can be more readily referred to the thing it stands for. The difference between these two modes of communication may become somewhat clearer if it is realized that no amount of listening to a foreign language on the radio, for example, will yield an understanding of the language, whereas some basic information can fairly easily be derived from watching sign language and from so-called intention movements, even when used by a person of a totally different culture. Analogic communication, we suggest, has its roots in far more archaic periods of evolution and is, therefore, of much more general validity than the relatively recent, and far more abstract, digital mode of verbal communication.

What then is analogic communication? The answer is relatively simple: it is virtually all nonverbal communication. This term, however, is deceptive, because it is often restricted to body movement only, to the behavior known as kinesics. We hold that the term must comprise posture, gesture, facial expression, voice inflection, the sequence, rhythm, and cadence of the words themselves, and any other nonverbal manifestation of which the organism is capable, as well as the communicational clues unfailingly present in any *context* in which an interaction takes place.[6]

2.53

Man is the only organism known to use both the analogic and

[6] The paramount communicational significance of context is all too easily overlooked in the analysis of human communication, and yet anyone who brushed his teeth in a busy street rather than in his bathroom might be quickly carted off to a police station or to a lunatic asylum—to give just one example of the pragmatic effects of nonverbal communication.

the digital modes of communication.[7] The significance of this is still very inadequately understood, but can hardly be overrated. On the one hand there can be no doubt that man communicates digitally. In fact, most, if not all, of his civilized achievements would be unthinkable without his having evolved digital language. This is particularly important for the sharing of information about *objects* and for the time-binding function of the transmission of knowledge. And yet there exists a vast area where we rely almost exclusively on analogic communication, often with very little change from the analogic inheritance handed down to us from our mammalian ancestors. This is the area of *relationship*. Based on Tinbergen (*153*) and Lorenz (*96*), as well as his own research, Bateson (*8*) has shown that vocalizations, intention movements, and mood signs of animals are analogic communications by which they define the nature of their relationships, rather than making denotative statements about objects. Thus, to take one of his examples, when I open the refrigerator and the cat comes, rubs against my legs, and mews, this does not mean "I want milk"—as a human being would express it—but invokes a specific relationship, "Be mother to me," because such behavior is only observed in kittens in relation to adult cats, and never between two grown-up animals. Conversely, pet lovers often are convinced that their animals "understand" their speech. What the animal does understand, needless to say, is certainly not the meaning of the words, but the wealth of analogic communication that goes with speech. Indeed, wherever relationship is the central issue of communication, we find that digital language is almost meaningless. This is not only the case between animals and between man and animal, but in many other contingencies in human life, e.g., courtship, love, succor, combat, and, of course, in all dealings with very young children or severely disturbed mental patients. Children, fools, and animals have always been credited with particular intuition regarding the sincerity or insincerity of human attitudes, for it is easy to profess something verbally, but difficult to carry a lie into the realm of the analogic.

[7] There is reason to believe that whales and dolphins may also use digital communication, but the research in this area is not yet conclusive.

In short, if we remember that every communication has a content and a relationship aspect, we can expect to find that the two modes of communication not only exist side by side but complement each other in every message. We can further expect to find that the content aspect is likely to be conveyed digitally whereas the relationship aspect will be predominantly analogic in nature.

2.54

In this correspondence lies the pragmatic importance of certain differences between the digital and analogic modes of communication which will now be considered. In order to make these differences clear, we can return to the digital and analogic modes as represented in artificial communication systems.

The performance, accuracy, and versatility of the two types of computers—digital and analogue—are vastly different. The analogues used in analogue computers in lieu of actual magnitudes can never be more than approximations of the real values, and this ever-present source of inaccuracy is further increased during the process of the computer operations themselves. Cogs, gears, and transmissions can never be built to perfection, and even when analogue machines rely entirely on discrete intensities of electrical currents, electrical resistances, rheostats, and the like, these analogues are still subject to virtually uncontrollable fluctuations. A digital machine, on the other hand, could be said to work with perfect precision if space for storing digits were not restricted, thus making it necessary to round off any results having more digits than the machine could hold. Anyone who has used a slide rule (an excellent example of an analogue computer) knows that he can only get an approximate result, while any desk calculator will supply an exact result, as long as the digits required do not exceed the maximum the calculator can handle.

Apart from its perfect precision, the digital computer has the enormous advantage of being not only an arithmetic, but also a *logical,* machine. McCulloch and Pitts (*101*) have shown that the sixteen truth functions of the logical calculus can be represented by combinations of all-or-none organs, so that, for instance, the summation of two pulses will represent the logical "and," the mutual exclusiveness of two pulses represents the logical "or," a pulse which inhibits the firing of an element represents negation, etc. Nothing even remotely comparable is possible in analogue computers. Since they operate only with discrete, positive quantities they are unable to represent any negative value, including negation itself, or any of the other truth functions.

Some of the characteristics of computers also apply to human communication: digital message material is of a much higher degree of complexity, versatility, and abstraction than analogic material. Specifically, we find that analogue communication has nothing comparable to the logical syntax of digital language. This means that in analogic language there are no equivalents for such vitally important elements of discourse as "if—then," "either—or," and many others, and that the expression of abstract concepts is as difficult, if not impossible, as in primitive picture writing, where every concept can only be represented by its physical likeness. Furthermore, analogic language shares with analogic computing the lack of the simple negative, i.e., an expression for "not."

To illustrate: there are tears of sorrow and tears of joy, the clenched fist may signal aggression or constraint, a smile may convey sympathy or contempt, reticence can be interpreted as tactfulness or indifference, and we wonder if perhaps all analogic messages have this curiously ambiguous quality, reminiscent of Freud's *Gegensinn der Urworte* (antithetical sense of primal words). Analogic communication has no qualifiers to indicate which of two discrepant meanings is implied, nor any indicators that would permit a distinction between past, present, or future.[8] These qualifiers

[8] By now the reader will have discovered for himself how suggestive a similarity there exists between the analogic and the digital modes of communication and the psychoanalytic concepts of *primary* and *secondary processes* respectively. If transposed from the intrapsychic to the interpersonal frame of reference, Freud's description of the id becomes virtually a definition of analogic communication:

> The *laws of logic—above all, the law of contradiction—do not hold for processes in the id.* Contradictory impulses exist side by side without neutralizing each other or drawing apart. . . . *There is nothing in the id which can be compared to negation,*

and indicators do, of course, exist in digital communication. But what is lacking in digital communication is an adequate vocabulary for the contingencies of relationship.

Man, in his necessity to combine these two languages, either as sender or receiver, must constantly *translate* from the one into the other, and in doing so encounters very curious dilemmas, which will be taken up in greater detail in the chapter on pathological communication (s. 3.5). For in human communication, the difficulty of translation exists both ways. Not only can there be no translation from the digital into the analogic mode without great loss of information (see s. 3.55 on hysterical symptom formation), but the opposite is also extraordinarily difficult: to *talk about* relationship requires adequate translation from the analogic into the digital mode of communication. Finally we can imagine similar problems when the two modes must coexist, as Haley has noted in his excellent chapter, "Marriage Therapy":

> When a man and a woman decide their association should be legalized with a marriage ceremony, they pose themselves a problem which will continue through the marriage: now that they are married are they staying together because they wish to or because they must? (*60*, p. 119)

In the light of the foregoing, we would say that when to the mostly analogic part of their relationship (courtship behavior) is added a digitalization (the marriage contract) an unambiguous definition of their relationship becomes very problematic.[9]

2.55

To summarize: *Human beings communicate both digitally and analogically. Digital language has a highly complex and powerful*

---

and we are astonished to find in it an exception to the philosophers' assertion that space and time are necessary forms of our mental acts (*49*, p. 104; italics ours)

[9] For the same reasons, it is possible to suggest that divorce would be experienced as something much more definite if the usually dry and uninspiring legal act of obtaining the final decree were implemented by some form of analogic ritual of final separation.

logical syntax but lacks adequate semantics in the field of relationship, while analogic language possesses the semantics but has no adequate syntax for the unambiguous definition of the nature of relationships.

2.6

Symmetrical and Complementary Interaction

2.61

In 1935 Bateson (6) reported on an interactional phenomenon which he observed in the Iatmul tribe in New Guinea and which, in his book *Naven* (10), published a year later, he dealt with in greater detail. He called this phenomenon *schismogenesis* and defined it as *a process of differentiation in the norms of individual behavior resulting from cumulative interaction between individuals.* In 1939 Richardson (125) applied this concept to his analyses of war and foreign politics; since 1952 Bateson and others have demonstrated its usefulness in the field of psychiatric research (Cf. *157*, pp. 7–17; also *143*). This concept, which, as we can see, has a heuristic value beyond the confines of any one discipline, was elaborated by Bateson in *Naven* as follows:

> When our discipline is defined in terms of the reactions of an individual to the reactions of other individuals, it is at once apparent that we must regard the relationship between two individuals as liable to alter from time to time, even without disturbance from outside. We have to consider, not only *A*'s reactions to *B*'s behaviour, but we must go on to consider how these affect *B*'s later behaviour and the effect of this on *A*.
>
> It is at once apparent that many systems of relationship, either between individuals or groups of individuals, contain a tendency towards progressive change. If, for example, one of the patterns of cultural behaviour, considered appropriate in individual

A, is culturally labelled as an assertive pattern, while *B* is expected to reply to this with what is culturally regarded as submission, it is likely that this submission will encourage a further assertion, and that this assertion will demand still further submission. We have thus a potentially progressive state of affairs, and unless other factors are present to restrain the excesses of assertive and submissive behavior, *A* must necessarily become more and more assertive, while *B* will become more and more submissive; and this progressive change will occur whether *A* and *B* are separate individuals or members of complementary groups.

Progressive changes of this sort we may describe as *complementary* schismogenesis. But there is another pattern of relationships between individuals or groups of individuals which equally contains the germs of progressive change. If, for example, we find boasting as the cultural pattern of behaviour in one group, and that the other group replies to this with boasting, a competitive situation may develop in which boasting leads to more boasting, and so on. This type of progressive change we may call *symmetrical* schismogenesis. (*10,* pp. 176–77)

2.62

The two patterns just described have come to be used without reference to the schismogenetic process and are now usually referred to simply as symmetrical and complementary interaction. They can be described as relationships based on either equality or difference. In the first case the partners tend to mirror each other's behavior, and thus their interaction can be termed *symmetrical.* Weakness or strength, goodness or badness, are not relevant here, for equality can be maintained in any of these areas. In the second case one partner's behavior complements that of the other, forming a different sort of behavioral Gestalt, and is called *complementary.* Symmetrical interaction, then, is characterized by equality and the minimization of difference, while complementary interaction is based on the maximization of difference.

There are two different positions in a complementary relationship. One partner occupies what has been variously described as the superior, primary, or "one-up" position, and the other the corresponding inferior, secondary, or "one-down" position. These terms are quite useful as long as they are not equated with "good" or "bad," "strong" or "weak." A complementary relationship may be set by the social or cultural context (as in the cases of mother and infant, doctor and patient, or teacher and student), or it may be the idiosyncratic relationship style of a particular dyad. In either case, it is important to emphasize the interlocking nature of the relationship, in which dissimilar but fitted behaviors evoke each other. One partner does not impose a complementary relationship on the other, but rather each behaves in a manner which presupposes, while at the same time providing reasons for, the behavior of the other: their definitions of the relationship (s. 2.3) fit.

2.63

A third type of relationship has been suggested—"metacomplementary," in which A lets or forces B to be in charge of him; by the same reasoning, we could also add "pseudosymmetry," in which A lets or forces B to be symmetrical. This potentially infinite regress can, however, be avoided by recalling the distinction made earlier (s. 1.4) between the observation of behavioral redundancies and their inferred explanations, in the form of mythologies; that is, we are interested in *how* the pair behave without being distracted by why (they believe) they so conduct themselves. If, though, the individuals involved avail themselves of the multiple levels of communication (s. 2.22) in order to express different patterns on different levels, paradoxical results of significant pragmatic importance may arise (s. 5.41; 6.42, ex. 3; 7.5, ex. 2d).

2.64

The potential pathologies (escalation in symmetry and rigidity in complementarity) of these modes of communication will be dealt with in the next chapter. For the present, we can state simply our last tentative axiom: *All communicational interchanges are either symmetrical or complementary, depending on whether they are based on equality or difference.*

2.7

Summary

Regarding the above axioms in general, some qualifications should be re-emphasized. First, it should be clear that they are put forth tentatively, rather informally defined and certainly more preliminary than exhaustive. Second, they are, among themselves, quite heterogeneous in that they draw from widely ranging observations on communication phenomena. They are unified not by their origins but by their *pragmatic* importance, which in turn rests not so much on their particulars as on their *interpersonal* (rather than monadic) reference. Birdwhistell has even gone so far as to suggest that

> an individual does not communicate; he engages in or becomes part of communication. He may move, or make noises . . . but he does not communicate. In a parallel fashion, he may see, he may hear, smell, taste, or feel—but he does not communicate. In other words, he does not originate communication; he participates in it. Communication as a system, then, is not to be understood on a simple model of action and reaction, however complexly stated. As a system, it is to be comprehended on the transactional level. (*28*, p. 104)

Thus, the impossibility of not communicating makes all two-or-more-person situations *interpersonal,* communicative ones; the relationship aspect of such communication further specifies this same point. The pragmatic, interpersonal importance of the digital and analogic modes lies not only in its hypothesized isomorphism with content and relationship, but in the inevitable and significant ambiguity which both sender and receiver face in problems of translation from the one mode to the other. The description of problems of punctuation rests precisely on the underlying metamorphosis of the classic action-reaction model. Finally, the symmetry-complementarity paradigm comes perhaps closest to the mathematical concept of *function,* the individuals' positions merely being variables with an infinity of possible values whose meaning is not absolute but rather emerges only in relation to each other.

Chapter 3

Pathological Communication

3.1

Introduction

Each of the axioms just described implies, as corollaries, certain inherent pathologies that will now be elaborated. In our opinion, the pragmatic effects of these axioms can be illustrated best by relating them to disturbances that can develop in human communication. That is, given certain principles of communication, we shall examine in what ways and with what consequences these principles can be distorted. It will be seen that the behavioral consequences of such phenomena often correspond to various individual psychopathologies, so that in addition to exemplifying our theory we will be suggesting another framework in which the behavior usually seen as symptomatic of mental illness may be viewed. (The pathologies of each axiom will be considered in the same sequence as in Chapter 2, except for some inevitable overlapping as our material rapidly becomes more complex.[1])

3.2

The Impossibility of Not Communicating

Mention has already been made in the foregoing (s. 2.23) of the schizophrenics' dilemma when it was pointed out that these pa-

---

[1] Transcripts of verbal interchanges simplify the material considerably but are for that very reason ultimately unsatisfactory, because they convey little more than lexical content and are devoid of most analogic material, such as voice inflection, rate of speech, pauses, the emotional overtones contained in laughing, sighing, etc. For a similar analysis of examples of interaction, produced both in written and sound-recorded form, cf. Watzlawick (157).

tients behave as if they tried to deny that they are communicating and then find it necessary to deny also that their denial is itself a communication. But it is equally possible that the patient may seem to *want* to communicate without, however, accepting the commitment inherent in all communication. For example, a young schizophrenic woman bounced into a psychiatrist's office for her first interview and cheerfully announced: "My mother had to get married and now I am here." It took weeks to elucidate some of the many meanings she had condensed into this statement, meanings that were at the same time disqualified both by their cryptic format and by her display of apparent humor and zestfulness. Her gambit, as it turned out, was supposed to inform the therapist that

(1) she was the result of an illegitimate pregnancy;
(2) this fact had somehow caused her psychosis;
(3) "had to get married," referring to the shotgun nature of the mother's wedding, could either mean that Mother was not to be blamed because social pressure had forced her into the marriage, or that Mother resented the forced nature of the situation and blamed the patient's existence for it;
(4) "here" meant both the psychiatrist's office and the patient's existence on earth, and thus implied that on the one hand Mother had driven her crazy while on the other hand she had to be eternally indebted to her mother who had sinned and suffered to bring her into the world.

3.21

"Schizophrenese," then, is a language which leaves it up to the listener to take his choice from among many possible meanings which are not only different from but may even be incompatible with one another. Thus, it becomes possible to deny any or all aspects of a message. If pressed for an answer to what she had meant by her remark, the patient above could conceivably have said casually: "Oh, I don't know; I guess I must be crazy." If asked for an elucidation of any one aspect of it, she could have answered: "Oh no, this is not at all what I meant. . . ." But even though condensed beyond immediate recognition, her statement is a cogent description of the paradoxical situation in which she finds herself, and the remark "I *must* be crazy" could be quite appropriate in view of the amount of self-deception necessary to adapt herself to this paradoxical universe. For an extensive discussion of negation of communication in schizophrenia, the reader is referred to Haley (*60*, pp. 89–99), where there is a suggestive analogy to the clinical subgroups of schizophrenia.

3.22

The converse situation exists in *Through the Looking Glass* when Alice's straightforward communication is corrupted by the Red and the White Queens' "brainwashing." They allege that Alice is trying to deny something and attribute this to her state of mind:

> "I'm sure I didn't mean—" Alice was beginning, but the Red Queen interrupted her impatiently.
>
> "That's just what I complain of! You should have meant! What do you suppose is the use of a child without any meaning? Even a joke should have a meaning—and a child is more important than a joke, I hope. You couldn't deny that, even if you tried with both hands."
>
> "I don't deny things with my hands," Alice objected.
>
> "Nobody said you did," said the Red Queen. "I said you couldn't if you tried."
>
> "She is in that state of mind," said the White Queen, "that she wants to deny something—only she doesn't know what to deny!"
>
> "A nasty, vicious temper," the Red Queen remarked; and then there was an uncomfortable silence for a minute or two.

One can only marvel at the author's intuitive insight into the pragmatic effects of this kind of illogical communication, for after some more of this brainwashing he lets Alice faint.

3.23

The phenomenon in question, however, is not limited to fairy tales or schizophrenia. It has much wider implications for human interaction. Conceivably the attempt not to communicate will exist in any other context in which the commitment inherent in all communication is to be avoided. A typical situation of this kind is the meeting of two strangers, one of whom wants to make conversation and the other does not, e.g., two airplane passengers sitting next to each other.[2] Let passenger A be the one who does not want to talk. There are two things he cannot do: he cannot physically leave the field, and he cannot *not* communicate. The pragmatics of this communicational context are thus narrowed down to a very few possible reactions:

3.231 *"Rejection" of Communication*

Passenger A can make it clear to passenger B, more or less bluntly, that he is not interested in conversation. Since by the rules of good behavior this is reproachable, it will require courage and will create a rather strained and embarrassing silence, so that a relationship with B has not in fact been avoided.

3.232 *Acceptance of Communication*

Passenger A may give in and make conversation. In all probability he will hate himself and the other person for his own weakness, but this shall not concern us. What is significant is that he will soon realize the wisdom of the army rule that "in case of capture give only name, rank, and serial number," for passenger B may not be willing to stop halfway; he may be determined to find out all about A, including the latter's thoughts, feelings, and beliefs. And once A has started to respond, he will find it increasingly difficult to stop, a fact that is well known to "brainwashers."

3.233 *Disqualification of Communication*

A may defend himself by means of the important technique of disqualification, i.e., he may communicate in a way that invalidates

---

[2] We want to emphasize once more that for the purposes of our communicational analysis, the respective *motivations* of the two individuals are quite beside the point.

his own communications or those of the other. Disqualifications cover a wide range of communicational phenomena, such as self-contradictions, inconsistencies, subject switches, tangentializations, incomplete sentences, misunderstandings, obscure style or mannerisms of speech, the literal interpretations of metaphor and the metaphorical interpretation of literal remarks, etc.[3] A splendid example of this type of communication is given in the opening scene of the motion picture *Lolita* when Quilty, threatened by the pistol-wielding Humbert, goes into a paroxysm of verbal and nonverbal gibberish while his rival tries in vain to get across his message: "Look, I am going to shoot you!" (The concept of motivation is of little use in deciding whether this is sheer panic or a clever defense.) Another example is that delightful piece of logical nonsense by Lewis Carroll, the poem read by the White Rabbit:

> They told me you had been to her,
>   And mentioned me to him:
> She gave me a good character,
>   But said I could not swim.
>
> He sent them word I had not gone
>   (We knew it to be true):
> If she should push the matter on,
>   What would become of you?
>
> I gave her one, they gave him two,
>   You gave us three or more;
> They all returned from him to you,
>   Though they were mine before.

And so on for three more stanzas. If we now compare this with an excerpt from an interview with a normal volunteer subject who is obviously uncomfortable in answering a question put to him by the interviewer but feels that he *should* answer it, we find that his communication is suggestively similar both in its form and in the paucity of its content:

[3] Internationally, the Italians lead the field with their inimitable response "*ma* . . ." which strictly speaking means "but," although it may be used as an exclamation to express doubt, agreement, disagreement, bewilderment, indifference, criticism, contempt, anger, resignation, sarcasm, denial, and maybe a dozen more things and therefore ultimately nothing, as far as content goes.

Interviewer: How does it work out, Mr. R.,
with your parents living in the same town
as you and your family?

Mr. R: Well we try, uh, very personally I mean
. . . uh, I prefer that Mary [his wife]
takes the lead with them, rather than my
taking the lead or what. I like to see them,
but I don't try too much to make it a
point to be running over or have them
. . . they know very definitely that . . .
oh, it's been always before Mary and I
ever met and it was a thing that was pretty
much just an accepted fact—in our family
I was an only child—and they preferred
that they would never, to the best of their
ability, not, ah, interfere. I don't think
there is . . . in any case I think there is
always a—an underlying current there in
any family, I don't care whether it's our
family or any family. And it is something
that even Mary and I feel when we . . .
both of us are rather perfectionists. And,
ah, yet again, we're very . . . we are . . .
we are st– rigid and . . . we expect that
of the children and we feel that if you got
to watch out—I mean, if ah . . . you can
have interference with in-laws, we feel,
we've seen others with it and we've just
. . . it's been a thing that my own family
tried to guard against, but ah . . . and,
uh, like here—why we've . . . I wouldn't
say we are standoffish to the folks. (*157,*
pp. 20–21)

It is not surprising that this kind of communication is typically
resorted to by anybody who is caught in a situation in which he
feels obliged to communicate but at the same time wants to avoid

the commitment inherent in all communication. From the communicational point of view there is, therefore, no essential difference between the behavior of a so-called normal individual who has fallen into the hands of an experienced interviewer and of a so-called mentally disturbed individual who finds himself in the identical dilemma: neither can leave the field, neither can *not* communicate but presumably for reasons of their own are afraid or unwilling to do so. In either case the outcome is likely to be gibberish, except that in the case of the mental patient the interviewer, if he be a symbol-minded depth psychologist, will tend to see it only in terms of unconscious manifestations, while for the patient these communications may be a good way of keeping his interviewer happy by means of the gentle art of saying nothing by saying something. Similarly, an analysis in terms of "cognitive impairment" or "irrationality" ignores the necessary consideration of *context* in the evaluation of such communications.[4] Let us once more point to the fact that at the clinical end of the behavioral spectrum, "crazy" communication (behavior) is not necessarily the manifestation of a sick mind, but may be the only possible reaction to an absurd or untenable communication context.

3.234 The Symptom As Communication

Finally, there is a fourth response passenger *A* can use to defend himself against *B*'s loquacity: he can feign sleepiness, deafness, drunkenness, ignorance of English, or any other defect or inability that will render communication justifiably impossible. In all these cases, then, the message is the same, namely, "*I* would not mind talking to you, but something stronger than I, for which I cannot be blamed, prevents me." This invocation of powers or reasons beyond one's control still has a rub: *A* knows that he really is cheating. But the communicational "ploy" becomes perfect once a person has convinced *himself* that he is at the mercy of forces beyond his control and thereby has freed himself of both censure by

---

[4] In this regard, the reader is referred to a communicational analysis of the psychoanalytic concept of "transference," which can be seen as the only possible response to a most unusual situation. Cf. Jackson and Haley (*76*), which is also discussed in s. 7.5, example 2.

significant others as well as the pangs of his own conscience. This, however, is just a more complicated way of saying that he has a (psychoneurotic, psychosomatic, or psychotic) symptom. Margaret Mead, in describing the difference between American and Russian personalities, remarked that an American might use the excuse of having a headache to get out of going to a party but the Russian would actually *have* the headache. In psychiatry, Fromm-Reichmann, in a little-known paper, pointed out the use of catatonic symptoms as communication (*51*), and in 1954 Jackson indicated the utility of the patient's use of hysterical symptoms in communicating with his family (*67*). For extensive studies of the symptom as communication the reader is referred to Szasz (*151*) and Artiss (*3*).

This communicational definition of a symptom may seem to contain a moot assumption, namely that one can convince oneself in this way. Instead of the rather unconvincing argument that everyday clinical experience fully supports this assumption, we should like to mention McGinnies' experiments on "perceptual defense" (*102*). A subject is placed in front of a tachistoscope, a device by which words can be made visible for very brief periods of time in a small window. The subject's threshold is determined for a few trial words and he is then instructed to report to the experimenter whatever he sees or thinks he sees on each subsequent exposure. The list of test words is composed of both neutral and "critical," emotionally-toned words, e.g., rape, filth, whore. A comparison between the subject's performance with the neutral and with the critical words shows significantly higher thresholds of recognition for the latter, that is, he "sees" fewer of these words. But this means that in order to produce more failures with the socially tabooed words, the subject must first identify them as such and then somehow convince himself that he was unable to read them. Thus he spares himself the embarrassment of having to read them out loud to the experimenter. (In this regard, we should mention that, in general, psychological testing must consider the communicational context of these tests. There can hardly be any doubt, for instance, that it must make quite a difference to the subject and his performance whether he has to communicate with a shriveled old professor, a robot, or a beautiful blonde. In fact Rosenthal's recent careful investigations into experimenter bias (e.g., *130*) have confirmed that complex and highly effective though as yet unspecifiable communication transpires even in rigidly controlled experiments.)

Let us recapitulate. Communication theory conceives of a symptom as a nonverbal message: It is not I who does not (or does) want to do this, it is something outside my control, e.g., my nerves, my illness, my anxiety, my bad eyes, alcohol, my upbringing, the Communists, or my wife.

3.3

The Level Structure of Communication
(Content and Relationship)

A couple in conjoint marriage therapy related the following incident. The husband, while alone at home, received a long-distance call from a friend who said he would be in the area for a few days. The husband immediately invited the friend to stay at their home, knowing that his wife would also welcome this friend and that, therefore, she would have done the same thing. When his wife came home, however, a bitter marital quarrel arose over the husband's invitation to the friend. As the problem was explored in the therapy session, both the husband and wife agreed that to invite the friend was the most appropriate and natural thing to do. They were perplexed to find that on the one hand they agreed and yet "somehow" disagreed on what seemed to be the same issue.

3.31

In actual fact there were two issues involved in the dispute. One involved the appropriate course of action in a practical matter, that is, the invitation, and could be communicated digitally; the other concerned the relationship between the communicants—the question of who had the right to take initiative without consulting the other—and could not be so easily resolved digitally, for it presupposed the ability of the husband and wife to *talk about* their relationship. In their attempt to resolve their disagreement this couple committed a very common mistake in their communication: they disagreed on the metacommunicational (relationship) level, but tried to resolve the disagreement on the content level, where it did not exist, which led them into pseudodisagreements. Another husband, also seen in conjoint therapy, managed to discover by himself and to state in his own words the difference between the content and the relationship levels. He and his wife had experienced many violent symmetrical escalations, usually based on the question of who was right regarding some trivial content matter. One day she was able to prove to him conclusively that he was factually wrong, and he replied, "Well, you may be right, but you are wrong *because you are arguing with me.*" Any psychotherapist is familiar with these confusions between the content and relationship aspects of an issue, especially in marital communication, and with the enormous difficulty of diminishing the confusion. While to the therapist the monotonous redundancy of pseudodisagreements between husbands and wives becomes evident fairly quickly, the protagonists usually see every one of them in isolation and as totally new, simply because the practical, objective issues involved may be drawn from a wide range of activities, from TV programs to corn flakes to sex. This situation has been masterfully described by Koestler:

> Family relations pertain to a plane where the ordinary rules of judgment and conduct do not apply. They are a labyrinth of tensions, quarrels and reconciliations, whose logic is self-contradictory, whose ethics stem from a cozy jungle, and whose values and criteria are distorted like the curved space of a self-contained universe. It is a universe saturated with memories—*but memories from which no lessons are drawn; saturated with a past which provides no guidance to the future. For in this universe, after each crisis and reconciliation, time always starts afresh and history is always in the year zero.* (86, p. 218; italics ours)

3.32

The phenomenon of disagreement provides a good frame of reference for the study of disturbances of communication due to confusion between content and relationship. Disagreement can arise on the content or the relationship level, and the two forms are contingent upon each other. For instance, disagreement over the truth value of the statement "Uranium has 92 electrons" can apparently be settled only by recourse to objective evidence, e.g., a textbook of chemistry, for this evidence not only proves that the uranium atom does indeed have 92 electrons, but that one of the contestants was right and the other wrong. Of these two results, the first resolves the disagreement on the content level, and the other creates a relationship problem. Now, quite obviously, to resolve this new problem the two individuals cannot continue to talk about atoms; they must begin to talk about themselves and their relationship. To do this they must achieve a definition of their relationship as symmetrical or complementary: for example the one who was wrong may admire the other for his superior knowledge, or resent his superiority and resolve to be one-up on him at the next possible occasion in order to re-establish equality.[5] Of course, if he could not wait until that next occasion, he could use the "to hell with logic" approach and try to be one-up by claiming that the figure 92 must be a misprint, or that he has a scientist friend who has just shown that the number of electrons is really quite meaningless, etc. A fine example of this technique is supplied by Russian and Chinese party ideologists with their hair-splitting interpretations of what Marx "really" meant in order to show what bad Marxists the others are. In such struggles words may eventually lose their last vestige of content meaning and become exclusively the tools of "one-upmanship," [6] as stated with admirable clarity by Humpty Dumpty:

[5] Either one of these possibilities could be appropriate or inappropriate, "good" or "bad," depending on the relationship involved.
[6] S. Potter, who may be credited with introducing the term, provides many insightful and amusing illustrations of this point (116).

"I don't know what you mean by 'glory,'" Alice said.

Humpty Dumpty smiled contemptuously. "Of course you don't—till I tell you. I meant 'there's a nice knock-down argument for you!'"

"But 'glory' doesn't mean 'a nice knock-down argument,'" Alice objected.

"When *I* use a word," Humpty Dumpty said, in a rather scornful tone, "it means just what I choose it to mean—neither more nor less."

"The question is," said Alice, "whether you *can* make words mean so many different things."

"The question is," said Humpty Dumpty, *"which is to be master*—that's all." (Last italics ours)

This, then, is merely another way of saying that, in the face of their disagreement the two individuals have to define their relationship as either complementary or symmetrical.

3.33—DEFINITION OF SELF AND OTHER

Now suppose that the same statement about uranium is made by one physicist to another. A very different kind of interaction may arise from this, for most probably the other's response will be anger, hurt, or sarcasm—"I know you think I am a complete idiot, but I did go to school for a few years . . ." or the like. What is different in this interaction is the fact that here there is no disagreement on the content level. The truth value of the statement is not contested; in fact, the statement actually conveys no information since what it asserts on the content level is known to both partners anyway. It is this fact—the agreement on the content level —that clearly refers the disagreement to the relationship level, in other words, to the metacommunicational realm. There, however, disagreement amounts to something that is pragmatically far more important than disagreement on the content level. As we have seen, on the relationship level people do not communicate about facts outside their relationship, but offer each other definitions of that relationship and, by implication, of themselves.[7] As already mentioned in s. 2.3, these definitions have their own hierarchy of complexity. Thus, to take an arbitrary starting point, person *P* may offer the other, *O*, a definition of self. *P* may do this in one or another of many possible ways, but whatever and however he may communicate on the content level, the prototype of his metacommunication will be "This is how I see myself." [8] It is in the nature of human communication that there are now three possible responses by *O* to *P*'s self-definition, and all three of them are of great importance for the pragmatics of human communication.

3.331 Confirmation

O can accept (confirm) *P*'s definition of self. As far as we can see, this confirmation of *P*'s view of himself by *O* is probably the greatest single factor ensuring mental development and stability that has so far emerged from our study of communication. Surprising as it may seem, without this self-confirming effect human communication would hardly have evolved beyond the very limited boundaries of the interchanges indispensable for protection and survival; there would be no reason for communication for the mere sake of communication. Yet everyday experience leaves no doubt that a large portion of our communications are devoted precisely to this purpose. The vast gamut of emotions that individuals feel for each other—from love to hate—would probably hardly exist, and we would live in a world devoid of anything except the most utilitarian endeavors, a world devoid of beauty, poetry, play, and humor. It seems that, quite apart from the mere exchange of

---

[7] Cf. Cumming:

> I have proposed that much of what Langer has spoken of as "the sheer expression of ideas" or symbolic activity for its own sake is, in normal people, the function of constantly rebuilding the self concept, of offering this self concept to others for ratification, and of accepting or rejecting the self-conceptual offerings of others.
>
> I have assumed, furthermore, that the self concept is continually to be rebuilt if we are to exist as people and not as objects, and in the main the self concept is rebuilt in communicative activity. (35, p. 113)

[8] Actually, this should read "This is how I see myself *in relation to you in this situation,*" but for the sake of simplicity we will in the following omit the italicized part.

information, man *has* to communicate with others for the sake of his own awareness of self, and experimental verification of this intuitive assumption is increasingly being supplied by research on sensory deprivation, showing that man is unable to maintain his emotional stability for prolonged periods in communication with himself only. We feel that what the existentialists refer to as the *encounter* belongs here, as well as any other form of increased awareness of self that comes about as the result of working out a relationship with another individual. "In human society," writes Martin Buber,

> at all its levels, persons confirm one another in a practical way, to some extent or other, in their personal qualities and capacities, and a society may be termed human in the measure to which its members confirm one another. . . .
>
> The basis of man's life with man is twofold, and it is one—the wish of every man to be confirmed as what he is, even as what he can become, by men; and the innate capacity of man to confirm his fellowmen in this way. That this capacity lies so immeasurably fallow constitutes the real weakness and questionableness of the human race: actual humanity exists only where this capacity unfolds. (*32*, pp. 101–2)

3.332 *Rejection*

The second possible response of *O* in the face of *P*'s definition of himself is to reject it. Rejection, however, no matter how painful, presupposes at least limited recognition of what is being rejected and, therefore, does not necessarily negate the reality of *P*'s view of himself. In fact, certain forms of rejection may even be constructive, as for instance a psychiatrist's refusal to accept a patient's definition of self in the transference situation in which the patient may typically try to impose his "relationship game" on the therapist. The reader is here referred to two authors who within their own conceptual frameworks have written extensively on this subject, Berne (*23, 24*) and Haley (*60*).

3.333 Disconfirmation

The third possibility is probably the most important one, from both the pragmatic and the psychopathological viewpoints. It is the phenomenon of disconfirmation, which, as we will see, is quite different from that of outright rejection of the other's definition of self. We are drawing here partly on the material presented by Laing (*88*) of the Tavistock Institute of Human Relations in London, in addition to our own findings in the field of schizophrenic communication. Laing quotes William James, who once wrote: "No more fiendish punishment could be devised, even were such a thing physically possible, than that one should be turned loose in society and remain absolutely unnoticed by all the members thereof" (*88*, p. 89). There can be little doubt that such a situation would lead to "loss of self," which is but a translation of the term "alienation." Disconfirmation, as we find it in pathological communication, is no longer concerned with the truth or falsity—if there be such criteria—of P's definition of himself, but rather negates the reality of P as the source of such a definition. In other words, while rejection amounts to the message "You are wrong," disconfirmation says in effect "You do not exist." Or, to put it in more rigorous terms, if confirmation and rejection of the other's self were equated, in formal logic, to the concepts of truth and falsity, respectively, then disconfirmation would correspond to the concept of undecidability, which, as is known, is of a different logical order.[9]

---

[9] Sometimes—admittedly rarely—literal undecidability may play an outstanding part in a relationship, as can be seen from the following transcript from a conjoint therapy session. The couple concerned had sought help because their sometimes violent quarrels left them deeply worried about their mutual failure as spouses. They had been married for twenty-one years. The husband was an eminently successful business man. At the beginning of this interchange, the wife had just remarked that in all these years she had never known where she stood with him.

> Psychiatrist: So what you are saying is that you don't get the clues from your husband that you need to know if you are performing well.
>
> Wife: No.
>
> Psychiatrist: Does Dan criticize you when you deserve criticism—I mean, positive or negative?
>
> Husband: Rarely do I criticize her . . .

To quote Laing:

> The characteristic family pattern that has emerged from the study of families of schizophrenics does not so much involve a child who is subject to outright neglect or even to obvious trauma, but a child whose authenticity has been subjected to subtle, but persistent, mutilation, often quite unwittingly. (p. 91)

> The ultimate of this is . . . when no matter how [a person] feels or how he acts, no matter what meaning he gives his situation, his feelings are denuded of validity, his acts are stripped of their motives, intentions and consequences, the situation is robbed of its meaning for him, so that he is totally mystified and alienated. (pp. 135–6)

And now a specific example that has been published in greater detail elsewhere (78). It is taken from a conjoint psychotherapy

---

Wife	(overlapping): Rarely does he criticize.
Psychiatrist:	Well, how—how do you know . . .
Wife	(interrupting): He compliments you. (Short laugh.) You see, that is the befuddling thing . . . Suppose I cook something and I burn it—well, he says it's really "very, very nice." Then, if I make something that is extra nice—well, it is "very, very nice." I told him I don't know whether something is nice—I don't know whether he is criticizing me or complimenting me. Because he thinks that by complimenting me he can compliment me into doing better, and when I deserve a compliment, he—he is always complimenting me—that's right, . . . so that I lose the value of the compliment.
Psychiatrist:	So you really don't know where you stand with someone who always compliments . . .
Wife	(interrupting): No, I don't know whether he is criticizing me or really sincerely complimenting me.

What makes this example so interesting is that although both spouses are evidently fully aware of the pattern they are caught in, this awareness does not help them in the least to do something about it.

session with an entire family composed of the parents, their twenty-five-year-old son Dave (who was first officially diagnosed schizophrenic while in military service at age twenty and had afterward lived at home until about a year before this interview, when he had been hospitalized), and their eighteen-year-old son, Charles. When the discussion focused on how the patient's weekend visits strained the family, the psychiatrist pointed out that it seemed as if Dave were being asked to bear the intolerable burden of the whole family's solicitude. Dave thus became the sole indicator of how well or poorly things went over the weekend. Surprisingly, the patient immediately took up this point:

1. Dave: Well, I feel that sometimes my parents, and Charles also, are very sensitive to how I might feel, maybe overly sensitive about how I feel, 'cause I don't—I don't feel I raise the roof when I go home, or . . .

2. Mother: Mhm. Dave, you haven't been like that either since you had your car, it's just—but *before* you did.

3. Dave: Well, I know I did . . .

4. Mother (overlapping): Yeah, but even —yeah, lately, the last twice since you had your car.

5. Dave: Yeah, OK, anyhow, ah (sigh), that's—ah, I wish I didn't have to be that way, I guess, it'd be nice if I could enjoy myself or somethin' . . . (sighs; pause)

6. Psychiatrist: You know, you change your story in mid-stream when

		your mother is nice to you. Which . . . is understandable, but in your position you just can't afford to do it.
7.	Dave	(overlapping): Mhm.
8.	Psychiatrist:	It makes you kookier. Then you don't even know what you're thinking.
9.	Mother:	What did he change?
10.	Psychiatrist:	Well, I *can't* read his mind so I don't know what he was going to say precisely—I have a general idea, I think, just from experience . . .
11.	Dave	(interrupting): Well, it's just, just the story that I'm the sick one in the family and so this gives everyone else a—a chance to be a good Joe and pick up Dave's spirits *whether Dave's spirits are necessarily down or not.* That's what it amounts to sometimes, I feel. In other words, I can't be anything but myself, and *if people don't like me the way they am—ah, the way I am*—then I appreciate when they—tell me or something, is what it amounts to. (*78*, p. 89)

The patient's slip of the tongue illuminates his dilemma: he says "I can't be anything but myself," but the question remains, is myself "I" or "they"? Simply to call this an evidence of "weak ego boundaries" or the like ignores the interactional fact of disconfirmation just presented, not only in Dave's report on his weekend visits but by the mother's immediate disconfirmation *in the present example* (statements 1–5) of the validity of Dave's impression. In the light of both present and reported disconfirmation of his self, the patient's slip emerges in a new aspect.

3.34—LEVELS OF INTERPERSONAL PERCEPTION

At last we are ready to return to the hierarchy of messages that is found when analyzing communications on the relationship level. We have seen that P's definition of self ("This is how I see myself . . .") can be met with one of three possible responses by O: confirmation, rejection, or disconfirmation. (This classification is, of course, virtually the same as the one used in sections 3.231–3.233). Now, these three responses have one common denominator, i.e., through any one of them O communicates "This is how I am seeing you." [10]

There is, then, in the discourse on the metacommunicational level, a message from P to $O:$ "This is how I see myself." It is followed by a message from O to $P:$ "This is how I am seeing you." To this message P will respond by a message asserting, among other things, "This is how I see you seeing me," and O in turn by the message "This is how I see you seeing me seeing you." As already suggested, this regress is theoretically infinite, while for practical purposes it must be assumed that one cannot deal with messages of a higher order of abstraction than the last one mentioned. Now, it should be noted that any one of these messages can be subjected by the recipient to the same confirmation, rejection, or disconfirmation described above, and that the same holds, of course, for O's definition of self and the ensuing simultaneous metacommunicational discourse with P. This leads to communicational contexts whose complexity easily staggers the imagination and yet which have very specific pragmatic consequences.

---

[10] At first sight this formula may not seem to fit the concept of disconfirmation as just described. However, in ultimate analysis even the message "For me you do not exist as an entity of your own" amounts to "This is how I am seeing you: you do not exist." The fact that this is paradoxical does not mean it cannot occur, as will be suggested in detail in Chapter 6.

Not very much is as yet known about these consequences, but very promising research in this area is being carried out by Laing, Phillipson and Lee, who have given us permission to quote here some of their results from an unpublished paper (*93*).[11] Disconfirmation of self by the other is mainly the result of a peculiar unawareness of interpersonal perceptions, called imperviousness and defined by Lee as follows:

> What we are concerned with is the aspect of awareness and unawareness. For smooth, adequate interaction to occur, each party must register the other's point of view. Since interpersonal perception goes on on many levels, so, too, can imperviousness go on on many levels. For there exists for each level of perception a comparable and analogous level of possible imperception or imperviousness. Where a lack of accurate awareness, or imperviousness, exists, the parties in a dyad relate about pseudo-issues. . . . They attain an assumed harmony which does not exist, or argue over assumed disagreements that similarly do not exist. It is this which I find to be the characteristic situation within the schizophrenic's family: they are constantly building harmonious relationships on the shifting sands of pseudo-agreements or else have violent arguments on the basis of pseudo-disagreements.

Lee then goes on to show that imperviousness can exist on the first level of the hierarchy, that is, to *P*'s message "This is how I see myself" *O* responds, "This is how I see you," in a way which is not congruent with *P*'s self-definition. *P* may then conclude that *O*

---

[11] Too recently to be included in this presentation, the above authors have published their findings on this subject in book form: R. D. Laing, H. Phillipson, and A. R. Lee, *Interpersonal Perception; A Theory and Method of Research.* New York, Springer Publishing Company, 1966. The full theoretical framework and an imaginative method of quantification are elaborated in this highly original work.

does not understand (or appreciate, or love) him while O, on the other hand, may assume that P feels understood (or appreciated, or loved) by him (O). In this case, O does not disagree with P, but ignores or misinterprets P's message, and thus is consistent with our definition of disconfirmation. A second-level imperviousness can be said to exist when P does not register that his message has not gotten through to O; that is, P does not convey accurately "This is how I see you seeing [in this case, misunderstanding] me." At this level, then, imperviousness to imperviousness occurs.

From their study of families with a schizophrenic member, Lee describes an important conclusion about the pragmatics of this kind of communication:

> The typical pattern is that the parental imperviousness exists on level No. 1, while the schizophrenic's imperviousness exists on level No. 2. That is, typically the parent fails to register his child's view, while the child does not register that his view has not been (and perhaps cannot be) registered.
>
> Most often the parent appears to remain impervious to the child's view because he feels it is uncomplimentary to him, or because it does not fit his value system. That is, the parent insists that the child does believe what he (the parent) feels the child "should" believe. The child, in turn, fails to recognize this. He believes that his message has gotten through and has been understood, and acts accordingly. In such a situation he is bound to be confused by the subsequent interaction. He feels as if he continuously runs into an invisible solid glass wall. This results in his experiencing a continuous sense of mystification which leads to dismay and eventually to despair. Ultimately he feels that life just does not make any sense.
>
> Such a schizophrenic child, during the course of therapy, finally realized this state of affairs, and stated his dilemma this way: "Whenever I disagree with my

mother she seems to say to herself, 'Oh, I know what you are saying out loud, but I know that isn't what you *really* think inside,' and then she proceeds to forget what I have just said."

A rich variety of clinical illustrations of imperviousness at the relationship level as just described can be found in Laing and Esterson (*90*). One example is given in Figure 1.

FIGURE 1
"IMPERVIOUSNESS" IN A SCHIZOPHRENIC FAMILY [12]

SOME ATTRIBUTIONS MADE BY PARENTS ABOUT PATIENT	PATIENT'S SELF-ATTRIBUTIONS
Always happy	Often depressed and frightened
Her real self is vivacious and cheerful	Kept up a front
No disharmony in family	Disharmony so complete that impossible to tell her parents anything
They have never kept her on a string	By sarcasm, prayer, ridicule, attempted to govern her life in all important respects
Has a mind of her own	True in a sense, but still too terrified of father to tell him her real feelings, still feels controlled by him

3.4

The Punctuation of the Sequence of Events

> He laughed because he thought that they could not hit him—he did not imagine that they were practicing how to miss him.— Brecht

A few examples of the potential complications inherent in this phenomenon have already been presented in the preceding chapter. They show that unresolved discrepancies in the punctuation of communicational sequences can lead directly into interactional im-

---

[12] Adapted from Laing and Esterson (*90*, p. 188).

passes in which eventually the mutual charges of madness or badness are proffered.

Discrepancies in the punctuation of sequences of events occur, of course, in all those cases in which at least one of the communicants does not possess the same amount of information as the other but does not know this. A simple example of such a sequence would be the following: *P* writes a letter to *O* proposing a joint venture and inviting *O*'s participation. *O* replies in the affirmative, but the letter is lost in the mail. After a while *P* concludes that *O* is ignoring his invitation and resolves to disregard him in turn. *O,* on the other hand, feels offended that his answer is ignored and also decides not to contact *P* any more. From this point their silent feud may last forever, unless they decide to investigate what happened to their communications, that is, unless they begin to metacommunicate. Only then will they find out that *P* did not know *O* had replied, while *O* did not know that his reply had never reached *P*. As can be seen, in this example a fortuitous outside event interfered with the congruency of punctuation.

One of the authors experienced this phenomenon of discrepant punctuation when he once applied for an assistantship with a psychiatric research institute. At the appointed hour he reported to the director's office for his interview and the following conversation took place with the receptionist:

Visitor:	Good afternoon, I have an appointment with Dr. H. My name is Watzlawick [VAHT-sla-vick].
Receptionist:	I did not say it was.
Visitor	(taken aback and somewhat annoyed): But I am telling you it *is.*
Receptionist	(bewildered): Why then did you say it wasn't?
Visitor:	But I *said* it was!

At this point the visitor was "certain" that he was being made the object of some incomprehensible but disrespectful joke, while, as it turned out, the receptionist had by then decided that the visitor must be a new psychotic patient of Dr. H's. Eventually it became clear that instead of "My name is Watzlawick" the receptionist had understood "My name is *not* Slavic," which, indeed, she had never said it was. It is interesting to see how even in this brief interchange in a rather impersonal context the discrepant punctuation, here due to a verbal misunderstanding, immediately led to mutual assumptions of badness and madness.

3.42

Generally speaking, it is gratuitous to assume not only that the other has the same amount of information as oneself but that the other must draw the same conclusions from this information. Communication experts have estimated that a person receives ten thousand sensory impressions (exteroceptive and proprioceptive) per second. Obviously, then, a drastic selection process is necessary to prevent the higher brain centers from being swamped by irrelevant information. But the decision about what is essential and what is irrelevant apparently varies from individual to individual and seems to be determined by criteria which are largely outside individual awareness. In all probability, reality is what we make it or, in Hamlet's words, ". . . there is nothing either good or bad, but thinking makes it so." We can only speculate that at the root of these punctuation conflicts there lies the firmly established and usually unquestioned conviction that there is only *one* reality, the world as *I* see it, and that any view that differs from mine must be due to the other's irrationality or ill will. So much for our speculations. What we can *observe* in virtually all these cases of pathological communication is that they are vicious circles that cannot be broken unless and until communication itself becomes the subject of communication, in other words, until the communicants are able to metacommunicate.[13] But to do this they have to step

[13] Such metacommunication need not necessarily be verbal, nor is it to be loosely equated with "insight" (cf. s. 7.32).

outside the circle, and this necessity to step outside a given contingency in order to resolve it will be a recurrent theme in later parts of this book.

3.43—CAUSE AND EFFECT

We typically observe in these cases of discrepant punctuation a conflict about what is cause and what is effect, when in actual fact neither of these concepts is applicable because of the circularity of the ongoing interaction. To return once more to Joad's example (s. 2.42), we can see that nation *A* arms *because* it feels threatened by nation *B* (that is, *A* sees its own behavior as the effect of *B*'s), while nation *B* calls *A*'s armaments the *cause* of its own "defensive" measures. Richardson points to essentially the same problem as he describes the arms race that began to escalate about 1912:

> The war-like preparations of the Entente and of the Alliance were both increasing. The usual explanation was then, and perhaps still is, that the motives of the two sides were quite different, for we were only doing what was right, proper and necessary for our own defense, whilst they were disturbing the peace by indulging in wild schemes and extravagant ambitions. There are several distinct contrasts in that omnibus statement. Firstly that their conduct was morally bad, ours morally good. About so national a dispute it would be difficult to say anything that the world as a whole would accept. But there is some other alleged contrast as to which there is some hope of general agreement. It was asserted in the years 1912–14 *that their motives were fixed and independent of our behaviour whereas our moitves were a response to their behaviour and were varied accordingly.* (*125*, p. 1244; italics ours)

From the pragmatic viewpoint there is little if any difference between the interactions of nations or of individuals once discrepant punctuation has led to different views of reality, including the

nature of the relationship, and thus into international or interpersonal conflict. The following example shows the same pattern
at work on the interpersonal level:

Husband (to therapist): From long experience I know that if I want peace at
home I must not interfere with the
way she wants things done.

Wife: That is *not* true—I wish you
showed a little more initiative and
did decide at least something every
once in a while, because . . .

Husband (interrupting): You'd never let me
do this!

Wife: I'd gladly let you—only if I do,
nothing ever happens, and then *I*
have to do everything at the last
moment.

Husband (to therapist): Can you see? Things
can't be taken care of if and when
they come up—they have to be
planned and organized a week ahead.

Wife (angrily): Give me *one* example in
the last few years when you did do
something.

Husband: I guess I can't—because it is better
for everybody, including the children, if I let you have your own
way. I found this out very early in
our marriage.

Wife: You have never behaved differently, right from the start you
didn't—you have always left everything up to me!

Husband: For heaven's sake, now listen to
this (pause, then to therapist)—I

97

> guess what she is talking about now
> is that I would always ask her what
> *she* wanted—like "where would
> you like to go tonight?" or "what
> would you like to do over the
> weekend?" and instead of seeing
> that I wanted to be nice to her,
> she would get mad at me . . .

Wife (to therapist): Yeah, what he still
doesn't understand is that if you
get this *"anything*-you-want-dear-is-
alright-with-me" stuff month after
month, you begin to feel that *nothing* you want matters to him. . . .

The same mechanism is contained in an example reported by
Laing and Esterson, involving a mother and her schizophrenic
daughter. Shortly before her hospitalization the daughter had made
a very ineffectual physical attack on her mother.

Daughter: Well, why did I attack you? Perhaps I was looking for something,
something I lacked—affection,
maybe it was greed for affection.

Mother: You wouldn't have any of that.
You always think it's soppy.

Daughter: Well, when did you offer it to me?

Mother: Well, for instance if I was to want
to kiss you, you'd say, "Don't be
soppy."

Daughter: *But I've never known you let me
kiss you.* (*90*, pp. 20–21)

3.44

This leads to the important concept of the *self-fulfilling prophecy*
which, from the interactional viewpoint, is perhaps the most interesting phenomenon in the area of punctuation. A self-fulfilling

prophecy may be regarded as the communicational equivalent of "begging the question." It is behavior that brings about in others the reaction to which the behavior would be an appropriate reaction. For instance, a person who acts on the premise that "nobody likes me" will behave in a distrustful, defensive, or aggressive manner to which others are likely to react unsympathetically, thus bearing out his original premise. For the purposes of the pragmatics of human communication, it is again quite irrelevant to ask *why* a person should have such a premise, how it came about, and how unconscious he may be of it. Pragmatically we can observe that this individual's interpersonal behavior shows this kind of redundancy, and that it has a complementary effect on others, forcing them into certain specific attitudes. What is typical about the sequence and makes it a problem of punctuation is that the individual concerned conceives of himself only as reacting to, but not as provoking, those attitudes.

3.5

Errors in the "Translation" Between Analogic and Digital Material

In trying to describe these errors, an anecdote from Daniele Varé's novel *The Gate of Happy Sparrows* comes to mind. The hero, a European living in Peking during the twenties, receives lessons in Mandarin script from a Chinese professor and is asked to translate a sentence composed of three characters that he correctly deciphers as the signs for "rotundity," "sitting," and "water." In his attempt to combine these concepts into an affirmative statement (into digital language, as we would say) he decides on "Somebody is taking a sitz bath," much to the disdain of the distinguished professor, for the sentence is a particularly poetic reference to a sunset at sea.

3.51

Like Chinese writing, analogic message material, as already mentioned, lacks many of the elements that comprise the morphology and syntax of digital language. Thus, in translating analogic into digital messages, these elements have to be supplied and inserted by the translator, just as in dream interpretation digital structure has to be introduced more or less intuitively into the kaleidoscopic imagery of the dream.

Analogic message material, as we have seen, is highly antithetical; it lends itself to very different and often quite incompatible digital interpretations. Thus not only is it difficult for the sender to verbalize his own analogic communications, but if interpersonal controversy arises over the meaning of a particular piece of analogic communication, either partner is likely to introduce, in the process of translation into the digital mode, the kind of digitalization in keeping with *his* view of the nature of the relationship. The bringing of a gift, for instance, is undoubtedly a piece of analogic communication. However, depending on the recipient's view of his relationship with the giver, he can see it as a token of affection, a bribe, or a restitution. Many a husband is dismayed to find himself suspected of an as yet unconfessed guilt if he breaks the rules of their marriage "game" by spontaneously presenting his wife with a bunch of flowers.

What is the digital meaning of growing pale, trembling, sweating, and stammering when displayed by a person under interrogation? It may be the ultimate proof of his guilt, or it may merely be the behavior of an innocent person going through the nightmarish experience of being suspected of a crime and realizing that his fear may be interpreted as guilt. Psychotherapy is undoubtedly concerned with the correct and the corrective digitalization of the analogic; in fact, the success or failure of any interpretation will depend both on the therapist's ability to translate from the one mode to the other and on the patient's readiness to exchange his own digitalization for more appropriate and less distressing ones. For discussion of these problems in schizophrenic communication, doctor-patient relations, and a wide variety of social and cultural phenomena, see Rioch (*127*, *128*).

Even where the translation appears to be adequate, digital

communication on the *relationship* level may remain curiously unconvincing. This fact is caricatured in the following "Peanuts" cartoon:

© *United Feature Syndicate, Inc. 1963*

3.52

In an unpublished report, Bateson hypothesizes that another of the basic mistakes made when translating between the two modes of communication is the assumption that an analogic message is by nature assertive or denotative, just as digital messages are. There is, however, good reason to believe that this is not so. He writes:

> When one octopus or one nation puts on a threatening gesture, the other might conclude "he is strong" or "he will fight," but this was not in the original message. Indeed, the message itself is non-indicative and may be better regarded as analogous to a *proposal* or a *question* in the digital world.

In this connection it should be remembered that all analogic messages are *invocations of relationship,* and that they are therefore proposals regarding the future rules of the relationship, to use another of Bateson's definitions. By my behavior, Bateson suggests, I can mention or propose love, hate, combat, etc., but it is up to you to attribute positive or negative future truth value to my proposals. This, needless to say, is the source of countless relationship conflicts.

3.53

Digital language, as explained in the preceding chapter, has a logical syntax and is therefore eminently suited for communication on the content level. But in translating analogic into digital material, logical truth functions must be introduced, which are absent in the analogic mode. This absence becomes most conspicuous in the case of negation, where it amounts to the lack of the digital "not." In other words, while it is simple to convey the analogic message "I shall attack you," it is extremely difficult to signal "I will *not* attack you," just as it is difficult if not impossible to introduce negatives into analogue computers.

In Koestler's novel *Arrival and Departure,* the hero, a young man who escaped from his Nazi-occupied homeland and whose face has been disfigured by torture, is in love with a beautiful girl. He has no hope that she will reciprocate his feelings, and all he wants is to be with her and stroke her hair. She resists these innocent advances, thereby arousing both his desperation and his passion, until he overpowers her.

> She lay turned to the wall, her head in a strangely twisted position, like a doll's head with a broken neck. And now at last he could caress her hair, gently, soothingly, as he had always meant to. Then he realized that she was crying, her shoulders shaking in dry, soundless sobs. He went on fondling her hair and shoulders and muttered:
> "You see, you wouldn't listen to me."
> She suddenly lay rigid, interrupting her sobbing:
> "What did you say?"
> "I said all I wanted was that you shouldn't go away and that you should allow me to stroke your hair and to give you iced drinks . . . Really, that was all I meant."
> Her shoulders shook in a slightly hysterical laughter. "By God, you are the biggest fool I have ever seen."

"Are you angry with me? Don't. I didn't mean to."

She drew her knees up, shrinking away from him, curling up against the wall. "Leave me alone. Please go away and leave me quiet for a while." She cried again, more quietly this time. He slid down from the couch, squatting on the carpet as before, but he got hold of one of her hands which lay limply on the cushion. It was a lifeless, humid hand, hot with fever.

"You know," he said, encouraged because she didn't withdraw her hand, "when I was a child we had a black kitten which I always wanted to play with, but she was too frightened and always ran away. One day with all sorts of cunning I got her into the nursery, but she hid under the cupboard and wouldn't come out. So I dragged the cupboard away from the wall, and got more and more angry because she wouldn't let me fondle her, and then she hid under the table and I upset the table and broke two pictures on the wall and turned the whole room upside down and chased the kitten with a chair all around the room. Then my mother came in and asked me what I was doing, and I told her I only wanted to fondle that stupid kitten, and I got a terrible thrashing. But I had told the truth . . ." (*85*, pp. 40–41)

Here the desperation of being rejected and unable to prove that he does *not* mean to harm leads to violence.

3.531

Now if, as Bateson did, one watches animal behavior for such contingencies, one finds that the only solution to this problem of signaling negation lies first in demonstrating or proposing the action to be denied, and then in not carrying it to its conclusion. This interesting and only apparently "irrational" behavior can be observed not only in animal interaction but on the human level as well.

We have observed a very interesting communication pattern for

the establishment of trust relationships between humans and bottle-
nosed porpoises. While this may be a ritual developed "privately"
by only two of the animals, it still provides an excellent example
for the analogic communication of "not." The animals had obviously concluded that the hand is one of the most important and
vulnerable parts of the human body. Each would seek to establish
contact with a stranger by taking the human's hand into his mouth
and gently squeezing it between his jaws, which have sharp teeth
and are powerful enough to bite the hand off cleanly. If the
human would submit to this, the dolphin seemed to accept it as
a message of complete trust. His next move was to reciprocate by
placing the forward ventral portion of his body (*his* most vulnerable part, roughly equivalent in location to the human throat)
upon the human's hand, leg, or foot, thereby signaling his trust in
the friendly intentions of the human. This procedure is, however,
obviously fraught with possible misinterpretation at every step.

On a poetic level, an essentially similar form of relationship,
here between man and the transcendental, is expressed in the
opening lines of Rilke's first Duino Elegy, where beauty is experienced as the negation of inherent, ever possible destruction:

> Who, if I cried would hear me among the angelic
> orders? And even if one of them suddenly
> pressed me against his heart, I should fade in the strength of his
> stronger existence. For Beauty's nothing
> but the beginning of Terror we are still just able to bear,
> and *we adore it so because it serenely*
> *disdains to destroy us.* (*126*, p. 21; italics ours)

3.532

As the dolphin example suggests, *ritual* may be the intermediary
process between analogic and digital communication, simulating
the message material but in a repetitive and stylized manner that
hangs between analogue and symbol. Thus we can observe that
animals such as cats routinely establish a complementary but non-
violent relationship through the following ritual. The "one-down"
animal (usually the younger or the one outside his own territory)

throws himself on his back, exposing his jugular vein, which is taken in the jaw of the other cat with impunity. This method of establishing an "I shall not attack you" relationship seems to be understood by both; what is even more interesting, this coding has been seen to be successful in interspecies (e.g., cats and dogs) communication as well. Analogic materials are often formalized in the rituals of human societies, and as such material is canonized it approaches symbolic or digital communication, revealing a curious overlap.

On a pathological plane, the same mechanism seems to be operative in sexual masochism. It would appear that the message "I shall *not* destroy you" is only convincing (and only allays, at least temporarily, the masochist's deep fear of terrible punishment) by means of the analogic denial inherent in the ritual of humiliation and punishment that he knows will eventually but certainly stop short of the imagined dread.

3·54

Those familiar with symbolic logic may by now appreciate that it is probably not necessary to prove the absence of *all* logical truth functions in analogic material but only a critical few. The logical truth function *alternation* (nonexclusive *or*), construed to mean "either one or both," can be seen to be similarly absent from analogic language. While it is easy to convey the meaning "one or the other or both will do" in digital language, it is not immediately obvious how this logical relation could be inserted into analogic material; indeed, it probably cannot. Symbolic logicians (e.g., *119*, pp. 9–12) have pointed out that to represent all the major truth functions (negation, conjunction, alternation, implication, and equivalence), two—negation and alternation (or, similarly, negation and conjunction)—are sufficient and, of the five, necessary to represent the remaining three. According to this reasoning, although we know almost nothing specific about the pragmatic importance of the absence of the other truth functions in analogic material, we can conclude that since these are but variations of "not" and "or" they will not escape similar difficulties of translation.

3.55

Bateson and Jackson have hypothesized the importance of analogic versus digital coding in hysterical symptom formation. According to them, a converse process from those we have been discussing takes place, a retranslation, as it were, from already digitalized message material back to the analogic mode:

> A converse—but much more complex—problem arises in regard to hysteria. No doubt this word covers a wide range of formal patterns, but it would appear that at least some cases involve errors of translation from the digital to the analogic. Stripping the digital material of its logical type markers leads to erroneous symptom formation. The verbal "headache" which was invented as a conventional excuse for not performing some task may become subjectively real and be endowed with real magnitudes in the pain dimension. (*19*, p. 282)

If we bear in mind that the first consequence of a breakdown in communication is usually a partial loss of the ability to metacommunicate digitally about the contingencies of the relationship, this "return to the analogic" appears as a plausible compromise solution.[14] The symbolic nature of conversion symptoms and, generally, their affinity with dream symbolism has been realized since the days of Liébault, Bernheim, and Charcot. And what is a sym-

---

[14] Again, there is little difference between the behavior of individuals and nations. When serious tension arises between two countries the customary step is to break off diplomatic relations, and consequently to resort to analogic communications like mobilizations, troop concentrations, and other analogic messages of this kind. What is so absurd about this procedure is that digital communication (diplomatic procedure) is broken off at the exact moment when it is more desperately needed than ever before. The "hot line" between Washington and Moscow may be prophylactic in this regard, even though its official rationale is only that of speeding up communications in times of crisis.

bol if not the representation, in real magnitudes, of something that is essentially an abstract function, an aspect of a relationship, as defined in s. 1.2? Throughout his work, C. G. Jung shows that the symbol appears where what we would call "digitalization" is not yet possible. But it seems to us that symbolization also takes place where digitalization is *no longer* possible and that this typically happens when a relationship threatens to grow into socially or morally tabooed areas such as incest.

3.6

Potential Pathologies of Symmetrical and Complementary Interaction

To avoid a frequent misunderstanding, it cannot be emphasized too strongly that symmetry and complementarity in communication are not in and by themselves "good" or "bad," "normal" or "abnormal," etc. The two concepts simply refer to two basic categories into which all communicational interchanges can be divided. Both have important functions, and from what is known about healthy relationships we may conclude that both must be present, although in mutual alternation or operation in different areas. As we will try to show, this means that each pattern can stabilize the other whenever a runaway occurs in one of them, and also that it is not only possible but necessary for two partners to relate symmetrically in some areas and complementarily in others.

3.61—SYMMETRICAL ESCALATION

Like any other pattern of communication, these two have their potential pathologies, which will first be described and then illustrated with clinical material. We have already suggested that in a symmetrical relationship there is an ever-present danger of competitiveness. As can be observed both in individuals and in nations, equality seems to be most reassuring if one manages to be just a little "more equal" than others, to use Orwell's famous phrase. This tendency accounts for the typical escalating quality of symmetrical interaction once its stability is lost and a so-called runaway occurs, e.g., quarrels and fights between individuals or wars between nations. In marital conflicts, for instance, it is easy to observe how the spouses go through an escalating pattern of frustration until they eventually stop from sheer physical or emotional exhaustion and maintain an uneasy truce until they have recovered enough for the next round. Pathology in symmetrical interaction is thus characterized by more or less open warfare, or *schism,* in Lidz's sense *(95)*.

In a healthy symmetrical relationship the partners are able to accept each other in their respective "suchness," which leads to mutual respect and trust in the other's respect and amounts to realistic, reciprocal confirmation of their selves. If and when a symmetrical relationship breaks down, we habitually observe the rejection rather than disconfirmation of the other's self.

3.62—RIGID COMPLEMENTARITY

In complementary relationships, there can be the same healthy, positive confirmation of each other. The pathologies of complementary relationships, on the other hand, are quite different, and tend to amount to disconfirmations rather than rejections of the other's self. They are, therefore, more important from a psycho-pathological point of view than the more or less open fights in symmetrical relations.

A typical problem arises in a complementary relationship when *P* demands that *O* confirm a definition of *P*'s self that is at variance with the way *O* sees *P*. This places *O* in a very peculiar dilemma: he must change his own definition of self into one that complements and thus supports *P*'s, for it is in the nature of complementary relationships that a definition of self can only be maintained by the partner's playing the specific complementary role. After all, there can be no mother without a child. But the patterns of a mother-child relationship change with time. The same pattern that is biologically and emotionally vital during an early phase of the infant's life becomes a severe handicap for his further development, if adequate change is not allowed to take place in the relationship. Thus, depending on the context, the same pattern may be highly self-confirming at one time and disconfirming at a later (or premature) stage in the natural history of a relationship. Because of their greater psychiatric flamboyance, the pathologies of complementary relationships have been given more attention in the literature than their symmetrical counterparts. Psychoanalysis refers to them as sadomasochistic and views them as the more or less fortuitous liaison of two individuals whose respective deviant character formations dovetail with each other. Among more recent and more interaction-oriented studies are Lidz's concept of marital skew (*95*), Scheflen's paper on the "gruesome twosome" (*136*), and the concept of "collusion" in Laing's sense (*88*). In these relationships we observe a growing sense of frustration and despair in one or both partners. Complaints of increasingly frightening feelings of self-estrangement and depersonalization, of abulia as well as compulsive acting-out are very frequently voiced by individuals who outside their homes (or otherwise in the absence of their partners) are perfectly capable of functioning satisfactorily, and who, when interviewed individually, may appear very well adjusted. This picture often changes dramatically when they are seen together with their "complements." The pathology of their *relationship* then becomes patent. Perhaps the most remarkable study of the pathology of complementary relationships is the famous paper, "La folie à deux," written by two French psychiatrists nearly a hundred years ago. How small a claim we have to the originality of our approach is, for instance, documented by the following passages from this paper. The authors first describe the patient and then continue:

> The above description belongs to the insane person, the agent who provokes the situation in "délire à deux." His associate is a much more complicated person to define and yet *careful research will teach one to recognize the laws which are obeyed by this second party in communicated insanity*. . . . Once the *tacit contract* that ties both lunatics is almost settled, the problem is not only to examine the influ-

ence of the insane on the supposedly sane man, *but also the opposite,* the influence of the rational on the deluded one, and to show how through mutual compromises the differences are eliminated. *(92,* p. 4; italics ours)

3.63

As already mentioned briefly at the beginning of this section, symmetrical and complementary relationship patterns can stabilize each other, and changes from the one to the other pattern and back again are important homeostatic mechanisms. This entails a therapeutic implication, namely that, at least in theory, therapeutic change can be brought about very directly by the introduction of symmetry into complementarity or vice versa during treatment. We say "at least in theory" advisedly, for it is only too well known how difficult it is in practice to induce any sort of change in rigidly defined systems whose participants, it seems, would "rather bear those ills we have than fly to others that we know not of."

3.64

To explain the foregoing, here are three exerpts from so-called Structured Family Interviews *(159).* All three of them are in reply to the interviewer's standard question to the spouses: "How, of all the millions of people in the world, did the two of you get together?" It should be made quite clear that the actual historic information contained in such an account is of only secondary importance, although it may be relatively accurate and may itself portray a symmetrical or complementary interaction which took place at that time. But it is not this historic information, often distorted by selective recall and wishful thinking, that is of interest here. Thus in considering the first couple one is struck by the symmetry of their interaction while responding to the interviewer's question. The story of their meeting, as told by them, is only the raw material, so to speak, which they manipulate in accordance with the rules of their game of "one-upmanship." For them, and for us, it is not important what *happened,* but rather *who has the right to say what to, and about, the other.* In other words, what is of the essence is not the content but the relationship aspect of their communication.

1) The first is an example of a typical symmetrical interchange.[15]

Transcript	*Comments*
Int: How, of all the millions of people in the world, did the two of you get together?	
H: We . . . both worked in the same place. My wife ran a comptometer, and I repaired comptometers, and . . .	H speaks first, offering a unilateral summary of the whole story, thereby defining his right to do so.
W: We worked in the same building.	W restates the same information in her own words, *not* simply agreeing with him, but instead establishing symmetry in regard to their discussion of this topic.
H: She worked for a firm which had a large installation, and I worked there most of the time because it was a large installation. And so this is where we met.	H adds no new information, but simply rephrases the same tautological sentence with which he began. Thus, he symmetrically matches her behavior of insisting on his right to give this information; on the relationship level they are sparring for the "last word." H attempts to achieve this by the finality of his second sentence.
W: We were introduced by some of the other girls up there. (Pause)	W does not let it drop; she modifies his statement, reasserting her right to participate equally in this discussion. Though this new twist is just as passive an interpretation as their "working in the same building" (in that neither is defined as having taken initiative), she establishes herself as "a little more equal" by referring to "the other girls," a group in which she was obviously the insider, not H. This pause ends the first cycle of symmetrical exchange with no closure.

[15] In the transcripts, the following abbreviations are used: H = husband, W = wife, Int = interviewer.

Transcript	Comments
H: Actually, we met at a party, I mean we first started going together at a party that one of the employees had. But we'd seen each other before, at work.	Though somewhat softened and compromising, this is a restatement which does not let her definition stand.
W: We never met till that night. (Slight laugh) (Pause)	This is a direct negation, not merely a rephrasing, of his statement, indicating perhaps that the dispute is beginning to escalate. (Notice however that "met" is quite an ambiguous term in this context—it could mean several things from "laid eyes on each other" to "were formally introduced"—so that her contradiction of him is disqualified; that is, she could not, if queried, be pinned down to it. Her laugh also enables her to "say something without really saying it.")
H (very softly): Mhm. (Long pause)	H puts himself one-down by agreeing with her—overtly; but "mhm" has a variety of possible meanings and is here uttered almost inaudibly, without any conviction or emphasis, so the result is quite vague. Even more, the previous statement is so vague that it is not clear what an agreement with it might mean. In any case, he does not go further, nor does he assert still another version of his own. So they reach the end of another round, again marked by a pause which seems to signal that they have reached the danger point (of open contradiction and conflict) and are prepared to end the discussion even without closure of the content aspect.
Int: But still, I have an image of dozens of people, or maybe more floating around; so how was it that the two of you, of all these people, got together?	Interviewer intervenes to keep the discussion going.

Transcript	Comments
H: She was one of the prettier ones up there. (Slight laugh) (Pause)	H makes a strong "one-up" move; this dubious compliment places her in comparison with the others, with him as the judge.

Transcript	*Comments*
W (faster): I don't know, the main reason I started going with him is because the girls—he had talked to some of the other girls before he talked to me, and told them he was interested in me, and they more or less planned this party, and that's where we met.	She matches his condescension with her own version: she was only interested in him because he was initially interested in her. (The subject around which their symmetry is defined has shifted from whose version of their meeting will be told and allowed to stand to who got the trophy, so to speak, in their courtship.)
H: Actually the party wasn't planned for that purpose—	A straightforward rejection of her definition.
W (interrupting): No, but it was planned for us to meet at the party. Meet formally, you might say. In person. (Slight laugh) We'd worked together, but I didn't make a habit of . . . well, I was around sixty women there, and ten or twelve men, and I didn't make it a habit of—	After agreeing with his correction, W repeats what she has just said. Her nonpersonal formulation has been weakened, and she now relies on a straight self-definition ("I am this kind of a person . . ."), an unassailable way to establish equality.
H (overlapping): She was certainly backward—bashful type of worker as far as associating with uh, uh strange men on the place, yeah but the women knew it. (Pause) And I was flirtin' with lots of 'em up there (slight laugh). Nothing meant by it I guess, but just . . . (sigh) just my nature I guess.	H gives a symmetrical answer based on *his* "nature," and another round ends.

This couple sought help because they feared that their constant bickering might hurt their children. As could almost be' predicted from the above excerpt, they also mentioned difficulties in their sexual relation, where, of course, their inability to relate complementarily made itself particularly felt.

2) The couple in the next example participated in a research project involving randomly selected families. It was generally felt by the investigators that they were emotionally quite distant and that the wife showed a good deal of depression. Their interaction is typically complementary, with husband in the "one-up" and wife in the "one-down" position. But, as already explained in the previous chapter, these terms must not be taken as indicators of relative strength or weakness. Quite obviously, this woman's am-

nesia and helplessness make it not only possible for him to play the role of the strong, realistic male, but they are also the very factors against which his strength and his realism are quite powerless. Thus we are again confronted by the interpersonal impact of any emotional symptom in the wider sense.

The excerpt starts a little after the interviewer has asked the standard question about their meeting and after the husband explained that she had come to work in an office next to his.

H: And—see, when'd you start there?

W: W—I haven't any i—

H (interrupting):—seems to me it was about, I came in October, the year before . . . and you probably started about . . . February uh, January or February —probably February or March 'cause your birthday was in December, that same year.

W: Mm, I don't even remember . . .

H (interrupting): So I happened to send her some flowers, you see, when—our first date out. And that never— we'd never gone anywhere had we?

W (with short laugh): No, I was very surprised.

H: And we just went from there. It was about a year later I guess we got married. Little over a year.

Int: What did you . . .

H (interrupting): Although Jane left the company very shortly after that. Mm, I don't think you worked there over a couple of months, did you?

W: You know, I'm sorry, I don't remember a thing about (slight laugh) how long it was or when I went—

H (interrupting): Yeah, a couple of months, and then you went back into teaching. (W: Mhm, mhm) 'Cause we—she found I guess that this war work was not contributing as much to the war effort as she thought it— was, when she went out there.

Int: So you—you went to a school?

W: Yes, I'd been working in it, before (Int: Mhm) I went to work there.

Int: And you continued the contact without interruption. (H: Oh yeah) What, uh, beside the fact that your wife is obviously attractive, what else do you think you have in common?

H: Absolutely nothing. (Laughing) We never have—had 'r we—(sharp breath). (Pause)

3) The third example is taken from the interview of a clinically normal couple who volunteered for the same type of interview. Here it can be seen how they manage to maintain a warm and mutually supportive relationship by a flexible alternation of symmetrical with complementary interchanges.[16] Thus, even though some of the details of their account could conceivably be felt to be depreciatory of each other, these do not seem to threaten the stability of their relationship and the mutual confirmation of their roles.

Transcript	*Comments*
Int: How of all the millions of people in the world did the two of you get together?	
W: How did we . . . ?	
Int: . . . get together.	
W: Well . . .	W starts to take over, thereby defining her right to do so.
H (interrupting): Well, I'll tell you (W laughs, H joins in)	H takes over in a highly symmetrical maneuver. This is softened by their mutual laughter.
W: Well, well, I'll tell it. Actually, I was working when I got out of high school, the Depression was on, so I got a job as a—ah, curb girl. I guess they used to call it then, and was . . .	W again takes over, rephrasing H exactly, then going a long way around to define the situation her way.
H: . . . drive-in restaurant . . .	W has gotten into trouble because "curb girl" could imply "street walk-

[16] An entirely different communicational contingency arises in the area of symmetrical and complementary interaction if a message defines the relationship as symmetrical *and* complementary *at the same time.* This is probably the most frequent and important way by which paradox can enter into human communication, and the pragmatic effects of this form of communicational inconsistency will, therefore, be taken up separately in Chapter 6.

er." H rescues her by making sure it is clear where she was working and in doing so strongly defines the situation *his* way. Up to this point, their interaction is symmetrical.

W: . . . working at—in a drive-in restaurant 'til I found another job. And he was working . . .

W accepts his definition and carefully follows the correction of connotation he indicated. She accepts the complementary one-down position.

H: I picked her up.

Complementary one-up.

W: Actually, I think he did. (Both laugh)

Complementary one-down (accepts H's definition).

H: That's about it.

Complementary one-up. Thus, the earlier symmetrical escalation has been cut off by a switch to complementarity and closure is possible; H sums up and the cycle ends.

W: But he was real bashful. He was the bashful type, and I thought, well—

W switches to a one-up maneuver about his having picked her up.

H: I've gotten over that—she says—I don't know.

Complementary one-down. H accepts her definition of him as bashful, i.e., not only that he was not the aggressor, but that she is still the judge of this. ("*She* says—*I* don't know")

W: So, so I felt . . .

H: This is all—

W: . . . he was harmless, so I—I did go home with him.

H (overlapping): The fact of the matter is it was more or less of a dare because I was out with another couple over a weekend and we were discussing on the way back to town, why, we decided it was high time that I found a steady girl friend.

H carries her interpretation even further, and goes on to say that he didn't have a girl friend, that his friends were influential in his actions, etc.

W (laughing): And I just happened to be there—

While the *content* sounds self-disparaging and thus complementary one-down, in this context her statement mirrors H's behavior in its passivity; W switches to symmetry. (Note the necessity of distinguishing between her motivation and the interpersonal effect, so that symmetry can be based on one-downness as well as other forms of competition.)

Transcript	*Comments*
H: So we stopped in at this place to have a root beer or something of the sort (both laugh) and there she was. So I—ah . . .	H symmetrically states both their phrasings of the situation and again laughter permits closure.
W: That was it.	W tops it off—just as H did at the end of the first cycle with "That's about it."

3.65

There are two points to be emphasized in the analysis of the preceding examples. First, content fades in importance as communicational patterns emerge. A group of second- and third-year psychiatric residents rated the couple in the third example as much "sicker" than other, clinically disturbed, couples. Upon inquiry, it was obvious that the basis of their judgment had been the relative social unacceptability of the meeting and the open "sparring" about details. In other words their erroneous judgment was based on content rather than on the interaction of their account.

More important, it should have become obvious that our analysis was of successive statements. No given statement in isolation can be symmetrical, complementary one-up, or whatever. It is the response of the partner that is of course necessary for the "classification" of a given message. That is, it is not in the nature of any of the statements as individual entities, but in the relation between two or more responses that the functions of communication are defined.

Chapter 4

The Organization of Human Interaction

4.1

Introduction

The relatively isolated examples presented in the previous chapters served to present, specifically and immediately, certain basic properties and pathologies of human communication. These are the elements out of which the complexity of communication is built. In turning now to the organization of interaction (as this unit of communication was defined in s. 2.22), we will consider the patterning of recurring, ongoing communications, that is, the *structure* of communication processes.

This level of analysis was implicit in earlier discussions, such as of cumulatively symmetrical or complementary interaction (s. 2.6 and 3.6). Similarly, the "self-fulfilling prophecy" (s. 3.44) encompasses more than the particular punctuation of a unique communicational sequence: repetition of this pattern of punctuation over time and over a variety of situations is a vital element. Thus the concept of pattern in communication can be seen as representing repetition or redundancy [1] of events. As there are certainly patterns of patterns and probably even higher levels of organization this hierarchy cannot be shown to be limited. However, for the moment, the unit of study will be the next higher level than that of our previous discussion: the organization of sequential messages, first

---

[1] The relevance of redundancy and constraint to our concept of pattern has been discussed in detail in s. 1.4; it is only necessary here to emphasize that a pattern is information conveyed by the occurrence of certain events and the *non*occurrence of other events. If all possible events of a given class occur randomly, there is no pattern and no information.

in general and then with specific consideration of ongoing interactional systems. This chapter is primarily theoretical, with the
complex problem of illustrating such macroscopic phenomena left
mostly for Chapter 5. Thus, these two chapters have essentially the
same relation (first theory and then illustration) as in Chapters 2
and 3.

4.2

Interaction as a System

Interaction can be considered as a system, and the general theory
of systems gives insight into the nature of interactional systems.
General System Theory is not only a theory of biological, economic,
or engineering systems. Despite their widely varying subject matter,
these theories of particular systems have so many common conceptions that a more general theory has evolved which structures the
similarities into formal isomorphies.[2] One of the pioneers in this
field, Ludwig von Bertalanffy, describes the theory as "the formulation and derivation of those principles which are valid for 'systems' in general" (25, p. 131). Von Bertalanffy has also anticipated
the concern of those who will shrink at our eagerness to treat
human relationships with a theory better known—which is not to
say better suited—for application to distinctly nonhuman, notably
computer, systems and has pointed out its faulty logic:

> The isomorphy we have mentioned is a consequence
> of the fact that in certain aspects, corresponding ab-
> stractions and conceptual models can be applied to
> different phenomena. It is only in view of these as-
> pects that system laws will apply. This does not mean
> that physical systems, organisms and societies are all
> the same. In principle, it is the same situation as when
> the law of gravitation applies to Newton's apple, the

[2] As will be noted, our focus herein is limited to certain aspects of ongoing
interactional systems, especially families. For a recent, comprehensive application
of this frame of reference to living systems in general, see Miller's series (*105*),
which signals the potentially fruitful integrative aspect of such an approach.

planetary system, and the phenomenon of tide. This
means that in view of some rather limited aspects a
certain theoretical system, that of mechanics, holds
true; it does not mean that there is a particular resemblance between apples, planets, and oceans in a
great number of other aspects. (*26*, p. 75)

4.21

Before any of the special properties of systems are defined, we
should point out that the obvious and very important variable
of time (with its companion, order) must be an integral part of
our unit of study. Communication sequences are not, to use Frank's
words, "anonymous units in a frequency distribution" (*45*, p. 510)
but the inseparable stuff of an ongoing process whose order and
interrelations, occurring over a period of time, shall be our interest
here. As Lennard and Bernstein have put it:

> Implicit to a system is a span of time. By its very
> nature a system consists of an interaction, and this
> means that a sequential process of action and reaction
> has to take place before we are able to describe any
> state of the system or any change of state. (*94*, pp.
> 13–14)

4.22—DEFINITION OF A SYSTEM

Initially, we can follow Hall and Fagen in defining a system as
"a set of objects together with relationships between the objects
and between their attributes" (*62*, p. 18), in which *objects* are the
components or parts of the system, *attributes* are the properties of
the objects, and *relationships* "tie the system together." These
authors further point out that any object is ultimately specified
by its attributes. Thus, while the "objects" may be individual humans, the attributes by which they are identified herein are their
communicative behaviors (as opposed to, say, intrapsychic attributes). The objects of interactional systems are best described not
as individuals but as persons-communicating-with-other-persons. By
pinning down the term "relationship" the present vagueness and

generality of the above definition can be considerably reduced. Conceding that there is always some kind of relationship, however spurious, between any objects whatever, Hall and Fagen are of the opinion

> that the relationships to be considered in the context of a given set of objects depend on the problem at hand, important or interesting relationships being included, trivial or unessential relationships excluded. The decision as to which relationships are important and which trivial is up to the person dealing with the problem, i.e., the question of triviality turns out to be relative to one's interest. (*62*, p. 18)

What is important here is not the content of communication per se but exactly the relationship (command) aspect of human communication, as defined in s. 2.3. Interactional systems, then, shall be *two or more communicants in the process of, or at the level of, defining the nature of their relationship.*[3]

4.23—ENVIRONMENT AND SUBSYSTEMS

Another important aspect of the definition of a system is the definition of its environment; again, according to Hall and Fagen: "For a given system, the environment is the set of all objects a change in whose attributes affect the system and also those objects whose attributes are changed by the behavior of the system" (*62*, p. 20). By the authors' own admission,

> the statement above invites the natural question of when an object belongs to a system and when it belongs to the environment; for if an object reacts with a system in the way described above should it not be considered a part of the system? The answer is by no means definite. In a sense, a system together with its environment makes up the universe of all things of

---

[3] While primary emphasis will be on human communicants, there is no theoretical reason to exclude the interaction of other mammals (*9*) or of groups, such as nations, which may interact much as two or more individuals do (*125*).

interest in a given context. Subdivision of this universe into two sets, system and environment, can be
done in many ways which are in fact quite arbitrary. . . .

It is clear from the definition of system and environment that any given system can be further subdivided into subsystems. Objects belonging to one
subsystem may well be considered as part of the environment of another subsystem. (*62*, p. 20)

The very elusiveness and flexibility of this system-environment or
system-subsystem concept in no small way accounts for the power
of systems theory in the study of living (organic) systems, be they
biological, psychological, or interactional as here. For

. . . organic systems are *open,* meaning they exchange materials, energies, or information with their
environments. A system is *closed* if there is no import
or export of energies in any of its forms such as information, heat, physical materials, etc., and therefore
no change of components, an example being a chemi-
cal reaction taking place in a sealed insulated container. (*62*, p. 23)

This distinction between closed and open systems can be said to
have freed the sciences concerned with life-phenomena from the
shackles of a theoretical model based essentially on classical physics
and chemistry: a model of exclusively *closed* systems. Because living
systems have crucial dealings with their environments, the theory
and methods of analysis appropriate to things which can be reasonably put in "a sealed insulated container" were significantly ob-
structive and misleading.[4]

[4] An interesting and relevant example of the indirect effect on diverse disciplines of the metatheory most articulated by classical physics can be found in
psychiatry: Pathologies of interaction were virtually unknown in the early days
of psychiatry with one exception, the *folie à deux* and related symbioses (s. 3.62).
These dramatic relationships were from the first considered interactional, not
individual, problems and, as such, were little more than nosological freaks.
Still, the fact that they were even admitted while many other relationship
problems were ignored is intriguing, especially since we can now see that only
the *folie à deux* fitted precisely the closed system model of the day.

With the development of the theory of hierarchically arranged open subsystems, the system and its environment need no longer be artificially isolated from one another; they fit meaningfully together within the same theoretical framework. Koestler describes the situation as follows:

> A living organism or social body is not an aggregation of elementary parts or elementary processes; it is an integrated hierarchy of semiautonomous sub-wholes, consisting of sub-sub-wholes, and so on. Thus the functional units on every level of the hierarchy are double-faced as it were: they act as whole when facing downwards, as parts when facing upwards. (*87*, p. 287)

With this conceptual model we can easily place a dyadic interactional system into larger family, extended family, community, and cultural systems. Also, such subsystems may (with theoretical impunity) overlap other subsystems, since each member of the dyad is involved in dyadic subsystems with other persons and even with life itself (see Epilogue). In short, communicating individuals are seen in both *horizontal* and *vertical* relations with other persons and other systems.

4.3

The Properties of Open Systems

Thus we have shifted our discussion from the most universal definition of general systems to focus on one of two basic kinds of systems, the open system. Now some of the macroscopic formal properties of open systems can be defined as they apply to interaction.

4.31—WHOLENESS

Every part of a system is so related to its fellow parts that a change in one part will cause a change in all of them and in the total system. That is, a system behaves not as a simple composite of independent elements, but coherently and as an inseparable whole. This characteristic is perhaps best understood in contrast with its polar opposite, summativity: if variations in one part do *not* affect the other parts or the whole, then these parts are independent of each other and constitute a "heap" (to use a term from systems literature) that is no more complex than the sum of its elements. This quality of summativity can be put on the other end of a hypothetical continuum from wholeness, and it can be said that *systems are always characterized by some degree of wholeness.*

While they were not at the time formalized into a metatheory, the mechanical theories of the nineteenth century can now be seen to have been primarily analytical and summative. "The mechanistic world-view found its ideal in the Laplacean spirit, i.e., in the conception that all phenomena are ultimately aggregates of fortuitous actions of elementary physical units" (25, p. 165). Thus it will be that historical contrasts will provide the best examples. As Ashby has noted:

> Science stands today on something of a divide. For two centuries it has been exploring systems that are either intrinsically simple or that are capable of being analyzed into simple components. The fact that such a dogma as "vary the factors one at a time" could be accepted for a century, shows that scientists were largely concerned in investigating such systems as allowed this method; for this method is often fundamentally impossible in the complex systems. Not until Sir Ronald Fisher's work in the '20's, with experiments conducted on agricultural soils, did it become clearly recognised that there are complex systems that just do not allow the varying of only one factor at a time—they are so dynamic and interconnected that the alteration of one factor immediately acts as cause to evoke alterations in others, perhaps in a great many others. Until recently, science tended to evade the study of such systems, focusing its attention on those that were simple and, especially, reducible.
> In the study of some systems, however, the com-

plexity could not be wholly evaded. The cerebral cortex of the free-living organism, the ant-hill as a functioning society, and the human economic system were outstanding both in their practical importance and in their intractability by the other methods. So today we see psychoses untreated, societies declining, and economic systems faltering, the scientists being able to do little more than to appreciate the full complexity of the subject he is studying. But science today is also taking the first steps towards studying "complexity" as a subject in its own right. (5, p. 5)

4.311

Nonsummativity, then, as a corollary of the notion of wholeness provides a negative guideline for the definition of a system. A system cannot be taken for the sum of its parts; indeed, formal analysis of artificially isolated segments would destroy the very object of interest. It is necessary to neglect the parts for the gestalt and attend to the core of its complexity, its organization. The psychological concept of gestalt is only one way of expressing the principle of nonsummativity; in other fields there is great interest in the *emergent quality* that arises out of the interrelation of two or more elements. The most obvious example is supplied by chemistry, where relatively few of the known elements produce an immense variety of complex new substances. Another example would be the so-called "Moiré patterns"—optical manifestations of the superposition of two or more lattices (*114*). In both cases, the result is of a complexity for which the elements, considered separately, could never account. Furthermore, it is very interesting that the slightest change in the relationship between the constituent parts is often magnified in the emergent quality—a different substance in the case of chemistry, a very different configuration in the Moiré pattern. In physiology, Virchowian cellular pathology contrasts in this regard with modern approaches such as Weiss's (*162*), and in psychology, classical association contrasts with Gestalt theory; so in the study of human interaction, we propose to contrast essentially individual-oriented approaches with communication theory. When interaction is considered a derivative of individual "properties" such as roles, values, expectations, and motivations, the composite— two or more interacting individuals—is a summative heap that can be broken into more basic (individual) units. In contrast, from the first axiom of communication—that all behavior is communication, and one cannot not communicate—it follows that communication sequences would be reciprocally inseparable; in short, that inter- action is nonsummative.

4.312

Another theory of interaction that is contradicted by the princi- ple of wholeness is that of *unilateral* relations between elements, i.e., that *A* may affect *B* but not vice versa. Recalling the example of the nagging wife and the withdrawing husband (s. 2.42), it was seen that although an interactional sequence may be *punctuated* (by the participants or the observer) into a pattern of one-way causality, such a sequence is in fact circular, and the apparent "response" must also be a stimulus for the next event in this inter- dependent chain. Thus, to assert that person *A*'s behavior causes *B*'s behavior is to ignore the effect of *B*'s behavior on *A*'s subse- quent reaction; it is, in fact, to distort the chronology of events by punctuating certain relations in bold relief while obscuring others. Especially when the relationship is complementary, as in leader- follower, strong-weak, or parent-child relationships, it is easy to lose the wholeness of the interaction and break it up into independent, linearly causal units. This fallacy has already been warned against in s. 2.62 and 2.63 and needs only to be made explicit in terms of long-term interaction here.

4.32—FEEDBACK

If the parts of a system are not summatively or unilaterally re- lated, then in what manner are they united? Having rejected these two classical conceptual models, we would seem to be left with what in the nineteenth and early twentieth centuries were their disreputable alternatives—vague, vitalistic, and metaphysical no- tions which, since they did not fit the doctrine of determinism, were branded teleological. However, as already shown in s. 1.3, the conceptual shift from energy (and matter) to information has finally led us away from the sterile choice between deterministic and teleological causal schemes. Since the advent of cybernetics and the "discovery" of feedback, it has been seen that circular and highly complex relatedness is a markedly different but no less scientific phenomenon than simpler and more orthodox causal notions. Feedback and circularity, as described in detail in Chapter 1 and as illustrated repeatedly in Chapters 2 and 3, are the appropriate causal model for a theory of interactional systems. The specific nature of a feedback process is of much greater interest than origin and, frequently, outcome.

4.33—EQUIFINALITY

In a circular and self-modifying system, "results" (in the sense of alteration in state after a period of time) are not determined so much by initial conditions as by the nature of the process, or the system parameters. Simply stated, this principle of equifinality means that the same results may spring from different origins, because it is the nature of the organization which is determinate. Von Bertalanffy has elaborated on this principle:

> The steady state of open systems is characterized by the principle of equifinality; that is, in contrast to equilibrium states in closed systems which are determined by initial conditions, the open system may attain a time-independent state independent of initial conditions and determined only by the system parameters. (27, p. 7)

If the equifinal behavior of open systems is based on their independence of initial conditions, then not only may different initial conditions yield the same final result, but different results may be produced by the same "causes." Again, this corollary rests on the premise that system parameters will predominate over initial conditions. So in the analysis of how people affect each other in their interaction, we will not consider the specifics of genesis or product to be nearly so important as the ongoing organization of inter-action.[5]

This issue is illustrated by the changing conceptions of the (psy-chogenic) etiology of schizophrenia. Theories of a unique trauma in childhood gave way to the postulation of a repetitive though unilateral and statically conceived relationship trauma inflicted by the schizophrenia-producing mother. As Jackson has pointed out, this is only the first phase in a larger revolution:

> Historically the place of psychogenic trauma in etiol-ogy appears to be shifting from Freud's original ideas of a single traumatic event to the concept of repeti-tive trauma. *The next step would be not who does what to whom, but how who does what.* Perhaps the next phase will include a study of schizophrenia (or schizophrenias) as a family-borne disease involving a complicated host-vector-recipient cycle that includes much more than can be connoted by the term "schizo-phrenogenic mother." (*68*, p. 184; italics ours) [6]

[5] Cf. Langer, who has put the choice another way:

> There is a widespread and familiar fallacy, known as the "ge-netic fallacy," which arises from the historical method in philos-ophy and criticism: the error of confusing the *origin* of a thing with its *import*, of tracing the thing to its most primitive form and then calling it "merely" this archaic phenomenon . . . e.g. words were probably ritualistic sounds before they were com-municative devices; that does not mean that language is now not "really" a means of communication, but is "really" a mere residue of tribal excitement. (*91*, p. 248) (Italics and quotation marks in original)

[6] There is evidence to support such an equifinal view of psychopathology; Kant (*82*) and Renaud and Estess (*124*) have found, respectively, no precipitat-ing traumatic factors in fifty-six consecutive cases of schizophrenia, and over-whelming reports of traumatic experiences in the life histories of men who were considered psychiatrically normal. Noting that their normal group was indistinguishable from clinical samples on this basis, Renaud and Estess go on to say:

> Such a conclusion is not incompatible with basic assumptions underlying twentieth century behavioral science (e.g., that in substantial degree human behavior is a product of life experi-ence); neither is it in conflict with the basic proposition that the early years of human life are crucial for later development. This view does question, however, elementalistic conceptions of

What has just been said about origins (etiology) can also be applied to the resultant clinical picture (nosology). To take schizophrenia as an example again, there are two ways to understand this term; as the label for a fixed disease entity or for a mode of interaction. It has already been proposed (s. 1.65 and 1.66) that the behavior traditionally classified as "schizophrenic" no longer be so reified but rather be studied only in the interpersonal context in which it occurs—the family, the institution—where such behavior is neither simply result nor cause of these usually bizarre environmental conditions but a complexly integrated part of an ongoing pathological system.

Finally, one of the most significant characteristics of open systems is found in equifinal behavior, especially in contrast to the closed-system model. The final state of the closed system is completely determined by initial circumstances that can therefore be said to be the best "explanation" of that system; in the case of the open system, however, organizational characteristics of the system can operate to achieve even the extreme case of total independence of initial conditions: *the system is then its own best explanation,* and the study of its present organization the appropriate methodology.[7]

4.4

Ongoing Interactional Systems

We are now ready to consider more closely systems characterized by stability, the so-called "steady state" systems. To return to Hall and Fagen, "a system is stable with respect to certain of its variables if these variables tend to remain within defined limits" (*62,* p. 23).

4.41—ONGOING RELATIONSHIPS

Almost inevitably such a level of analysis turns the focus to ongoing relationships, that is, to those which are (1) important to both parties and (2) long-lasting; generalized examples are friend-

---

simple, direct causal relations insistently presumed to exist between certain kinds of events and later development of mental illness. (*124,* p. 801)

[7] The same point has been made by writers as scientific as Wieser (*167,* p. 33) and as facetious yet realistic as C. Northcote Parkinson (*115*).

ships, some business or professional relationships, and, especially, marital and familial relationships (73). Besides their practical importance as social or cultural institutions, such vital-groups-with-histories are of particular heuristic significance to the pragmatics of communication. Under the above conditions there is not only the opportunity but the necessity for repetition of communicational sequences leading to the long-range consequences of the axioms and pathologies previously discussed. Stranger groups or chance encounters may provide interesting idiosyncratic material, but unless one is interested in singular, artificial, or novel phenomena, such interaction is not so valuable as that of a "natural" network in which we assume the properties and pathologies of human communication will be manifested with clearer pragmatic impact.[8]

4.411

The question usually arises, why does a given relationship exist? That is, why, especially in the face of pathology and distress, do these relationships ultimately perdure, with the participants not only not leaving the field but—more positively stated—accommodating themselves to a continuation of the relationship? The question evokes answers based on motivation, need satisfaction, social or cultural factors, or other determinants which, while clearly implicated, are tangential to the present exposition. Still, the issue cannot be summarily dismissed, and in fact we have already suggested, with Buber and others, the importance of confirmation as a social purpose (s. 3.331).

However, since our aim is intensive rather than extensive, it is necessary to explore the interactional explanations first, before the integration of premises from other frames of reference. Thus, we will hold with an answer which is descriptive rather than explanatory,[9] that is, on *how* and not why the interactional system oper-

---

[8] This is not to deny either the usefulness or possibility of experimental (that is, controlled) investigation of these phenomena, although as Bateson (*11*), Haley (*59*), Scheflen (*138, 139*), and Schelling (*140*) have suggested in widely differing contexts, such experimentation is likely to be of a fundamentally new order. See also Ashby's comments in s. 4.31.

[9] For example, phenomenologically the ongoing relationship can be seen as a mixed-motive nonzero-sum game (*140*) in which any solution within the relationship seems preferable to any outside it. Such a model is proposed and illustrated in s. 6.446.

ates. A highly simplified analogy can be made to the operation of a favorite model, the computer. How the machine works can be described in terms of its language, feedback loops, input-output system, and so forth. The proverbial man from Mars could conceivably observe the operation of such a system long enough to understand how it works, but he still would not know "why," which is a different question and not a simple one. The computer may operate, ultimately, because it is plugged into a power source; it may operate in a certain manner because of the nature of its component parts; in the teleological sense, it may operate as it does because it was designed for a certain purpose. In the over-all view, the *why* of power and purpose (drive and need, in psychological terms) cannot be ignored; but neither can the nature of the operation, the *how*. Moreover, these issues can be considered separately, at least for the present, as are similar issues in other fields; a well-known discontinuity of models exists in physics:

> It may not be time, for example, to ask why electrons and photons act like particles as well as like waves and expect an answer; theoretical physics has not yet advanced this far. On the other hand, it is possible to ask whether a wave-like property could explain why a particle electron is restricted to certain orbits as it spins around the nucleus of an atom. (2, p. 269)

4.42—LIMITATION

One reason, as stated above, to take such a confined position is that there may well be identifiable factors intrinsic to the communication process—that is, aside from motivation and simple habit—that serve to bind and perpetuate a relationship.

We can tentatively subsume these factors under the notion of the limiting effect of communication, by noting that *in a communicational sequence, every exchange of messages narrows down the number of possible next moves.* At the most superficial extreme, this point amounts to a restatement of the first axiom, that in an interpersonal situation one is limited to communicating; the stranger who accosts or ignores you must be answered at the least by ignoring-behavior. In more complicated circumstances, the restriction of response possibilities is even narrower. It was shown, for instance, in s. 3.23, that given relatively few contextual modifications of the stranger situation, a general outline of all possibilities could be given. *Context,* then, can be more or less restricting, but always determines the contingencies to some extent. But context does not consist only of institutional, external (to the communicants) factors. The manifest messages exchanged become part of the particular interpersonal context and place their restrictions on subsequent interaction (*144*). To return to the game analogy, in any interpersonal game—not only the mixed-motive models mentioned above—a move changes the configuration of the game at that stage, affecting the possibilities open from that point on and thereby altering the course of the game. The definition of a relationship as symmetrical or complementary, or the imposition of a particular punctuation, by and large restricts the vis-à-vis. That is, not only the sender but the relationship, including the receiver, is affected in this view of communication. Even to disagree, reject, or redefine the previous message is not only to respond but thereby to engender an involvement that need not have any other basis except the relationship definition and the commitment inherent in *any* communication. The hypothetical airline passenger of s. 3.23, who might choose to exchange banalities, could find himself increasingly involved—trapped, we would suggest, by his initial moves, however innocuous. Quasiclinical illustration will be found in Chapter 5, and examples of perhaps the most rigid limitation, that imposed by paradox, will be taken up in Chapter 6, where it will be suggested that interpersonal paradoxes are reciprocal and interlocking, so that what systems engineers call oscillation occurs, with both parties in a complex, untenable, yet apparently inescapable bind.

4.43—RELATIONSHIP RULES

With consideration of limitation phenomena, we can return to issues directly related to ongoing interactional systems. It will be recalled that in every communication the participants offer to each other definitions of their relationship, or, more forcefully stated, each seeks to determine the nature of the relationship. Similarly, each responds with his definition of the relationship, which may confirm, reject, or modify that of the other. This process warrants close attention, for in an ongoing relationship it cannot be left unresolved or fluctuating. If the process did not stabilize, the wide variations and unwieldiness, not to mention the inefficiency of re-defining the relationship with every exchange, would lead to run-away and dissolution of the relationship. The pathological families so frequently seen in therapy arguing endlessly over relationship issues (s. 3.31) illustrate this necessity, though we suggest that there are limits even to their disputes and often very dramatic regularity in their chaos.

> Couples, . . . who may engage in wondrously var-
> ied behavioral ploys during courtship, undoubtedly
> achieve considerable economy after a while in terms
> of what is open to dispute, and how it is to be dis-
> puted. Consequently they seem . . . to have mutu-
> ally excluded wide areas of behavior from their inter-
> actional repertoire and never quibble further about
> them. . . . (74, p. 13)

This stabilization of relationship definition has been called the *rule* of the relationship by Jackson (73, 74); it is a statement of the redundancies observed at the relationship level, even over a diverse range of content areas. This rule may regard symmetry or comple-mentarity, a particular punctuation (such as scapegoating), recip-rocally matching interpersonal imperviousness (s. 3.35), or some other—undoubtedly many—aspects of the relationship. In any case, an extreme circumscription of possible behaviors along any partic-ular dimension into one redundant configuration is observed, which prompted Jackson further to characterize families as rule-governed systems (74). Obviously, this does not mean that a priori laws govern family behavior. Rather, as Mach has said for science in general,

> . . . rules for the reconstruction of great numbers of
> facts may be embodied in a *single* expression. Thus,

instead of noting individual cases of light-refraction, we can mentally reconstruct all present and future cases, if we know that the incident ray, the refracted ray, and the perpendicular lie in the same plane and that $\sin \alpha / \sin \beta = n$. Here, instead of the numberless cases of refraction in different combinations of matter and under all different angles of incidence, we have simply to note the rule above stated and the values of n,—which is much easier. The economical purpose is here unmistakable. In nature there is no *law* of refraction, only different cases of refraction. The law of refraction is a concise compendious rule, devised by us for the mental reconstruction of a fact, and only for its reconstruction in part, that is, on its geometrical side. (*99*, pp. 485–6)

4.44—THE FAMILY AS A SYSTEM

The family-rules theory fits the initial definition of a system as "stable with respect to certain of its variables if these variables tend to remain within defined limits," and in fact this suggests a more formal consideration of the family as a system.

Such a model for family interaction was proposed by Jackson when he introduced the concept of *family homeostasis* (*69*). Observing that the families of psychiatric patients often demonstrated drastic repercussions (depression, psychosomatic attacks, and the like) when the patient improved, he postulated that these behaviors and perhaps therefore the patient's illness as well were "homeostatic mechanisms," operating to bring the disturbed system back into its delicate balance. This brief statement is the core of a communication approach to the family, which can now be enumerated in terms of some principles already introduced.

4.441 Wholeness

The behavior of every individual within the family is related to and dependent upon the behavior of all the others. All behavior is communication and therefore influences and is influenced by others. Specifically, as noted above, changes for better or worse in the family member identified as the patient will usually have an effect on other family members, especially in terms of their own psychological, social, or even physical health. Family therapists who relieve the labeled complaint are often faced with a new crisis. The following example is typical in principle, although it was selected because of the unusual clarity of the depiction of the complaint.

A couple enters marriage therapy at the insistence of the wife, whose complaint appears more than justified: her husband, a neat, likable, and mentally alert young man has somehow managed to complete grammar school without ever learning to read or write. During his military service he also successfully withstood a special remedial course for illiterate soldiers. After his discharge he started work as a laborer and was precluded from any advancement or pay raise. The wife is an attractive, energetic, and extremely conscientious person. As a result of her husband's illiteracy she carries the burden of the family responsibilities and on many occasions has to drive her husband to new work sites because he cannot read street signs or city maps.

Relatively soon in the course of therapy the husband enrolls in an evening course for illiterates, enlists his father's help as a kind of study supervisor, and acquires a rudimentary reading proficiency. From a therapeutic point of view everything seems to proceed extremely well, when one day the therapist receives a telephone call from the wife, informing him that she would no longer come to the joint sessions and that she had filed for divorce. As in the old joke, "the operation was a success, but the patient died." The therapist had overlooked the interactional nature of the presenting complaint (illiteracy), and by removing it had altered their complementary relationship, although this outcome was exactly what the wife had expected from therapy in the first place.

4.442 Nonsummativity

The analysis of a family is not the sum of the analyses of its individual members. There are characteristics of the system, that is, interactional patterns, that transcend the qualities of individual members—for instance, the complements of s. 3.62 or the mutually double-binding communication to be described in s. 6.432. Many of

the "individual qualities" of members, especially symptomatic behavior, are in fact particular to the system. For example, Fry (52)
has concisely and clearly examined the marital context in which a
group of patients exhibited a syndrome of anxiety, phobias, and
stereotyped avoidance behavior. In no case was there a successfully
functioning spouse, but of even more interest to the present theory
is the subtle and pervasive interlocking of behavior seen in each
couple. Fry notes that

> the spouses reveal, upon careful study, a history of
> symptoms closely resembling, if not identical to, the
> symptoms of the patient. Usually they are reluctant to
> reveal this history. For example, a wife was not only
> unable to go out alone, but even in company she
> would panic if she entered a brightly lighted and/or
> crowded place or had to stand in line. Her husband
> disclaimed any emotional problems of his own at first,
> but then revealed he experienced occasional episodes
> of anxiety and so avoided certain situations. The situ-
> ations he avoided were: being in crowds, standing in
> line, and entering brightly lighted public places. How-
> ever, both marriage partners insisted the wife should
> be considered the patient because she was *more* afraid
> of these situations than he was.
>
>   In another case the wife was labeled the patient
> because she was afraid of enclosed places and could
> not ride in elevators. Therefore, the couple could not
> visit a cocktail lounge on the top of a tall building.
> However, it was later revealed that the husband had
> a fear of high places which he never needed to face
> because of the marital agreement that they never went
> to the tops of buildings because of the wife's fear of
> elevators. (52, p. 248)

The author goes on to suggest that the patient's symptoms seem to
be protective of the spouse, and in support of this notes that the
onset of symptoms typically correlates with a change in the spouse's

life situation, a change that might be anxiety-producing for the spouse:

> [A] lawyer, with a previously rather desultory employ-
> ment history, was given a better position in another
> city. He uprooted his family and took the position,
> which was unusual self-assertion for him. At this time
> the couple also began to sleep in the same bedroom
> again after sleeping in different rooms for over a year.
> The wife developed severe anxiety attacks and was
> unable to venture forth from the new house.
>
> [A] city employee, on a small salary, largely completed
> building a rather elaborate house by himself. His wife
> shortly developed anxiety attacks which kept her at
> home. Another husband finally received his graduate
> degree and obtained a job. His wife, who had previ-
> ously been supporting him, collapsed with anxiety.
> (52, pp. 249–50)

The interactional pattern and problem characteristic of such couples Fry calls "dual control," that is,

> The patient's symptoms put her in the position, as
> the ailing member, to demand that the marriage part-
> ner always be at her beck and call and do what she
> says. The partner cannot make a move without con-
> sulting the patient and clearing it with her. Yet at the
> same time the patient is constantly supervised by the
> spouse. He may have to be near the telephone so she
> can contact him, but he is also checking up on all her
> activities. Both patient and spouse will often report
> that the *other* is always getting his or her own way.
> The patient's difficulties function to permit the
> spouse to avoid many situations in which he might
> experience anxiety or other discomfort, without being
> confronted with the possibility of symptoms. She can
> be an elaborate excuse for him. He may avoid social

life, ostensibly because the patient is uneasy. He may limit his work, ostensibly because he must attend the ailing patient. He may deal inadequately with his children because of his withdrawal and over-reaction tendencies. But he is spared self-confrontation by the suspicion that the children's problems are caused by the patient's symptoms. He may avoid sexual experiences with the patient ostensibly because she is ill and wouldn't be up to it. He may be uneasy about being alone but since the patient is afraid to be alone, he can always have her with him without it being emphasized that *he* has this symptom.

The discontented patient may indicate some desire for an extramarital relationship, but her phobia symptoms prevent her association with other men. Because of his personality characteristics and his reaction to the patient's illness, an affair does not become a serious possibility for the spouse. Both the patient and spouse are relatively protected from this exigency by the patient's symptoms.

Usually the marriage is miserable and the couple distant and discontented, but the symptoms function to keep the couple united. This type of marriage might be called a compulsory marriage. . . .

As long as the symptoms persist, there is no way out of this dilemma. The patient, uneasy about whether her spouse wants her, demands more and more that he stay with her—because she is sick. He stays with her, but this does not reassure her because he is apparently staying with her because of the illness, not because he wants to be with her. Since he feels compelled to associate with her for the sake of her illness, he can never reassure her or himself that he might voluntarily seek her company.

The spouse cannot resolve this problem. If he stays with the patient, it seems to be only because she is so

ill. If he leaves her, he is a cad who does not care for
her misfortune. Furthermore, if he left her or if she
recovered, he would have to face his own anxiety and
his symptoms. He cannot be openly sympathetic because of his resentment, nor openly unsympathetic.
The patient, in turn, cannot be appreciative of the
sacrifices the husband makes for her, nor can she be
openly unappreciative of them. (52, pp. 250–2)

4.443 *Feedback and Homeostasis*

Inputs (actions of family members or of the environment) introduced into the family system are acted upon and modified by the
system. The nature of the system and its feedback mechanisms
must be considered as well as the nature of the input (equifinality).
Some families can absorb large reverses and even turn them into
rallying points; others seem unable to handle the most insignificant
crises. Still more extreme are those families of schizophrenic patients who seem unable to accept the inevitable manifestations of
maturity in their child, and who counteract these "deviations" by
labeling them sick or bad. Laing and Esterson (90) describe the
reaction of the mother ("Mrs. Field") of a fifteen-year-old schizophrenic ("June") to the daughter's increased independence. From
age two until ten, June had suffered a congenital dislocation of
the hip, which required elaborate and cumbersome corrective devices and which almost totally restricted her activities.

> Mother: Oh, yes, she was *always* with me, al-
> ways. Well naturally I wouldn't
> leave her because of her irons in case
> she fell or anything. She did fall as
> a matter of fact, she knocked her
> front teeth out. But she played with
> the other children too you see . . .
> we all used to take June out because
> I always took her everywhere with
> me, always. Naturally I would. I
> didn't ever leave her. You see when

June was in plaster I didn't put her
on the ground because the plaster
would have been quickly worn out
(smiling). I put her on the bed, you
see, like that (demonstrates)—and
then I had—she had a good leather
straps on because she's always been
a very strong child and I had a dog-
lead there and a dog-lead there, then
June could move freely up and
down and across, not very far, but
always up and down. And she
jumped on this bed *so* hard that
(laughing) in a matter of two years
all the springs had gone. She wasn't
there all the time because as I say I
always took her out with me. And
then we used to put her in the garden and I put her on the ground in
the garden under the trees if it was
summer time, on the rug you see, and
I tied her to the tree which meant
that June could get all round the
tree but not on the concrete. Because
the plaster's—well they're not so ter-
ribly strong, you know what friction
is on concrete, they very quickly go
through. And you see there was this
bar between, it was a butterfly plaster
and each time it extended more.
And once she got it off, of course
June used to get hold of this plaster
you see, this bar, and really almost
rock herself on it, she could do, quite
easily. And early one morning she
got it out, I had to take her back to

> hospital to have another one put in.
> As I say, she was always a boisterous
> child, she's always been such a happy
> little girl—haven't you June?
>
> June: Mmm
> Mother: Yes you have dear.

Mrs. Field's story was told in a cheerful brisk manner. As much is revealed in the manner of telling as in the remarkable content. . . .

Not only does Mrs. Field never express one word to the effect that June might have been a painful sight at times to her mother, as well as "lovely"; unhappy, wretched, miserable perhaps, as well as very happy; quiet as well as boisterous; and not necessarily always affectionate, but her repertoire of positive attributes never varies. This picture of June up to the age of fourteen is held with certitude and with rigidity, and is surely an extraordinarily constricted view of any human being. It is impervious to direct confrontations from June to the contrary. Powerful pressure is put on June to accept this picture as her own, and attacks are made on her life if she dissents. It is timeless. As Mrs. Field says repeatedly: "That isn't my June. I can't understand June now. She was always a very happy child. She was always a very boisterous child."

> (*90*, pp. 135–6)

Note the denial of any evidence to the contrary. When evidence began to come from June herself, however, the dyad entered a new phase, characterized by Mrs. Field's massive efforts to counteract the changes, efforts which increasingly took the form of labeling June as sick:

> In the summer before the winter of her admission,
> June was separated from her mother for the first time
> since admission to hospital for six weeks at the age of

two, for her hip condition. This was when she went to a girls' camp run by the Church. Alone of all the girls' mothers, Mrs. Field accompanied June to the camp. During the month she was away, she made a number of discoveries about herself and others and unhappily fell out with her best friend. She became aware of herself sexually with much greater force than before.

In her mother's view, when she came back from camp she was "not my June. I did not know her."

The following is a list of June's qualities before and after her separation from her mother, as described by Mrs. Field.

BEFORE	AFTER
a lovely girl	looked hideous
	put on terrible make-up
	had got fat
a very happy girl	was unhappy
boisterous	withdrawn
always told me everything	wouldn't tell me her thoughts
would sit in room at night with mother, father, and grandad	went to her own room
used to love to play cards with mother, father, and grandad	preferred to read, or played, but without spirit
worked too hard at school	worked less hard—didn't work hard enough
was always obedient	became truculent and insolent (e.g., called mother a liar on one occasion)
was well-mannered	gobbled her food
	wouldn't wait at table until everyone was finished
believed in God	said she didn't believe in God; said she has lost faith in human nature
was good	looked at times evil

Her mother was very alarmed at these changes and between August and December had consulted two doctors and her head mistress about her. None of these other people saw anything abnormal in June, nor did her sister or her father. However, Mrs. Field could not leave her alone.

It is important to realize that Mrs. Field's picture of June was, of course, never true. June's whole life was totally unknown to her mother. She felt shy and self-conscious, unsure of herself, but big for her age and active in swimming and other sports that she had undertaken to master her prolonged childhood crippled condition (she was not finally out of calipers until she was ten years old). Although active, she was not independent for, as she told us, she had largely complied with her mother, and had seldom dared to contradict her. She did however begin to go out with boys when she was thirteen while pretending to be at Church Club.

When she came back from camp, she began for the first time to give some expression to how she really felt about herself, her mother, her school work, God, other people, and so on, by ordinary standards, to a very subdued extent indeed.

This change was actively welcomed by her schoolteachers, was regarded with a certain amount of ordinary sisterly cattiness by Sylvia, and seemed part of the upset of having a daughter to her father. Only her mother saw it as an expression of *illness*, and felt confirmed in this opinion when June began to become more withdrawn at home over the Christmas vacation and thereafter.

This view held by her mother as to the events leading to June's state of almost complete immobile passivity can be put as follows: June was becoming ill from August onwards. She underwent insidious changes in her personality, becoming rude, aggressive, truculent, and insolent at home, while at school

she became withdrawn and self-conscious. According
to this view, a mother knows her own daughter best,
and she may detect the beginnings of schizophrenia
before others (father, sister, teachers, doctors). (*90*, pp.
137–9)

In this unusually intensive investigation, the period of hospitalization and recovery were directly observed:

> The phase in which June was clinically catatonic and
> in which her mother nursed her like an infant lasted
> three weeks, and was the most harmonious phase di-
> rectly observed by us in their relationship.
>
> Conflict only began when June, from our point of
> view, began to recover.
>
> In the period of recovery, almost every advance
> made by June (in the viewpoint of nursing staff, psy-
> chiatric social worker, occupational therapists, and
> ourselves) was opposed vehemently by her mother,
> who consistently regarded as steps back what to us
> and to June were steps forward.
>
> Here are a few examples.
>
> June began to take some initiative. Her mother
> expressed great alarm at any such show either on the
> grounds that June was irresponsible, or that it was
> not like June to do anything without asking. It was
> not that there was anything wrong in what June did,
> it was that she did not ask permission first. . . .
>
> [An] example her mother gave that alarmed her was
> how June ate a threepenny bar of chocolate after
> breakfast, once more without asking. . . .
>
> June was allowed no pocket money by her parents,
> but was told that they would give her money if she ex-
> plained why she wanted it. Not surprisingly, she pre-
> ferred to borrow small sums from others. The smallest
> amount in her possession had to be accounted for.

This control was taken to extraordinary lengths. Once June helped herself to sixpence from her father's money-box to buy ice-cream, without asking him. He told her mother that if June was stealing, she was lost to him. Another time she had found a shilling in a cinema and her parents insisted that she should hand it in at the desk. June said that this was ridiculous and taking honesty too far as she herself would not expect to get a shilling back if she lost it. But her parents kept on about it all the next day and late that evening her father came into her bedroom once again to admonish her.

The above examples can be multiplied many times over. They epitomize the intense reactions of her parents to June's emergent, but brittle, autonomy. Mrs. Field's term for this growing independence was "an explosion."

So far June has held her own. Her mother continues to express herself in extremely ambivalent terms over evidences of June's greater independence. She tells her she looks hideous when wearing ordinary make-up, she actively ridicules her expectancy that any boy is interested in her, she treats any expressions of irritation or exasperation on June's part as symptoms of the "illness," or construes them as tokens of "evil." . . .

[June] has to keep a tight control on herself however because if she shouts, screams, cries, swears, eats too little, or eats too much, eats too fast, or eats too slowly, reads too much, sleeps too much or too little, her mother tells her that she is ill. It takes a lot of courage on June's part to take the risk of not being what her parents call "well." (*90,* pp. 139–45)

It is when we come to the issue of feedback that a review of terminology is necessary for the clarification of the theory. The term homeostasis has come to be equated with stability or equilibrium, not only as applied to the family but in other fields as well. But, as Davis (*36*) and Toch and Hastorf (*154*) have emphasized, two definitions of homeostasis have existed from the time of Bernard on: (1) as an *end,* or state, specifically the existence of a certain constancy in the face of (external) change; and (2) as a *means:* the negative feedback mechanisms which act to minimize change. The ambiguity of this double usage and subsequent wide-ranging, often equally vague applications of the term have dulled its usefulness as a precise analogy or explanatory principle. It is presently clearer to refer to the *steady state* or *stability* of a system, which is generally maintained by *negative feedback* mechanisms.

All families that stay together must be characterized by some degree of negative feedback, in order to withstand the stresses imposed by the environment and the individual members. Disturbed families are particularly refractory to change and often demonstrate remarkable ability to maintain the status quo by predominantly negative feedback, as Jackson [10] observed, and as Laing and Esterson's example illustrates.

However, there is also learning and growth in the family, and it is exactly here that a pure homeostasis model errs most, for these effects are closer to *positive* feedback. The differentiation of behavior, reinforcement, and learning (of both adaptive and symptomatic behavior), and the ultimate growth and departure of children all indicate that while from one view the family is balanced by homeostasis, on the other hand, there are important simultaneous

---

[10] Cf. Jackson:

> It is significant in the development of family theory that it was the observation of homeostatic mechanisms in the families of psychiatric patients that led to the hypothesis of the family as a homeostatic, and eventually specifically as a rule-governed system. For [rules] become quickly apparent if one can observe the reaction to their abrogation and infer therefrom the rule which was broken. Tiresome long-term observation of the beaten path, with careful noting of possible routes which were *not* taken, can eventually yield a fair guess about the rules of the game. But the observable counteraction of a single deviation is like a marker to our goal. (*74*, pp. 13–14)

factors of change in operation,[11] and a model of family interaction must incorporate these and other principles into a more complex configuration.

4.444 Calibration and Step-Functions

Implicit in the above are a pair of more basic assumptions: of *constancy* within a *defined range*. The importance of change and variation (in terms of positive feedback, negative feedback, or other mechanisms) rests on the implicit premise of some fundamental stability of variation, a notion already shown to have been obscured by the dual use of "homeostasis." The more accurate term for this fixed range is *calibration* (*14*), the "setting" of the system, which will be seen to be equivalent to the more specific concept of *rule*, defined above. The classic analogy to the household furnace thermostat will illustrate these terms. The thermostat is set, or calibrated, at a certain temperature for the room, fluctuations below which will activate the furnace until the deviation is corrected (negative feedback) and the room temperature is again within the calibrated range. Consider, however, what happens when the thermostat setting is changed—set higher or lower; there is a difference in the behavior of the system as a whole though the mechanism of negative feedback remains exactly the same. This change in calibration, such as changing the setting of a thermostat or shifting gears in a car, is a *step-function* (*4*).

It should be noted that a step-function often has a stabilizing effect. Lowering the setting on a thermostat reduces the necessity for negative feedback and lightens the work and expense of the furnace. Also, more adaptive effects can be achieved by step-functions. The feedback loop of driver-gas pedal-speed of the car has certain limits in each gear, and in order to increase over-all speed or climb a hill, a recalibration (shifting of gear) is necessary. It appears that in families, too, step-functions have a stabilizing effect: psychosis is a sharp change that recalibrates the system and may even be adaptive (*77;* note also the catatonic period in the Laing and Esterson example above). Virtually inevitable internal changes

---

[11] Here, again, we can refer to Pribram's suggestion (s. 1.3) that constancy may lead to new sensitivities and necessitate new coping mechanisms.

(age and maturation both of parents and of children) may change the setting of the system, either gradually from within or drastically from without as the social environment impinges on these changes (with demands for higher education, military service, retirement, and so forth).

In this light, the homeostatic mechanisms noted clinically by Jackson (*69, 70*) may in fact be even more complex phenomena than those discussed here. If certain homeostatic mechanisms typically occur in response to deviation from the family rules, then these constitute a higher-order pattern of breaking and restoring a pattern over larger units of time.

Applying this model to family life or larger social patterns such as law enforcement, we propose that there is a calibration of customary or acceptable behavior, a family's rules or society's laws, within which individuals or groups operate for the most part. At one level these systems are quite stable, for a deviation in the form of behavior outside the accepted range is counteracted (disciplined, sanctioned, or even replaced by substitute, as when another family member becomes the patient). At another level, change occurs over time, which we propose is at least in part due to amplification of other deviations, and may eventually lead to a new setting for the system (step-function).

4.5

Summary

Human interaction is described as a communication system, characterized by the properties of general systems: time as a variable, system-subsystem relations, wholeness, feedback, and equifinality. Ongoing interactional systems are seen as the natural focus for study of the long-term pragmatic impact of communicational phenomena. Limitation in general and the development of family rules in particular lead to a definition and illustration of the family as a rule-governed system.

Chapter 5

A Communicational Approach
to the play
"Who's Afraid of Virginia Woolf?"

5.1

Introduction

The general problem of adequately illustrating the theory of interactional systems described in the previous chapter, as well as our choice of a fictitious system rather than actual clinical data (such as in earlier chapters), deserves some special comment. Having described a unit of recurring, ongoing processes with no single important incident or variable but rather redundant patterns over time and over a wide variety of situations, the first difficulty of providing examples becomes one of sheer size. In order to demonstrate exactly what is meant by the various abstractions that define a system—rules, feedback, equifinality, and so forth—an enormous number of messages, their analysis, and their configurations must be available. Transcripts of hours and hours of family interviews, for instance, would be prohibitively bulky and would be biased by both the therapist's point of view and by the therapeutic context. Unedited "natural history" data would carry the lack of limits to unusable extreme. Selecting and summarizing is not a ready answer either, for this would be biased in such a way as to deny the reader the right to observe this very process of selection. The second major goal, in addition to manageable size, is thus reasonable independence of the data, that is, independence of the authors themselves, in the sense of being publicly accessible.

Edward Albee's unusual and well-known play seems to satisfy both these criteria. The limits of the data presented in the play are fixed by artistic license, though the play is possibly even more real than reality, a "fire in the sogggy ashes of naturalism" (*145*); and all the information is available to the reader. A consequence of this last fact is that many other interpretations can and have been made of this play, and indeed many are possible. Focusing on one interpretation, as here, does not imply disagreement with others. It is simply that our purpose is to illustrate the thesis at hand and not to exhaustively analyze the play as an independent unit. After a synopsis of the line of action, this chapter will follow as closely as possible the major section structure of Chapter 4, with at least the first decimal headings (5.2, .3, and .4) referring to their counterparts in that chapter.

5.11—PLOT SYNOPSIS

This play, which according to one critic depicts "a limbo of domestic cantankerousness" (*107*, p. 58), has little concrete action. Most of its movement is contained in fast, detailed verbal interchanges. Through these interchanges the communicational complexity of the four actors' interaction is more starkly developed than would perhaps have been possible if the author had relied more on "real" events in the orthodox dramatic sense.

The entire play takes place during the small hours of a Sunday morning in the living room of George and Martha's house on a New England college campus. Martha is the only child of the college president, and her husband, George, is an associate professor in the history department. She is a large, boisterous woman of fifty-two, looking somewhat younger; he is a thin, graying intellectual of about forty-six. They are childless. According to Martha, she and her father expected George, who came to the college as a young man, to take over the history department and eventually become the next president of the college. George never lived up to this expectation and has remained an associate professor.

As the play opens, George and Martha are returning home from a faculty party held at the home of Martha's father. It is two o'clock in the morning, but, unbeknown to George, Martha has invited a couple they met at the party to join them. These visitors are Nick, a new man in the biology department, about thirty years old, blond and good-looking, and his wife, Honey, twenty-six, a petite, insipid, mousy blonde. As it is later revealed, Nick married Honey because he thought she was going to have a baby, but her condition turned out to be a hysterical pregnancy, which of course disappeared as soon as they were married; and perhaps he was also motivated by thoughts of her father's wealth. Whether for these or other reasons, Nick and Honey maintain, to each other, an extremely overconventional style of communication.

George and Martha have secrets of their own. There is above all their shared fiction that they have a son who is just coming of age, and a rule related to this imaginary child, namely that they must not disclose his "existence" to anybody. There is also a very dark chapter in George's earlier life. It appears that he accidentally fatally shot his mother and that a year later, while receiving driving instructions from his father, he lost control of the car and his father was killed; but the audience is somehow left wondering if this is not simply another fantasy.

Act One is called "Fun and Games" and provides an introduction to the older couple's style of verbal brawling and to their mythical son, as well as to Martha's (obviously stereotyped) seductive attitude toward Nick. It is climaxed by Martha's scathing attack on George's professional failure.

Act Two, "Walpurgisnacht" (Witches' Sabbath), begins with George and Nick alone in the room, almost competing in the revelation of confidences—George talking about the death of his parents, although this is disguised as the sad life story of a third person, and Nick explaining why he got married. When the women return, Martha begins to dance brazenly with Nick for George's benefit and the first overtly labeled game, "Humiliate the Host," is played. Martha reveals to their guests how George's parents died, whereupon George attacks her physically. He then initiates the next game, "Get the Guests," and relates, to Nick's extreme mortification and Honey's horror, the secret of their shotgun marriage. In the bitter aftermath, Martha and George exchange challenges and vow further battle. The next game becomes "Hump the Hostess" and leads to Martha's open seduction of Nick, whose ability to cooperate, however, turns out to have been impaired by the constant drinking, which has been going on since the early evening.

Act Three, "Exorcism," opens with Martha alone, regretting yet complaining about her would-be infidelity. George has meanwhile prepared the last game ("Bringing Up Baby") and gathers the other three for this final round. He reveals the full story of the myth about their son and then announces to the helplessly enraged Martha that the boy was "killed" in an auto accident. The nature of this exorcism dawns on Nick ("Jesus Christ, I think I understand this" [p. 236 [1]]). He and Honey leave, and the play ends on an exhausted, ambiguous note that makes it unclear whether George and Martha will go on playing the game of parents bemoaning the death of their only child in the prime of his youth, or whether a complete change of their relationship patterns has now become possible.

5.2

Interaction As a System

The characters in this play, especially George and Martha, can be seen as comprising an interactional system, characterized, *mutatis mutandis,* by many of the properties of general systems. There is no harm in emphasizing once more that such a model is neither

---

[1] Page references, in brackets, are to the Atheneum edition (*1*).

literal nor comprehensive; that is, these characters, as those in
real ongoing relationships, are not considered in any sense mechanical, automated, or completely defined by their interactional
aspects. Indeed, the power of a model as a scientific device rests in
this deliberately simplified representation and organization of the
subject of discourse (2).

5.21—TIME AND ORDER, ACTION AND REACTION

Gregory Bateson defined social psychology as "the study of the
reactions of individuals to the reactions of other individuals," adding, "We have to consider, not only A's reactions to B's behavior,
but we must go on to consider how these affect B's later behavior
and the effect of this on A" (10, pp. 175-6). This is the underlying
principle of the present analysis. George and Martha are interesting
individuals, but they will not be abstracted from their social context
(which is, primarily, each other) and considered as "types." Rather
the unit of analysis will be what goes on, sequentially, between
them: Martha as she reacts to George and he to her. These transactions accumulate, over larger time periods, taking on an order that,
though abstracted, is still essentially comprised of sequential processes.

5.22—DEFINITION OF THE SYSTEM

An interactional system was defined in s. 4.22 as two or more
communicants in the process of, or at the level of, defining the
nature of their relationship. As we have tried to explain in the
preceding chapters, relationship patterns exist independently from
content although, of course, in actual life they are always manifested by and through content. If attention is limited to the content of what people communicate to each other, then indeed there
often seems to be hardly any continuity in their interaction—
"time always starts afresh and history is always in the year zero."
And so it is with Albee's play: for three painful hours the spec-
tator witnesses a kaleidoscopic sequence of ever-changing events.
But what is their common denominator? Alcoholism, impotence,

childlessness, latent homosexuality, sadomasochism—all these have been proposed as explanations of what is taking place between these two couples during the small hours of a Sunday morning. In his Stockholm production, Ingmar Bergman stressed "the christological reference in the sacrifice of the son by the father—the son who was a gift of the father to the mother, of heaven to earth, of God to mankind" (*109*). As long as the *content* of communication is the criterion, all these viewpoints, contradictory as some of them are, appear justified to a certain degree.

But Albee himself supplies an altogether different viewpoint. Act One is called "Fun and Games": games of relationships are being played throughout the play, and rules are constantly invoked, followed, and broken. They are terrifying games, devoid of all playful characteristics, and their rules are their own best explanation. Neither the games nor the rules answer the question *why?* As Schimel, too, points out:

> It is appropriate that the first act is entitled "Fun and Games," a study of repetitious, although destructive, *patterns of behavior between people*. Albee graphically represents the "how" of games and leaves the "why" up to the audience and critics. (*141*, p. 99; italics ours)

It little matters then if, for instance, George is really an academic failure and for the reasons Martha describes, or if Nick is really the Scientist of the Future who threatens history and historians. Consider, for instance, the latter—George's frequent references [e.g., pp. 36–40, 65–68] to history and the biology of the future (eugenics, conformity). This may be seen as a personal, rather peevish preoccupation, as he terms it; as social commentary; even as an allegory of the struggle of traditional Western man (George) against the wave of the future (Nick), with the "Earth Mother" (as Martha calls herself [p. 189]) as the prize; or as all of these and more. But seen in terms of George and Nick's *relationship*, this topic is another "bean bag" (as George later describes the mythical son [p. 98]), that is, a toy, often a missile—the medium through which their game is manifested. In this sense, George's digressions on history and biology can be seen as provocations disguised as defense and, thus, as a very interesting communicational phenomenon involving disqualification, denial of communication (with the effect of progressive involvement), and a punctuation that leads to a self-fulfilling prophecy in which Nick really does take George's wife.

Similarly, it appears that George and Martha are so caught up in their relationship struggle that they do not take the content of their insults personally (in fact Martha will not permit Nick to call George the same things she calls him nor to interfere with their game [e.g., p. 190, p. 204]); they seem to respect each other *in the system.*

5.23—SYSTEMS AND SUBSYSTEMS

The main focus of the play, and of this commentary, is on the dyad George-and-Martha. They are, however, an "open system," and the concept of hierarchical structure is appropriate here. Each of them forms a subdyad with Nick and, to a far lesser extent, with Honey. Nick-and-Honey are of course another dyadic system which moreover stands in a notable relation to George-and-Martha by virtue of the formers' starkly contrasting complementarity. George, Martha, and Nick comprise a triangle of shifting dyads.[2] The four as a whole are the total visible system of the drama, although the structure is not limited to the cast present but also involves, and on occasion invokes, the unseen son, Martha's father, and the campus milieu. Present purposes will not permit exhaustive classification and analysis of all the possibilities, and we are left with what Lawrence Durrell (*41*) called "Workpoints"—a virtual infinity of revolutions and new views as other facets of the structure are elaborated; for example, Nick and Honey's peculiar complementarity; Martha's aggressive boldness fitting Nick's narcissism;

[2] In which any two are a unit against the third, as when Martha and Nick dance or otherwise mock George [e.g., pp. 130–6], or George and Martha team up against Nick [e.g., pp. 196–7].

George and Nick's tense rapprochement;[3] Martha and George's competition for her father; and so forth.

As a final comment, it is instructive that Albee works almost exclusively with smaller units, at most shifting dyads into a triangle or (in the men versus women aspect and perhaps spuriously) two against two. The use of three or four units at once would probably be too complicated.

5.3

The Properties of an Open System

The general characteristics of systems can be illustrated by restating them in terms of George and Martha's system, especially with contrast, for clarity, with individual approaches.

5.31—WHOLENESS

Ideally, we would describe the gestalt, the emergent quality of this cast of characters. Their relationships are both something more and something other than what the individuals bring into them. That which is George or Martha, individually, does not explain what is compounded between them, nor how. To break this whole into individual personality traits or structures is essentially to separate them from each other, to deny that their behaviors have special meaning in the context of this interaction—that in fact the pattern of the interaction perpetuates these. Phrased in other terms, wholeness is a description of the overlapping triadic links of stimulus-response-reinforcement described by Bateson and Jackson (*19*) and discussed in s. 2.41. So instead of focusing on the motivations of the individuals involved, it is possible, at another level, to describe the system *as workable,* with any emphasis on individuals directed to the appropriateness of their behavior to

---

[3] Which gives an interactional meaning to the title "Walpurgisnacht," in which George shows Nick the orgy [p. 115] just as Mephistopheles showed Faust.

this system. All the conclusions of Chapter 1—the Black Box approach, consciousness versus unconsciousness, present versus past, circularity, and the relativity of "normal" and "abnormal"—should be kept in mind as corollaries of the principle of system wholeness.

The *unilateral* view of this dyad is taken almost unanimously by journalistic reviewers, who seem to "favor" George as the victim in the situation. But the only difference between George's and Martha's recriminations is that he accuses her of strength while she accuses him of weakness. If the reviewers acknowledge his part in the battle at all, George is seen as resorting to his tactics after hard provocation. In our view, this is a system of mutual provocation that neither party can stop. It is, however, enormously difficult to describe such circularity with the balance it justifies and requires, mostly because of the lack of an adequate vocabulary to describe mutually causal relations,[4] and also because one must start somewhere, and wherever the circle is broken analytically, a starting point is implied.

Because Martha's offenses are obvious and unmistakable and because she so easily fits the stereotype of an emasculating harridan, George's actions tend to be more emphasized here. This is, of course, not simply to shift the blame, for blame is not the issue; it is rather that Martha and George both make her contribution obvious: it is, in fact, their shared punctuation that she is the active and he the passive one (though they put different values on activity and passivity, with George, for instance, seeing himself as restrained and Martha calling this weakness). But this is a tactic of their game; what should be seen as basic is that they are playing the game together.

This emphasis on circularity will also neglect more than cursory mention of their individual redeeming qualities, although in fact both are quite bright and perceptive, both show compassion on occasion, and both seem aware, at different points, of the fearful destructiveness of their game and apparently want to stop it.

[4] Maruyama has created the term "multilateral mutual simultaneous causal relations" (*100*).

5.32—FEEDBACK

The feedback processes in this perhaps simplified system correspond precisely to symmetry (positive, deviation-amplifying feedback) and complementarity (negative, stabilizing feedback). The "everything you can do I can do better" format of symmetrical competition inexorably leads to more of the same, with increment piling on augmentation in runaway proportions. Conversely, a switch to complementarity in this system—acceptance, compliance, laughter, sometimes even inaction—usually brings closure and at least temporary surcease of struggle.

There are, however, exceptions to this general pattern. As the tempo increases in both acrimony and cycle size (from brief, almost playful banter to more significant and larger patterns such as "Humiliate the Host"), similarly larger deviation-corrections are required to counteract this tendency, and, as Martha and George demonstrate, their skills in conciliation contrast sadly with those for combat. Metacommunication, a possible stabilizer, proves to be subject to the same rule of symmetry (s. 5.43), and, instead of stopping the conflagration, further ignites it. There are even more problems when complementarity in the service of symmetry (s. 5.41) leads to paradox and further precludes resolution.

In s. 5.42, the son myth will be considered as a strictly controlled paradigm of their system, with built-in homeostatic mechanisms of a different sort.

5.33—EQUIFINALITY

Considering a system as something developed over a period of time, achieving a certain state, or changing from one state to another, there emerge two very different ways to account for the present state. One common approach is to observe or, as is more common and necessary in human study, to infer the initial conditions (etiology, past causes, history) that presumably led to the present conditions. In an interactional system such as George and Martha's, these initial conditions may be either shared experiences in courtship or early marriage or, even earlier, they may be individual personality patterns fixed in the early life of each or both. Of the former, a causal role could be assigned, for example, to Martha's accidental knockout of George, about which she says, "I think it's colored our whole life. Really I do. It's an excuse, anyway" [p. 57]; or, less superficially, to the circumstances surrounding this event including the failure of George to materialize as "heir-apparent" to the father's presidency; or to Martha's loss of innocence and/or alcoholism (from "real ladylike little drinkies" to "rubbing alcohol" [p. 24]) that George has long endured; or other such problems dating from the early history of their marriage. Of the individual "initial conditions," the possible explanations are even more varied.[5] George could be seen as a latent homosexual who despises Martha, using and subtly encouraging her affair with the beautiful young man (and, presumably, others) for his own vicarious satisfaction. Or, Martha and George with the fantasy son or Nick form a classic Oedipal situation, in which not only does Nick attempt to sleep with the mother and find himself impotent, unable to break the taboo, but also the maturing son is killed by the father in exactly the same manner in which George as a boy reportedly killed his own father [compare pp. 95–96 and p. 231]; further, his mock killing of Martha with the toy shotgun [p. 57] duplicates the manner in which he is said to have shot his own mother [p. 94]. These are only suggestions of possible directions of analysis, in all of which the interaction is seen as determined by previous, often individual, conditions which thus would make the best explanation of that interaction.

Several comments have been made earlier (s. 1.2; 1.63; 3.64) about the nature and use of anamnestic data, and a trend toward a more complex conceptualization than one-to-one relationships between past and present has been commented on in the previous chapter (s. 4.33). So it will suffice here, as a critique of the above-described historical approaches, to note again that in this case, as in many— perhaps most—others in human study, the past is not available

---

[5] But they are also clearly *summative,* with no explicit explanation of how the other fits into the situation.

except as reported in the present and therefore is not pure content but has a relationship aspect as well. Occurring in an actual interaction in present time, the past-as-reported can also be material for the present game. Truth, selection, and distortion are less important for the understanding of present interaction than how the material is used and what kind of relationship is defined. The view proposed here aims to explore the extent to which system parameters—the rules and limitations observed in the ongoing interaction—can account for both perpetuation and change in the system; that is the extent to which a lawfulness that does not depend on the past can be offered as an explanation of the system.[6]

5.4

An Ongoing Interactional System

At this point, in order to illustrate what is meant by present interaction, a sketch of the rules and tactics of George and Martha's interactional game, as we see it, should be given; then some of the specific aspects of ongoing relationships can be considered.

5.41

Their game can be described as *symmetrical escalation* (s. 3.61) with each keeping up with the other or trying to outdo the other, depending on whose punctuation one accepts. This struggle is established at the very beginning when George and Martha run through several quick symmetrical escalations, almost as if practicing, "merely . . . exercising," as George claims [p. 33]. The content is entirely different in each case, but their structure is virtually identical and momentary stability is reached by joint laughter. For instance, at one point Martha tells her husband, "You make me puke!" George considers this with facetious detachment:

[6] This issue is not, at this stage of knowledge, a dichotomous one, where a choice must be made between total dependence or total independence of initial conditions. It is rather the simpler one of examining in some detail the power of the reciprocal behavioral effects of a communication system such as the family, and questioning—no matter how they started—whether they can stop.

> That wasn't a very nice thing to say, Martha.

Martha: That wasn't *what?*

George: . . . a very nice thing to say. [p. 13]

Martha persists less elegantly:

> I like your anger. I think that's what I like about
> you most . . . your anger. You're such a . . .
> such a simp! You don't even have the . . . the
> what? . . . .

George: . . . guts? . . .

Martha: Phrasemaker! (Pause) [pp. 13–14]

Then they both laugh—at their teamwork, perhaps—and closure
has been reached. Laughter seems to signal acceptance and so has
a homeostatic, stabilizing effect. But it is by now apparent how
pervasive is their symmetry, for even the slightest directive by one
precipitates further struggle, with the other immediately retaliating
in such a way as to define his equality. Thus Martha tells George
to put more ice in her drink, and George, while complying, likens
her to a cocker spaniel always chewing ice cubes with her "big
teeth," and they are off again:

Martha: THEY'RE MY BIG TEETH!

George: Some of them . . . some of them.

Martha: I've got more teeth than you've got.

George: Two more.

Martha: Well, two more's a lot more. [p. 14]

And George, quickly switching to a known vulnerability:

> I suppose it is. I suppose it's pretty remarkable
> . . . considering how old you are.

Martha: YOU CUT THAT OUT! (Pause) You're not so
young yourself.

George (With boyish pleasure . . . a chant): I'm six
years younger than you are. . . . I always have
been and I always will be.

Martha (Glumly): Well . . . you're going bald.

161

> George: So are you. (Pause . . . they both laugh) Hello,
>   honey.
> Martha: Hello. C'mon over here and give your Mommy a
>   big sloppy kiss. [pp. 14–15]

And another escalation starts. George sarcastically refuses to kiss
her:

>   Well, dear, if I kissed you I'd get all excited . . .
>   I'd get beside myself, and I'd take you, by force,
>   right here on the living room rug [. . . .]
> Martha: You pig!
> George   (Haughtily): Oink! Oink!
> Martha: Ha, ha, ha HA! Make me another drink . . .
>   lover. [pp. 15–16]

The subject now switches to her drinking, the escalation becomes
bitter and leads into a power struggle over who is to open the door
for the guests who have meanwhile arrived and keep ringing the
bell.

Note here that just as neither will take an initiative or command
from the other, so neither does anything *but* command or control.
Martha does not say, "You can give me some more ice," much less
"May I please have . . . ?" but "Hey, put some more ice in my
drink, will you?" [p. 14]; similarly she orders him to kiss her and
to open the door. Nor is she simply rude and ill-mannered, for not
to act so is to put herself at a considerable disadvantage, as George
shows later in the play with a well-executed maneuver before their
guests, after Martha has openly ridiculed him:

> George   (With a great effort controls himself . . . then,
>   as if she had said nothing more than "George,
>   dear." . . .): Yes, Martha? Can I get you some-
>   thing?
> Martha   (Amused at his game): Well . . . uh . . . sure,
>   you can light my cigarette, if you're of a mind to.
> George   (Considers, then moves off): No . . . there are
>   limits, I mean, man can put up with only so much

without he descends a rung or two on the old evolutionary ladder . . . (Now a quick aside to Nick) . . . which is up your line . . . (Then back to Martha) . . . sinks, Martha, and it's a funny ladder . . . you can't reverse yourself . . . start back up once you're descending. (Martha blows him an arrogant kiss) Now . . . I'll hold your hand when it's dark and you're afraid of the bogey man, and I'll tote your gin bottles out after midnight, so no one'll see . . . but I will not light your cigarette. And that, as they say, is that. (Brief silence)

Martha (Under her breath): Jesus! [pp. 50–1]

Similarly, if George is polite or otherwise accepts the one-down position, Martha either calls him spineless or, with some justification, suspects a trap.

Part of a game is its *tactics;* though George's and Martha's styles differ greatly, each is highly consistent and, what is most important, their respective tactics interlock neatly. Martha is crass, overtly insulting, and very directly, almost physically, aggressive. Her language is coarse, her insults seldom eloquent but always straight. Even her most pain-producing thrust ("Humiliate the Host") amounts to a simple exposé.

George, on the other hand, adroitly sets traps, using passivity, indirectness, and civilized restraint as weapons. While Martha insults him along customary lines (with vulgar epithets, or belaboring his professional failure), he invokes subtler values, insulting her articulately and with control, but more often making certain that her behavior in insulting him does not go unnoticed. By quietly framing it, he uses her behavior against her as if with a mirror, delicately turning it back on her—as above, "That wasn't a very nice thing to say, Martha," or, with clearer instigation, when he mimics the simpering Honey:

Hee, hee, hee, hee.

Martha (Swinging on George): Look, muckmouth . . . you cut that out!

George   (Innocence and hurt): Martha! (To Honey and Nick) Martha's a devil with language; she really is. [p. 21]

It would have been quite effective, perhaps, if Martha had said nothing and let George's rudeness show instead. But she does not use his very tactic, as he must know she will not, and he takes her neatly. Clearly, the behavior of each is predicated on that of the other, with Martha's insults turned into barbs that make her howl the louder.[7] Thus they fight at entirely different levels, so closure or resolution is effectively prevented: *the tactics themselves serve not only to implement but to perpetuate the game.*

There is in this state of affairs some inherent instability. Martha may, and sometimes does, intensify her attacks beyond manageable limits. George may then switch to her level, as he does in the extreme case by bodily assault after her revelation of his apparent accidental parricides in "Humiliate the Host":

George   (On her): I'LL KILL YOU! (Grabs her by the throat. They struggle)

Nick: HEY! (Comes between them)

Honey   (Wildly): VIOLENCE! VIOLENCE! (George, Martha, and Nick struggle . . . yells, etc.)

Martha   [persisting with her aggravation]: IT HAPPENED! TO ME! TO ME!

George: YOU SATANIC BITCH!

Nick: STOP THAT! STOP THAT!

Honey: VIOLENCE! VIOLENCE! (The other three struggle. George's hands are on Martha's throat. Nick grabs him, tears him from Martha, throws him on the floor. George, on the floor; Nick over him; Martha, to one side, her hand on her throat) [pp. 137–8]

[7] The formulation "sadomasochistic symbiosis" may spring to mind here, but there are two inadequacies in this view: first, the circularity of their pattern makes it difficult and perhaps arbitrary to decide which role to assign which partner. Even more, such a label is a speculation on *why*, but it is not definitively descriptive; it does not even hint *how* the dyad operates, because it is of course a summative formulation.

Still, he cannot win at that level and must then redouble his response in his own style, as he indicates in the lull that follows this attack:

> All right . . . all right . . . very quiet now . . . we will all be . . . very quiet.

Martha   (Softly, with a slow shaking of her head): Murderer. Mur . . . der . . . er.

Nick   (Softly to Martha): O.K. now . . . that's enough. (A brief silence. They all move around a little, self-consciously, like wrestlers flexing after a fall)

George   (Composure seemingly recovered, but there is a great nervous intensity): Well! That's one game. What shall we do now, hunh? (Martha and Nick laugh nervously) Oh come on . . . let's think of something else. We've played Humiliate the Host . . . we've gone through that one . . . what shall we do now?

Nick: Aw . . . look . . .

George: AW LOOK! (Whines it) AWWW . . . looooook. (Alert) I mean, come on! We must know other games, college-type types like us . . . that can't be the . . . limit of our vocabulary, can it? [pp. 138–9]

And he immediately suggests the variation that will occupy them until the final denouement. It is "Hump the Hostess," a game of *coalitions* that requires Nick's participation. Now, the addition of a third party to an already tangled interaction, with consequent shifting subdyads, considerably increases the complexity of the game. Previously the use of the guests was only quasi-coalitional, in which they served as backboards, so to speak, for George and Martha's shots.[8] In this last-but-one round, however, the third party (Nick) is more directly involved. Since the latter

---

[8] Ogden Nash has contributed to the formalization of this method in his poem "Don't Wait, Hit Me Now!" which goes, in part:

> Here is the formula, in which the presence of a third person is the only essential extra ingredient; . . .

does not rise to the game at first, George lays the groundwork with another game, "Get the Guests," after which Nick is ready:

> Nick   (To George, as he moves toward the hall): You're going to regret this.
>
> George: Probably. I regret everything.
>
> Nick: I mean, I'm going to make you regret this.
>
> George   (Softly): No doubt. Acute embarrassment, eh?
>
> Nick: I'll play the charades like you've got 'em set up . . . I'll play in your language . . . I'll be what you say I am.
>
> George: You are already . . . you just don't know it. [pp. 149–50]

Yet the most remarkable aspect of the ensuing events is their conformity to George and Martha's basic rules and respective tactics. For each, again, is out to get the other, Martha by the flagrant insult of unconcealed adultery, George by in fact setting this up and then, again, thrusting her own behavior upon her. Thus, instead of entering with her into another symmetrical escalation, he suddenly not only agrees (complementarily) with her threat of betraying him with Nick, but even suggests that she go ahead and sets up the situation accordingly. This is no simple outage, and is not painless to George [p. 173]. Martha is prepared for a new escalation, but not for this kind of communication (which will be considered in greater detail in s. 7.3 under the heading "Prescribing the Symptom"), which leaves her defenseless and,

---

Suppose you think your Gregory danced too often with Mrs. Limbworthy at the club, you don't say to him directly, "Gregory, I'll smack you down if you don't lay off that platinum-plated hussy,"

No, you wait till a friend drops in and then with a glance at Gregory say to her, "Isn't it funny what fools middle-aged men can make of themselves over anything blonde and slithery, do you understand how anybody sober and in their right mind could look twice at that Limbworthy job, but then of course darling, Gregory wasn't altogether in his right mind last night, was he?"

This is indeed more excruciating to Gregory than Shakespearian excursions and alarums,

Because there is no defense against caroms. . . .

Because the hit direct doesn't compare with the ricochet in deadly unanswerability. (*110*, pp. 99–101)

as Albee puts it, "oddly furious" [p. 168]. In the face of her threat, George quietly announces that he is going to read a book:

> Martha: You're gonna do *what?*
>
> George   (quietly, distinctly): I am going to read a book. Read. Read. Read? You've heard of it? (Picks up a book)
>
> Martha: Whaddya mean you're gonna read? What's the matter with you? [p. 168]

Now Martha is faced with the alternatives of stopping or continuing in order to see how seriously George means what he says. She takes the second alternative and begins to kiss Nick. George is immersed in his reading:

> Martha: You know what I'm doing, George?
>
> George: No, Martha . . . what are you doing?
>
> Martha: I'm entertaining. I'm entertaining one of the guests. I'm necking with one of the guests. [p. 170]

But George does not rise to the challenge. Martha has used up the challenges that might ordinarily call George's reactions into play. She tries once more:

> Martha: . . . I said I was necking with one of the guests.
>
> George: Good . . . good. You go right on.
>
> Martha   (Pauses . . . not knowing quite what to do): Good?
>
> George: Yes, good . . . good for you.
>
> Martha   (Her eyes narrowing, her voice becoming hard): Oh, I see what you're up to, you lousy little. . . .
>
> George: I'm up to page a hundred and . . . [p. 171]

Uncertain what to do, Martha sends Nick into the kitchen, then turns to George again:

> Martha: Now you listen to me . . .
>
> George: I'd rather read, Martha, if you don't mind . . .
>
> Martha   (Her anger has her close to tears, her frustration

> to fury): Well, I do mind. Now, you pay attention
> to me! You come off this kick you're on, or I swear
> to God I'll do it. I swear to God I'll follow that
> guy into the kitchen, and then I'll take him up-
> stairs, and . . .

George   (Swinging around to her again . . . loud . . .
> loathing): SO WHAT, MARTHA? [p. 173]

Similarly, he turns on Nick:

> Nick: You don't . . . you don't even . . .
> George: Care? You're quite right . . . I couldn't care less.
> So, you just take this bag of laundry here, throw
> her over your shoulder, and . . .
> Nick: You're disgusting.
> George   (Incredulous): Because *you're* going to hump
> Martha, *I'm* disgusting? (He breaks down in ridi-
> culing laughter) [p. 172]

Later, it is not even necessary for George to point this out to
Martha, as she comments on her own behavior:

> I disgust me. I pass my life in crummy, totally
> pointless infidelities . . . (Laughs ruefully) *would-
> be* infidelities. Hump the Hostess? That's a laugh.
> [p. 189]

5.411

George and Martha's competitive game is not, as it may seem on
the surface or in specific instances, simply one of open conflict in
which the object is solely to destroy the other. Rather, in its more
general aspects, it appears to be collaborative conflict, or conflictive
collaboration: there may be some "upper limit" to their escalation,
and there are shared rules, as already implied, on how the game
is played. These rules qualify the basic rule of symmetry and give
winning (or losing) its value within the game; without them, winning and losing have no meaning.

Without excessive formalization, it can be said that the constraint on their symmetry (which in itself, would logically lead to murder—directly and literally, not metaphorically as in the play) is that they must be not only effective but witty and daring. Paradigmatic is the following perfectly symmetrical exchange of insults:

George: Monstre!
Martha: Cochon!
George: Bête!
Martha: Canaille!
George: Putain! [p. 101]

There is a certain off-beat stylishness to their articulate though vicious deportment, which makes Nick and especially Honey the blander by comparison. Neither of the latter makes a suitable sub-partner in the game; Martha's disappointment with Nick is not only sexual but that he is passive and rather unimaginative, and George, who tries Nick out as a sparring partner at times, seems also to find him poor competition:

George (Toying with him): I asked you how you liked that for a declension: Good; better; best; bested. Hm? Well?

Nick (With some distaste): I really don't know what to say.

George (Feigned incredulousness): You really don't know what to *say?*

Nick (Snapping it out): All right . . . what do you want me to say? Do you want me to say it's funny, so you can contradict me and say it's sad? or do you want me to say it's sad so you can turn around and say no, it's funny. You can play that damn little game any way you want to, you know!

George (Feigned awe): Very good! Very good!

Nick (Even angrier than before): And when my wife comes back [to the living room], I think we'll just. · · · [pp. 32–3]

169

Besides their colorfulness, then, George and Martha find, even demand in each other a certain strength, an ability to take anything into the game without flinching. In the last act, George teams with Martha to ridicule Nick, even when the material of the joke is his cuckoldry:

> Martha   (To Nick): Ach! You just stay where you are. Make my hubby a drink.
>
> Nick: I don't think I will.
>
> George: No, Martha, no; that would be too much; he's your houseboy, baby, not mine.
>
> Nick: I'm nobody's houseboy.
>
> George and Martha: . . . (Sing) I'm nobody's houseboy now . . . (Both laugh).
>
> Nick: Vicious . . .
>
> George   (Finishing it for him): . . . children. Hunh? That right? Vicious children, with their oh-so-sad games, hopscotching their way through life, etcetera, etcetera. Is that it?
>
> Nick: Something like it.
>
> George: Screw, baby.
>
> Martha: Him can't. Him too fulla booze.
>
> George: Weally? (Handing the snapdragons to Nick) Here; dump these in some gin. [pp. 196–7]

This callous daring is also seen in their "brinkmanship," in which outdoing or "getting" the other requires less and less restraint and more and more imagination. For instance, Martha is delighted at a particularly terrifying riposte of George's: she is ridiculing George to Nick and Honey when he returns to the scene, his hands behind his back, at first in sight only of Honey; Martha continues with the story of her knocking out George:

> And it was an *accident* . . . a real, goddamn accident! (George takes from behind his back a short-barreled shotgun, and calmly aims it at the back of Martha's head. Honey screams . . . rises. Nick

> rises, and, simultaneously, Martha turns her head
> to face George, George pulls the trigger)
>
> George: POW!!!
>   (Pop! From the barrel of the gun blossoms a large
>   red and yellow Chinese parasol. Honey screams
>   again, this time less, and mostly from relief and
>   confusion) You're dead! Pow! You're dead!
>
> Nick   (Laughing): Good Lord.
>   (Honey is beside herself. Martha laughs too . . .
>   almost breaks down, her great laugh booming.
>   George joins in the general laughter and confu-
>   sion. It dies, eventually)
>
> Honey: Oh! My goodness!
>
> Martha   (Joyously): Where'd you get that, you bastard?
>   [. . .]
>
> George   (A trifle abstracted): Oh, I've had it awhile. Did
>   you like that?
>
> Martha   (Giggling): You bastard. [pp. 57–8]

Martha's joy and giggling may be in part sheer relief, but there is
also an almost sensual delight in the game well played, a delight
which they both share:

> George   (Leaning over Martha): You liked that, did you?
>
> Martha: Yeah . . . that was pretty good. (Softer) C'mon
>   . . . give me a kiss.

The result, however, cannot be closure, for just as their rivalry has
sexual aspects, their sexual behavior is also rivalry, and when
Martha persists with direct advances, George demures; she will not
be dissuaded, and he eventually gains a "Pyrrhic victory" [p. 59]
in refusing her and commenting, for their guests to hear, on the
impropriety of her behavior.

Thus their shared style represents a further restriction, another
regularity in their game. Further, it is apparent that there is some
mutual confirmation of their selves in the excitement of the risk.

However, there is also extreme rigidity that prevents either from more than briefly appreciating or building on this confirmation.

5.42—THE SON

The imaginary son is a unique topic deserving of separate treatment. Many reviewers, while enthusiastic about the play in general, have reservations about this issue. Malcolm Muggeridge feels "the play falls to pieces in the third act, when the lamentable business of the imaginary child is developed" (*107*, p. 58); and Howard Taubman protests that

> Mr. Albee would have us believe that for 21 years his older couple have nurtured a fiction that they have a son, that his imaginary existence is a secret that violently binds and sunders them and that George's pronouncing him dead may be a turning point. This part of the story does not ring true, and its falsity impairs the credibility of his central characters. (*152*)

We do not agree, first, on the basis of psychiatric evidence. The credibility of the existence of the fiction is not precluded by its delusional proportions, nor by the fact that it must be shared between them. Since the classic *folie à deux,* other shared, reality-distorting experiences have been described. Ferreira has referred to the "family myth" as

> a series of fairly well-integrated beliefs shared by all family members, concerning each other and their mutual position in the family life, beliefs that go unchallenged by everyone involved in spite of the reality distortions which they may conspicuously imply. (*42*, p. 457)

What is noteworthy in this formulation is that (1) the issue of literal belief is not central and (2) the function of the deception is relational.

Considering the first point, Ferreira comments, "The individual family member may know, and often does, that much of the image is false and represents no more than a sort of official party line" (*42*, p. 458). Nowhere does Albee suggest that George and Martha "really" believe they have a son. When they speak *about* this, their usage is clearly impersonal, referring not to a person but to the myth itself. When the fiction of the son is first mentioned, early in the play, George speaks of "the bit . . . the bit about the kid," [p. 18]. Later he even puns about their double-reference system:

> George: . . . you brought it out into the open. When is he coming home, Martha?
> Martha: I said never mind. I'm sorry I brought it up.
> George: Him up . . . not it. You brought *him* up. Well, more or less. When's the little bugger going to appear, hunh? I mean, isn't tomorrow meant to be his birthday, or something?
> Martha: [. . . .] I DON'T WANT TO TALK ABOUT IT!
> George: I bet you don't. (To Honey and Nick) Martha does not want to talk about it . . . him. Martha is sorry she brought it up . . . him. [p. 70]

This distinction between the "son" and the "son-game" is so consistently maintained, even to Martha's immediate reaction to George's announcement of the death—"You can't decide that for yourself" [p. 232]—that it is not possible to assume that they literally believe they have a son.

If this is so, then why do they play the game of pretending to have a son? Again, *what for* is a better question than *why*. As Ferreira describes it:

> The family myth represents nodal, resting points in the relationship. It ascribes roles and prescribes behavior which, in turn, will strengthen and consolidate those roles. Parenthetically we may observe that, in its content, it represents a group departure from reality, a departure that we could call "pathology." But at the same time it constitutes *by its very existence,* a frag-

> ment of life, a piece of reality that faces, and thus
> shapes [any] children born into it and the outsiders
> that brush by. (*42*, p. 462; italics ours)

This last point is most important. While the son is imaginary, their interaction about him is not, and the nature of this interaction, then, becomes the fruitful question.

The primary requirement of interaction about the son is a coalition between George and Martha; they *must* be together on this fiction in order to maintain it for, unlike a real child who, once procreated, exists, here they must constantly unite to create their child. And, changing the focus slightly, in this one area they *can* get together, collaborating without competition. The story is so "far-out" and private that they can perhaps afford to be together in it precisely because it is not real. In any case, they can and do fight about him just as about everything else, but there is a built-in limit to their game of symmetrical escalation in the necessity to share this fiction. *Their child-myth is a homeostatic mechanism.* In what appears to be a central area of their life they have a stable symmetrical coalition. And thus Martha, in her dreamlike recitation of the child's life, describes him in what could be metaphor:

> . . . and as he grew . . . oh! so wise! . . . he walked evenly
> between us . . . (She spreads her hands) . . . a hand out
> to each of us for what we could offer [. . .] and these hands,
> still, to hold us off a bit, for mutual protection [. . .] to pro-
> tect himself . . . and *us*. [pp. 221–2]

There is every reason to assume that a real child, had they had one, would have faced the same task. Although we do not actually observe it, because the play centers on the misuse of the myth, we can conjecture the following, with Ferreira:

> Seemingly, the family myth is called into play when-
> ever certain tensions reach predetermined thresholds
> among family members and in some way, real or
> fantasied, threaten to disrupt ongoing relationships.
> Then, the family myth functions like the thermostat

that is kicked into action by the "temperature" in the family. Like any other homeostatic mechanism, the myth prevents the family system from damaging, perhaps destroying, itself. It has therefore the qualities of any "safety valve," that is, a *survival* value. . . . It tends to maintain and sometimes even to increase the level of organization in the family by establishing patterns that perpetuate themselves with the circularity and self-correction characteristic of any homeostatic mechanism. (*42*, p. 462)

Real children, too, can be both salve and excuse for a marriage; so, as Fry pointed out (s. 4.442), can symptomatic behavior serve the same function.

But the play does not concern this use of the myth, but rather, ostensibly, the process of destruction of the myth. As noted, anything regarding the son's very existence is not fair ammunition in their warfare. To act otherwise, even in the heat of the battle, is considered truly wrong:

Martha: George's biggest problem about the little . . . ha, ha, ha, HA! . . . about our son, about our great big son, is that deep down in the privatemost pit of his gut, he's not completely sure it's his own kid.

George (Deeply serious): My God, you're a wicked woman.

Martha: And I've told you a million times, baby . . . I wouldn't conceive with anyone but you . . . you know that, baby.

George: A deeply wicked person.

Honey (Deep in drunken grief): My, my, my, my. Oh, my.

Nick: I'm not sure that this is a subject for . . .

George: Martha's lying. I want you to know that, right now. Martha's lying. (Martha laughs) There are very few things in this world that I *am* sure of . . . national boundaries, the level of the ocean, political allegiances, practical morality . . . none

of these would I stake my stick on any more . . .
but the one thing in this whole sinking world that
I am sure of is my partnership, my chromosomo-
logical partnership in the . . . creation of our
. . . blond-eyed, blue-haired [sic] . . . son. [pp.
71–2]

Yet it is George who, as far as can be determined, makes the move
which sets into motion the system change. In the first moments of
the play, apparently caught between Martha's ordering him to answer the door and the guests waiting outside, he concedes but,
typically, adds a retort of his own to keep even: he tells her not to
mention the son [p. 18]. They have, as George explicitly states later,
a rule not to mention him to others [p. 237], so George's comment
may seem unnecessary but also unimportant. However, there is a
higher "rule"—their entire game—that neither will be permitted to
determine the behavior of the other; so any order must be disqualified or disobeyed. In this sense, it little matters who made the
first wrong move, for the predictable result of this confusion of the
boundaries of the game is Martha's defiance and incorporation of
this material into their symmetrical competition. Thus,

George: Just don't start in on the bit about the kid, that's
          all.
Martha: What do you take me for?
George: Much too much.
Martha   (Really angered): Yeah? Well, I'll start in on the
          kid if I want to.
George: Just leave the kid out of this.
Martha   (Threatening): *He's mine as much as he is yours.*
          I'll talk about him if I want to.
George: I'd advise against it, Martha.
Martha: Well, good for you. (Knock) C'mon in. Get over
          there and open the door!
George: You've been advised.
Martha: Yeah . . . sure. Get over there! [pp. 18–19; italics
          ours]

As soon as the occasion permits, Martha tells Honey about their son and his birthday.[9] Now their homeostatic mechanism is mere fuel on the fire, and George will ultimately destroy the son altogether, invoking an implicit right of either ("I have the right, Martha. We never spoke of it; that's all. I could kill him any time I wanted to." [p. 236])

What we witness on the stage, then, is the beginning of a symmetrical runaway that eventually leads to the overthrow of a long-lasting relationship pattern. More than anything else, the play is the case history of a systemic *change,* a change in the rules of a relationship game that comes, we feel, from a small but perhaps inevitable confounding of those rules. The play does not define a new pattern, the new rules; it merely depicts the sequence of states through which the old pattern proceeds to its own destruction. (In s. 7.2 the *general* aspects of systemic change from within and without a system will be considered.) What might happen next is not clear:

George	(Long silence): It will be better.
Martha	(Long silence): I don't . . . know.
George:	It will be . . . maybe.
Martha:	I'm . . . not . . . sure.
George:	No.
Martha:	Just . . . us?

[9] It is interesting that later, after the "death," she pleads amnesia for this:

George: You broke our rule, baby. You mentioned him . . . you mentioned him to someone else.
Martha (Tearfully): I did *not.* I never did.
George: Yes, you did.
Martha: Who? WHO?
Honey (Crying): To me. You mentioned him to me.
Martha (Crying): I FORGET! Sometimes . . . sometimes when it's night, when it's late, and . . . and everybody else is . . . talking . . . I forget and I . . . want to mention him . . . but I . . . HOLD ON . . . I hold on . . . but I've wanted to . . . so often . . . [pp. 236–7]

Neither she nor George sees the conflict of relationship rules which led to this.

George: Yes.
Martha: I don't suppose, maybe, we could . . .
George: No, Martha.
Martha: Yes. No. [pp. 240–1]

Excluding the unassessable fact that Nick and Honey are now involved by their knowledge, Ferreira makes a cogent summary and prediction in terms of the family myth:

> . . . a family myth . . . subserves important homeostatic functions in the relationship. . . . [P]erhaps better than anywhere else, these functions of the family myth come to the fore in Edward Albee's well-known play, "Who's Afraid of Virginia Woolf?", where a family myth of psychotic proportions dominates the whole action. Throughout the play, a husband and wife talk, fight, and cry about their absent son. In an orgy of vilifications, they dispute every incident in their son's life, the color of his eyes, his birth, upbringing, etc. However, we learn much later, the son is fictitious, an agreement between the two, a tale, a myth—but a myth that they both cultivated. At the height of the play, the husband, seething with anger, announces that the son is dead. With this gesture, of course, he "kills" the myth. However, their relationship goes on, seemingly undisturbed by the announcement, and there transpires no notion of impending change or dissolution. In fact, nothing had changed. *For the husband had destroyed the myth of a living son only to initiate the myth of a dead one.* Obviously, the family myth had only evolved in its content which became, perhaps, more elaborate, more "psychotic"; its function, we surmise, remained intact. And so did the relationship. (*43*)

On the other hand, perhaps the death of the son is a recalibration, a step-functional change to a new level of operation. We cannot know.

5.43—METACOMMUNICATION BETWEEN GEORGE AND MARTHA

Metacommunication, as defined in s. 1.5, describes our discourse on George and Martha's rules of communication. But insofar as George and Martha talk or attempt to talk *about* their game, they metacommunicate within the play itself. This is of interest for a number of reasons, for instance regarding the issue of George and Martha's apparent "game-consciousness." That is, their numerous references to, naming of, and citing rules for games may seem to make them an unusual couple whose pattern of interaction is more basically an obsessive-compulsive preoccupation with playing and labeling bizarre and cruel games—really, as George suggests, "Vicious children, with their oh-so-sad games, hopscotching their way through life, etcetera, etcetera" [p. 197]. But this implies both that their game behavior is fully deliberate (or governed by different metarules) and that therefore perhaps the principles they demonstrate, being essentially only the idiosyncratic *content* of their game, cannot be applied to other couples, especially real ones. The nature of their metacommunication bears directly on this question, for it will be seen that *even their communication about their communication is subject to the rules of their game.*

In two striking instances of some length [pp. 150–9, 206–9], George and Martha discuss their interaction explicitly. The first of these metacommunicative exchanges indicates how differently each views the interaction and how, when these differences are revealed, mutual charges of madness or badness are immediately made (s. 3.4). Martha has objected to "Get the Guests," which she apparently sees as out of order or not in the rules:

> George   (Barely contained anger now): You can sit there in that chair of yours, you can sit there with the gin running out of your mouth, and you can humiliate me, you can tear me apart . . . ALL NIGHT . . . and that's perfectly all right . . . that's O.K. . . .
>
> Martha: YOU CAN STAND IT!
>
> George: I CANNOT STAND IT!

Martha: YOU CAN STAND IT!! YOU MARRIED ME
            FOR IT!! (A silence)
George   (Quietly): That is a desperately sick lie.
Martha: DON'T YOU KNOW IT, EVEN YET?
George   (Shaking his head): Oh . . . Martha.
Martha: My arm has gotten tired whipping you.
George   (Stares at her in disbelief): You're mad.
Martha: For twenty-three years!
George: You're deluded . . . Martha, you're deluded.
Martha: IT'S NOT WHAT I'VE WANTED!
George: I thought at least you were . . . on to yourself.
            I didn't know. I . . . didn't know. [pp. 152–3]

This is an unusually clear instance of pathology in the punctuation
of the sequence of events, in which George sees himself as justifiably
retaliating for Martha's attacks, and Martha sees herself almost as
a prostitute hired to "whip" him; each sees himself as responding
to the other but never also as a stimulus to the other's actions.
They do not see the full nature of their game, its true circularity.
These discrepant views become material for further symmetrical
escalation. Continuing the above episode:

George: I thought at least you were . . . on to yourself.
            I didn't know. I . . . didn't know.
Martha   (Anger taking over): I'm on to myself.
George   (As if she were some sort of bug): No . . . no
            . . . you're . . . sick.
Martha   (Rises—screams): I'LL SHOW YOU WHO'S
            SICK! [p. 153]

The competition over who is sick, wrong, or misunderstood continues to a by-now familiar ending, in which they demonstrate their
inability to "come together" by the very way in which they handle
the issue of their inability to come together:

George: Once a month, Martha! I've gotten used to it
            . . . once a month and we get misunderstood
            Martha, the good-hearted girl underneath the

barnacles, the little Miss that the touch of kind-
ness'd bring to bloom again. And I've believed it
more times than I want to remember, because I
don't want to think I'm that much of a sucker.
I don't believe you . . . I just don't believe you.
There is no moment . . . there is no moment
any more when we could . . . come together.

Martha   (Armed again): Well, maybe you're right, baby.
You can't come together with nothing, and you're
nothing! SNAP! It went snap tonight at Daddy's
party. (Dripping contempt, but there is fury and
loss under it) I sat there at Daddy's party, and I
watched you . . . I watched you sitting there,
and I watched the younger men around you, the
men who were going to go somewhere. And I sat
there and I watched you, and *you* weren't *there!*
And it snapped! It finally snapped! And I'm going
to howl it out, and I'm not going to give a damn
what I do, and I'm going to make the damned
biggest explosion you ever heard.

George   (Very pointedly): You try it and I'll beat you at
your own game.

Martha   (Hopefully): Is that a threat, George? Hunh?
George: That's a threat, Martha.
Martha   (Fake-spits at him): You're going to get it, baby.
George: Be careful, Martha . . . I'll rip you to pieces.
Martha: You aren't man enough . . . you haven't got the
guts.
George: Total war?
Martha: Total. (Silence. They both seem relieved . . .
elated.) [pp. 157–9]

Again George has quietly challenged Martha, which is not to say
that he starts this round any more than any other; there is no real
beginning to these rounds. She counterattacks frontally, and he
tops this with a dare that she cannot refuse. So it becomes, as we

have frequently pointed out, a new round of the same old game, with the stakes pushed even higher, leaving them relieved, even elated, but none the wiser or different. For there is nothing to distinguish their metacommunication from their ordinary communication; a comment, a plea, an ultimatum *about* their game is no exception to the rules of the game and therefore cannot be accepted or, in a sense, even heard by the other. In the end, when Martha, pleading and pathetic, takes a completely one-down position and repeatedly begs George to stop, the result is inexorably the same:

> Martha   (Tenderly; moves to touch him): Please, George, no more games; I . . .
>
> George   (Slapping her moving hand with vehemence): Don't you touch me! You keep your paws clean for the undergraduates!
>
> Martha   (A cry of alarm, but faint)
>
> George   (Grabbing her hair, pulling her head back): Now, you listen to me, Martha; you have had quite an evening . . . quite a night for yourself, and you can't just cut it off whenever you've got enough blood in your mouth. We are going on, and I'm going to have at you, and it's going to make your performance tonight look like an Easter pageant. Now I want you to get yourself a little alert. (Slaps her lightly with his free hand) I want a little life in you, baby. (Again)
>
> Martha   (Struggling): Stop it!
>
> George   (Again): Pull yourself together! (Again) I want you on your feet and slugging, sweetheart, because I'm going to knock you around, and I want you up for it. (Again; he pulls away, releases her; she rises)
>
> Martha: All right, George. What do you want, George?
>
> George: An equal battle, baby; that's all.
>
> Martha: You'll get it!
>
> George: I want you mad.

Martha: I'M MAD!!
George: Get madder!
Martha: DON'T WORRY ABOUT IT!
George: Good for you, girl; now, we're going to play this
            one to the death.
Martha: Yours!
George: You'd be surprised. Now, here come the tots; you
            be ready for this.
Martha   (She paces, actually looks a bit like a fighter): I'm
            ready for you. [pp. 208–9]

Nick and Honey re-enter and the Exorcism begins.

They are thus playing what will be described in detail as the "game without end" (s. 7.2), in which the self-reflexiveness of the rules leads to a paradox precluding resolution within the system.

5.44—LIMITATION IN COMMUNICATION

It was noted in s. 4.42 that every exchange of messages in a communicational sequence narrows the number of possible next moves. The interlocking nature of George and Martha's game, their shared myth, and the pervasiveness of their symmetry have illustrated the stabilized limitation which has been called relationship rules.

Examples of limitation in a new relationship are provided by a number of exchanges between George and Nick. The latter, by his initial behavior and his own protests, does not want to become involved with George or Martha or their quarrel. Still, as in the sample above (s. 5.411 [pp. 32–3]), he is increasingly drawn in even while staying out. At the beginning of Act Two, the by-now wary Nick encounters the same sort of escalation from small talk to intense anger again:

George: [. . .] It gets pretty bouncy around here some-
            times.
Nick   (Coolly): Yes . . . I'm sure.
George: Well, you saw an example of it.

Nick: I try not to . . .

George: Get involved. Um? Isn't that right?

Nick: Yes . . . that's right.

George: I'd imagine not.

Nick: I find it . . . embarrassing.

George   (Sarcastic): Oh, you do, hunh?

Nick: Yes. Really. Quite.

George   (Mimicking him): Yes. Really. Quite. (Then aloud, but to himself) IT'S DISGUSTING!

Nick: Now look! I didn't have anything . . .

George: DISGUSTING! (Quietly, but with great intensity) Do you think I like having that . . . whatever-it-is . . . ridiculing me, tearing me down, in front of . . . (Waves his hand in a gesture of contemptuous dismissal) YOU? Do you think I *care* for it?

Nick   (Cold—unfriendly): Well, no . . . I don't imagine you care for it at all.

George: Oh, you don't imagine it, hunh?

Nick   (Antagonistic): No . . . I don't. I don't imagine you do!

George   (Withering): Your sympathy disarms me . . . your . . . your compassion makes me weep! Large, salty, unscientific tears!

Nick   (With great disdain): I just don't see why you feel you have to subject *other* people to it.

George: *I?*

Nick: If you and your . . . wife . . . want to go at each other, like a couple of . . .

George: *I!* Why *I* want to!

Nick: . . . animals, I don't see why you don't do it when there aren't any . . .

George   (Laughing through his anger): Why, you smug, self-righteous little . . .

Nick   (A genuine threat): CAN . . . IT . . . MIS-TER! (Silence) Just . . . watch it! [pp. 90–2]

In this sequence, George's sarcastic attack on Nick's lack of involve-ment pushes Nick further into disdainful aloofness. But this ap-parently infuriates George, who, although perhaps seeking sym-pathy, finishes by insulting Nick until the latter threatens him. On Nick's side, the attempt not to communicate leads to intense involvement, while George's effort to convince Nick of his punctu-ation of his and Martha's game ends with his demonstrating how infuriating he (George) can be. A pattern for the future is clearly set.

5.45—SUMMARY

It should by now be clear that description of even a fairly simple, artificial family system requires a considerably bulky elaboration, for the variations in content on a few relationship rules are in-numerable and often highly detailed. (Reminiscent of this problem is Freud's interpretation of the dream of Irma [50], in which a half-page dream grows into eight pages of interpretation.) The fol-lowing is a very general summary of George and Martha's inter-actional system.

5.451

A system is said to be stable along certain of its variables if those variables remain within defined limits, and this is true of George and Martha's dyadic system. "Stability" may seem the least appro-priate term to describe their indoor commando games, but the issue rests on the variables intended. Their conversations are mercurial, noisy, shocking; restraint and social graces are quickly left behind, as it seems that anything goes. Indeed it would be extremely diffi-cult at any point to guess what will happen next. It would, how-ever, be fairly easy to describe *how* it will happen between George and Martha. For the variables that here define stability are those of relationship, not content, and in terms of their relationship pattern the couple demonstrate an extremely narrow range of be-havior.[10]

---

[10] We would even suggest, on the basis of clinical observation and some ex-perimental evidence (61), that pathogenic families generally demonstrate *more constrained* patterns of interaction than do normogenic families. This is in marked contrast to the traditional sociological view of disturbed families as

5·452

This range of behavior is the calibration, the "setting," of their system. The symmetry of their behavior defines the quality and a highly sensitive "lower limit" of this range, that is, nonsymmetrical behavior is rarely and only briefly seen. The "upper limit," as already indicated, is marked by their particular style, some negative feedback in complementarity, and the myth of the son, which, in requiring both of them, sets a limit to how much they can attack each other and enforces a reasonably stable symmetry—until, of course, the distinction between son-myth and other behavior breaks down, and this area is no longer sacrosanct nor homeostatic. Even within the range of symmetrical behaviors, they are limited: their symmetry is almost exclusively that of the potlatch,[11] featuring destruction rather than accumulation or accomplishment.

5·453

With the escalation that leads to the destruction of the son, the system is dramatically ended for us at what may be a recalibration, a step-function, in George and Martha's system. They have escalated almost without limitation until their very limitations were destroyed. Unless the son-myth is continued in the manner Ferreira suggests, a new order of interaction is required; both George and Martha openly express their fear and insecurity, mixed with hope, about the outcome.

---

chaotic and disorganized; but again the difference resides in the level of analysis and definition of variables. Extreme rigidity of interfamily relationships can appear as—and perhaps even account for—chaos in the family-society interface.

[11] A ritual of certain northwestern Indian tribes, in which the chiefs compete in the *destruction* of possessions, symmetrically burning their material goods (*21*).

Chapter 6

Paradoxical Communication

6.1

The Nature of Paradox

Paradox has fascinated the human mind for the last two thousand years, and it continues to do so in the present day. In fact, some of this century's most important achievements in the areas of logic, mathematics, and epistemology deal, or are intimately linked, with paradox, notably the development of metamathematics or the theory of proof, the theory of logical types, and problems of consistency, computability, decidability, and the like. As uninitiated outsiders, frustrated by the complex and esoteric nature of these subjects, we are inclined to dismiss them as too abstract to be of importance for our lives. Some may recall the classical paradoxes from school days, though probably as little more than amusing oddities. The purpose of this and the following chapters, however, is to show that there is something in the nature of paradox that is of immediate pragmatic and even existential import for all of us; paradox not only can invade interaction and affect our behavior and our sanity (s. 6.4), but also it challenges our belief in the consistency, and therefore the ultimate soundness, of our universe (s. 8.5 and 8.63). Furthermore, in section 7.4 we will try to show that deliberate paradox, in the spirit of Hippocrates' maxim "Likes are cured by likes," has significant therapeutic potential; and section 7.6 will touch briefly on the role of paradox in some of the noblest pursuits of the human mind. We hope that from this treatment of paradox it will be seen that consideration of the concept of paradox is of central importance and by no means a retreat into an ivory tower, although we will first have to examine its *logical* foundation.

6.11—DEFINITION

Paradox may be defined as a *contradiction that follows correct deduction from consistent premises.* This definition allows us to exclude immediately all those forms of "false" paradoxes that are based on a concealed error in reasoning or some fallacy deliberately built into the argument.[1] However, already at this point the definition becomes fuzzy, for the division of paradoxes into real and false ones is relative. Today's consistent premises are not at all unlikely to be tomorrow's errors or fallacies. For instance, Zeno's paradox of Achilles and the turtle he could not overtake was undoubtedly a "true" paradox until it was discovered that infinite, converging series (in this case the constantly diminishing distance between Achilles and the turtle) have a finite limit.[2] Once this discovery was made and a hitherto trusted assumption proved fallacious, the paradox no longer existed. This point is made clear by Quine:

> Revision of a conceptual scheme is not unprecedented. It happens in a small way with each advance in science, and it happens in a big way with the big advances, such as the Copernican revolution and the shift from Newtonian mechanics to Einstein's theory of relativity. We can hope in time even to get used to the biggest such changes and to find the new schemes natural. There was a time when the doctrine that the

---

[1] A typical example of this kind of paradox is the story about the six men who wanted six single rooms, while the innkeeper only had five. He "solved" the problem by taking the first man to room No. 1 and asking another man to wait there with the first for a few minutes. He then took the third man to room No. 2, the fourth man to room No. 3, and the fifth man to room No. 4. Having done this, the innkeeper returned to room No. 1, got the sixth gentleman who had been waiting there and put him up in room No. 5. Voilà! (The fallacy lies in the fact that the second and sixth men are treated as one.)

[2] For an explanation of this paradox and its fallacy, see Northrop (*112*).

earth revolves around the sun was called the Coperni-
can paradox, even by the men who accepted it. And
perhaps a time will come when truth locutions without implicit subscripts, or like safeguards, will really
sound as nonsensical as the antinomies show them to
be. (*120*, pp. 88–89)

6.12—THE THREE TYPES OF PARADOXES

"Antinomies," a term contained in the last sentence of this quotation, requires explanation. "Antinomy" is sometimes used interchangeably with "paradox," but most authors prefer to limit its
use to paradoxes arising in formalized systems such as logic and
mathematics. (The reader may wonder where else paradoxes could
arise; this chapter and the next will be devoted to showing that
they can equally well occur in the fields of semantics and pragmatics, and Chapter 8 will consider how and where they also enter
into man's experience of existence.) An antinomy, according to
Quine (*120*, p. 85), "produces a self-contradiction by accepted ways
of reasoning." Stegmüller (*147*, p. 24) is more specific and defines
an antinomy as a statement that is both contradictory *and* provable. Thus if we have a statement S_j and a second statement that
is the negation of the first, $-S_j$ (which means *not* S_j, or "S_j is false"),
then the two can be combined to a third statement S_k where
$S_k = S_j \,\&\, -S_j$. We thereby obtain a formal contradiction, for nothing can be both itself and not itself, that is, both true and false.
But, as Stegmüller continues, if it can be shown, by deduction, that
both S_j and its negation $-S_j$ are provable, then also S_k is provable
and we have an antinomy. Thus every antinomy is a logical contradiction, although, as will be seen, not every logical contradiction is an antinomy.

Now there exists a second class of paradoxes that differ from the
antinomies only in one important aspect: they do not occur in
logical or mathematical systems—and, therefore, are not based on
terms such as formal class and number—but rather arise out of
some hidden inconsistencies in the level structure of thought and

language.[3] This second group is frequently referred to as the *semantical antinomies* or *paradoxical definitions*.

Finally, there is a third group of paradoxes that is the least explored of all. These are of the greatest interest for our study, because they arise in ongoing interactions, where they determine behavior. We shall call this group the *pragmatic paradoxes* and shall later see that they can be divided into *paradoxical injunctions* and *paradoxical predictions*.

In summary, there are three types of paradoxes:

(1) logico-mathematical paradoxes (antinomies),
(2) paradoxical definitions (semantical antinomies),
(3) pragmatic paradoxes (paradoxical injunctions and paradoxical predictions),

clearly corresponding, within the framework of the theory of human communication, to the three main areas of this theory—the first type to logical syntax, the second to semantics, and the third to pragmatics. We shall now present examples of each type and endeavor to show how the little-known pragmatic paradoxes grow, so to speak, out of the other two forms.

6.2

Logico-Mathematical Paradoxes

The most famous paradox of this group is about "the class of all classes which are not members of themselves." It is based on the

---

[3] In making this distinction we are following Ramsey (*121*, p. 20), who introduced this classification:

    Group A: (1) The class of all classes which are not members of themselves.
           (2) The relation between two relations when one does not have itself to the other.
           (3) Burali Forti's contradiction of the greatest ordinal.

    Group B: (4) "I am lying."
           (5) The least integer not nameable in fewer than 19 syllables.
           (6) The least indefinable ordinal.
           (7) Richard's contradiction.
           (8) Weyl's contradiction about "heterological."

(It should be noted that Ramsey prefers the term "contradiction in the theory of aggregates" rather than "paradox.") All these paradoxes are described in Bochénski (*29*).

following premises. A class is the totality of all objects having a certain property. Thus, all cats, past, present, and future, comprise the class of cats. Having established this class, the remainder of all other objects in the universe can be considered the class of noncats, for all these objects have one definite property in common: they are *not* cats. Now any statement purporting that an object belongs to both these classes would be a simple contradiction, for nothing can be a cat and not a cat at the same time. Here nothing extraordinary has happened; the occurrence of this contradiction simply proves that a basic law of logic has been violated, and logic itself is none the worse for it.

Leaving individual cats and noncats alone now, and stepping one logical level higher, let us look at what sort of things the classes themselves are. We see readily that classes can be members of themselves or not. The class of all concepts, for instance, is obviously itself a concept, whereas our class of cats is not itself a cat. Thus, on this second level, the universe is again divided in two classes, those which are members of themselves and those which are not. Again, any statement purporting that one of these classes *is and is not* a member of itself would amount to a simple contradiction to be dismissed without further ado.

However, if the analogous operation is repeated once more on the next higher level, disaster suddenly strikes. All we have to do is to unite all classes that are members of themselves into one class, to be called M, and all classes that are not members of themselves into class N. If we now examine whether class N is or is not a member of itself, we run straight into Russell's famous paradox. Let us remember that the division of the universe into self-membership and non-self-membership classes is exhaustive; there cannot, by definition, be any exceptions. Therefore, this division must apply equally to class M and class N themselves. Thus, if class N is a member of itself, it is *not* a member of itself, for N is the class of classes which are *not* members of themselves. On the other hand, if N is not a member of itself, then it satisfies the condition of self-membership: it is a member of itself, precisely because it is *not* a member of itself, for non-self-membership is the essential distinction of all classes composing N. This is no longer a simple contradiction, but a true antinomy, because the paradoxical outcome is based on rigorous logical deduction and not on a violation of the laws of logic. Unless there is somewhere a hidden fallacy in the whole notion of class and membership, the logical conclusion is inescapable that class N is a member of itself if and only if it is not a member of itself, and vice versa.

In point of fact there *is* a fallacy involved. It was made apparent by Russell through the introduction of his *theory of logical types.* Very briefly, this theory postulates the fundamental principle that, as Russell (*164*) puts it, *whatever involves* all *of a collection must not be one of the collection.* In other words: the Russellian paradox is due to a confusion of logical types, or levels. A class is of a higher type than its members; to postulate it, we had to go one level up in the hierarchy of types. To say, therefore, as we did, that the class of all concepts is itself a concept is not false, but *meaningless,* as we shall presently see. This distinction is important, for if the statement were simply false, then its negation would have to be true, which is plainly not the case.

6.3

Paradoxical Definitions

This example of the class of all concepts provides a convenient bridge over which we can now cross from the logical to the semantical paradoxes (the paradoxical definitions or semantical antinomies). As we have seen, "concept" on the lower (member) level and "concept" on the next higher (class) level are not identical. The same *name,* "concept," is however used for both, and a linguistic illusion of identity is thus created. To avoid this pitfall, *logical type markers*—subscripts in formalized systems, quotation marks or italics in more general usage—must be used whenever there is a chance that a confusion of levels might arise. It then becomes clear that in our example $concept_1$ and $concept_2$ are not identical and that the idea of self-membership of a class must be thrown out.

Moreover, it becomes clear that in these cases inconsistencies of language rather than of logic are the root of the evil.

Perhaps the most famous of all semantical antinomies is that of the man who says of himself, "I am lying." On following this statement to its logical conclusion, we find again that it is true only if it is not true; in other words, the man is lying only if he is telling the truth and, vice versa, truthful when he is lying. In this case, the theory of logical types cannot be used to eliminate the antinomy, for words or combinations of words do not have a logical-type hierarchy. To the best of our knowledge, it was again Bertrand Russell who first thought of a solution. In the last paragraph of his introduction to Wittgenstein's *Tractatus Logico-Philosophicus* he suggests, in an almost incidental fashion, "that every language has, as Mr. Wittgenstein says, a structure concerning which, *in the language,* nothing can be said, but that there may be another language dealing with the structure of the first language and having itself a new structure, and that to this hierarchy of languages there may be no limit" (*133*, p. 23). This suggestion was developed, mainly by Carnap and by Tarski, into what is now known as the theory of levels of language. In analogy to the theory of logical types, this theory safeguards against a confusion of levels. It postulates that at the lowest level of language statements are made about objects. This is the realm of the *object language.* The moment, however, we want to say something *about* this language, we have to use a metalanguage, and a metametalanguage if we want to speak about this metalanguage, and so forth in theoretically infinite regress.

Applying this concept of levels of language to the semantical antinomy of the liar, it can be seen that his assertion, although composed of only three words, contains two statements. One is on the object-level, the other is on the metalevel and says something *about* the one on the object-level, namely that it is not true. At the same time, almost by a conjuror's trick, it is also implied that this statement in the metalanguage is itself one of the statements about which the metastatement is made, that it is itself a statement in the object language. In the theory of levels of language this kind of self-reflexiveness of statements involving their own truth or falsehood (or analogous properties, like demonstrability, definability, decidability, and the like) are the equivalent of the concept of self-membership of a class in the theory of logical types; both are meaningless assertions.[4]

Of course, it is only with reluctance that we follow the logicians' proof that the liar's statement is meaningless. Somewhere there seems to be a catch, and this feeling is even stronger for another famous paradoxical definition. In a small village, so the story goes, there is a barber who shaves all the men who do not shave themselves. Again, this definition is exhaustive on the one hand, but on the other it leads straight into paradox if one tries to assign the barber himself to either the self-shavers or the non-self-shavers. And again, rigorous deduction proves that there can be no such barber; yet we are left with the uneasy feeling, why not? With this stubborn doubt in mind let us now take a look at the behavioral—pragmatic—consequences of paradox.

6.4

Pragmatic Paradoxes

6.41—PARADOXICAL INJUNCTIONS

While the Barber paradox is almost always presented in the above-mentioned form, there exists at least one slightly different version of it. It is the one used by Reichenbach (*123*) in which, apparently for no particular reason, the barber is a soldier who is ordered by his captain to shave all the soldiers of the company who do not shave themselves, but no others. Reichenbach, of course, arrives at the only *logical* conclusion "that there is no such thing as the barber of the company, in the sense defined."

Whatever this author's reason may have been for presenting the story in this somewhat unusual form, it provides an example par excellence of a pragmatic paradox. There is ultimately no reason

---

[4] A delightful example, in an interactional context, of a self-reflexive statement that negates its own assertion is provided by the cartoon facing page 224.

why such an injunction could not in fact be given—its logical absurdity notwithstanding. The essential ingredients of this contingency are the following:

(1) A strong complementary relationship (officer and subordinate).
(2) Within the frame of this relationship, an injunction is given that must be obeyed but must be disobeyed to be obeyed (the order defines the soldier as a self-shaver if and only if he does not shave himself and vice versa).
(3) The person occupying the one-down position in this relationship is unable to step *outside* the frame and thus dissolve the paradox by commenting on, that is, metacommunicating about, it (this would amount to "insubordination").

A person caught in such a situation is in an *untenable position.* Thus, while from a purely logical point of view the captain's order is meaningless and the barber allegedly nonexisting, the situation looks very different in real life. Pragmatic paradoxes, especially paradoxical injunctions, are in fact far more frequent than one would be inclined to believe. As soon as we begin to look at paradox in interactional contexts, the phenomenon ceases to be merely a fascinating pursuit of the logician and the philosopher of science and becomes a matter of stark practical importance for the sanity of the communicants, be they individuals, families, societies, or nations. Following are several examples, ranging from a purely theoretical model, through others taken from literature and related fields, to clinical cases.

6.42—EXAMPLES OF PRAGMATIC PARADOXES

Example 1: It is syntactically and semantically correct to write *Chicago is a populous city.* But it would be incorrect to write *Chicago is a trisyllabic,* for in this case quotation marks must be used: *"Chicago" is a trisyllabic.* The difference in these two uses of the word is that in the first statement the word refers to an object (a city), while in the second instance the same word refers to a name (which is a word) and therefore to itself. The two uses of the word "Chicago" are, therefore, clearly of a different logical type (the first statement is in the object language, the second in the metalanguage), and the quotation marks function as logical type markers (cf. *108*, pp. 30–1 fn.).[5]

Let us now imagine the odd possibility of someone's condensing the two statements about Chicago into one (*Chicago is a populous city and a trisyllabic*), dictating it to his secretary, and threatening her with dismissal if she cannot or will not write it down correctly. Of course, she cannot (and neither could we in the foregoing). What, then, are the behavioral effects of this communication?—for this is the concern of the pragmatics of human communication. The inanity of the present example should not detract from its theoretical significance. There can be no doubt that communication of this kind creates an untenable situation. Since the message is paradoxical, any reaction to it within the frame set by the message must be equally paradoxical. It simply is not possible to behave consistently and logically within an inconsistent and illogical context. As long as the secretary stays within the frame set by her employer, she has only two alternatives: to try to comply, and, of course, fail, or to refuse to write anything down. In the first case she can be accused of incompetence, in the second of insubordination. It should be noticed that of these two charges the first alleges intellectual impairment, the second ill will. This is not too far from the typical charges of madness or badness referred to in the preceding chapters. In either case she is likely to react emotionally, for example, by crying or getting angry. To all this it may be objected that no person in his right mind would behave like this imaginary boss. This, however, is a non sequitur. For at least in theory—and

---

[5] Tribute must at this point be paid to the mathematician Frege, who as early as 1893 warned:

> Probably the frequent use of inverted commas will seem strange; by means of them I differentiate between the cases in which I am speaking about the *sign itself* and those in which I am speaking about *its meaning*. However pedantic this may seem, I nevertheless hold it to be necessary. *It is remarkable how an inexact manner of speech or of writing,* which may have been used originally only for the sake of convenience and brevity, with full awareness of its inexactitude, *can eventually confuse thought,* once this awareness has vanished. (*48,* p. 4; italics ours)

very likely also in the secretary's view—there exist two possible reasons for such behavior: either the boss wants a pretext to dismiss her and is using a nasty trick for this purpose, or he is *not* in his right mind. Notice that, again, badness or madness seem to be the only explanations.

An entirely different situation arises if the secretary does not stay within the frame set by the injunction, but comments about it; in other words, if she does not react to the content of the boss's direction but communicates about his communication. She thereby steps outside the context created by him and is thus not caught in the dilemma. This, however, is usually not easy. For one reason, it is— as has been repeatedly illustrated in earlier chapters—difficult to communicate about communication. The secretary would have to point out why the situation is untenable and what this does to her, yet this in itself would be no mean accomplishment. Another reason metacommunication is not a simple solution is that the boss, using his authority, can quite easily refuse to accept her communication on the metalevel and can label it as further evidence for her incapacity or insolence.[6]

Example 2: Paradoxical self-definitions of the Liar type are quite frequent, at least in our clinical experience. Their pragmatic import is more obvious if we hold in mind that these statements not only convey logically meaningless content but define the relationship of the self to the other. Therefore, when presented in human interaction, it does not matter so much that the content (report) is

---

[6] This experience of blocking metacommunications to prevent somebody from getting out of an untenable situation was well known to Lewis Carroll. We return to Alice after the Red and White Queens have driven her to distraction with their questions (see s. 3.22); they fan her head with bunches of leaves until she comes to again, and the brainwashing continues:

> "She's all right again now," said the Red Queen. "Do you know languages? What's the French for fiddle-de-dee?"
> "Fiddle-de-dee's not English," Alice replied gravely.
> "Who ever said it was," said the Red Queen.
> *Alice thought she saw a way out of the difficulty,* this time. "If you tell me what language 'fiddle-de-dee' is, I'll tell you the French for it!" she exclaimed triumphantly.
> But the Red Queen drew herself up rather stiffly, and said, *"Queens never make bargains."* (Italics ours)

meaningless as that the relationship (command) aspect can neither be evaded nor clearly understood. The following variations of this problem are taken almost at random from recently held interviews:

(a.) Interviewer: What would you say, Mr. X, are the main problems in your family?

Mr. X: My contribution to our problem is that I'm a habitual liar . . . a lot of people will use the expression— uhm—oh, falsehood or exaggeration or bull-slinger, many things— but actually it's lying . . .

We have reason to believe that this man has never come across the Liar paradox, and that he was not deliberately trying to pull the interviewer's leg. He did, however, for how can one proceed in the face of such a paradoxical relationship message?

(b.) A family, composed of the parents and their rather obese twenty-year-old son who is allegedly mentally retarded, are interpreting together the proverb "A rolling stone gathers no moss" as part of a Structured Family Interview *(159):*

Father: Used as a proverb it means to us, to Mom and me, that if we are busy and active like a rolling stone, you know, moving, then, ah, we are not going to be too—fat, you're going to be more alert mentally . . .

Son: It does?

Mother: Now do you understand?

Son: I catch on.

Mother (overlapping): —do you understand?

Son (overlapping): Yeah, I DO.

Father (overlapping): —that it would be GOOD for—

Son (interrupting): *Mental retardation.*

Father (continuing): —keep busy—

Mother: Ohh—does that seem like it means that to you, "a rolling stone gathers . . ."

Son   (interrupting): *Well, getting over mental retarda-*
tion, it does.
Mother: Well—
Father   (interrupting): Well, keeping busy would HELP,
that's—I think that's right.

How do his parents, or a therapist, deal with a "mental retar-
date"[7] who speaks about ways of overcoming his mental retardation, and even uses the term? Like the liar, he jumps in and out of
the frame set by the diagnosis (a definition of self), thereby leading
the diagnosis ad absurdum in a truly schizophrenic way. The use
of the term excludes the condition which the term denotes.

(c.) In a conjoint marital session, a discussion of the couple's
sexual relations and of their individual attitudes about different
sexual behaviors led to evidence of the husband's extreme discomfort with regard to masturbation. He said that, "to be perfectly
frank," although he was frequently "forced" to masturbate by his
wife's rebuffs, he was tortured by fears of abnormality and sin (the
husband was Catholic and held that masturbation was a mortal
sin). The therapist replied that he could not speak to the question
of sin, but that as far as abnormality or deviance went, numerous
surveys indicated that this group did report lower frequency than
any other religious group, although there was a higher incidence
of masturbation among Catholics than many would expect. The
husband scoffed at such findings, saying, "Catholics always lie
about sex."

Example 3: Perhaps the most frequent form in which paradox
enters into the pragmatics of human communication is through an
injunction demanding specific behavior, which by its very nature
can only be spontaneous. The prototype of this message is, therefore, *"Be spontaneous!"* Anybody confronted with this injunction

---

[7] This patient had been repeatedly diagnosed through psychological testing as
having an IQ of about 50–80. On a test just prior to this interview he refused
to participate on the grounds that he was unable to comprehend what was
being asked. (In the course of the therapy he was later rediagnosed as schizophrenic; his recovery proceeded satisfactorily, and his performance in many
areas exceeds by far the expectations of the above tests.)

is in an untenable position, for to comply he would have to be spontaneous within a frame of compliance, of nonspontaneity. Some variations of this kind of paradoxical injunction are:

(a) "You ought to love me";
(b) "I want you to dominate me" (request of a wife to her passive husband);
(c) "You should enjoy playing with the children, just like other fathers";
(d) "Don't be so obedient" (parents to their child whom they consider too dependent on them);
(e) "You know that you are free to go, dear; don't worry if I start crying" (from a novel by W. Styron, *150*, p. 33).

The patrons of the microcosmic superbrothel in Genet's *Balcony* are all caught in this dilemma. The girls are paid to perform the complementary roles necessary for the clients to live their dreams of self, but it all remains a sham, for they know that the sinner is not a "real" sinner, the thief is not a "real" thief, etc. Similarly, this is also the problem of the homosexual who longs for an intense relationship with a "real" male, only to find that the latter is always, must always be, another homosexual. In all these instances, the other at worst refuses to comply or at best does the right thing for the wrong reason, and the "wrong reason" is then compliance itself. In terms of symmetry and complementarity, these injunctions are paradoxical, because they demand symmetry in the frame of a relationship defined as complementary. Spontaneity thrives in freedom and vanishes under constraint.[8]

Example 4: Ideologies are particularly liable to get entangled

---

[8] Freedom itself is similar to paradox. For Sartre the only freedom we do not have it not to be free. In a similar vein, the Swiss Civil Code, one of the most enlightened of Europe, states (article 27): ". . . Nobody can abdicate his freedom or limit it to a degree which violates law or morality." And Berdyaev, summarizing Dostoevsky's thought, writes

> Freedom cannot be identified with goodness or truth or perfection: it is by nature autonomous, it is freedom and not goodness. Any identification or confusion of freedom with goodness and perfection involves a negation of freedom and a strengthening of methods of compulsion; obligatory goodness ceases to be goodness by the fact of its constraint. (22, pp. 69–70)

in the dilemmas of paradox, especially if their metaphysics consist in antimetaphysics. The thoughts of Rubashov, the hero in Koestler's *Darkness at Noon,* are paradigmatic in this connection:

> The Party denied the free will of the individual—and at the same time it exacted his willing self-sacrifice. It denied his capacity to choose between two alternatives—and at the same time it demanded that he should always choose the right one. It denied his power to distinguish between good and evil—and at the same time it spoke accusingly of guilt and treachery. The individual stood under the sign of economic fatality, a wheel in a clockwork which had been wound up for all eternity and could not be stopped or influenced—and the Party demanded that the wheel should revolt against the clockwork and change its course. There was somewhere an error in the calculation; the equation did not work out. *(84 p. 257)*

It is in the nature of paradox that "equations" based on it do not work out. Where paradox contaminates human relations, disease appears. Rubashov has realized the symptoms, but looks in vain for the cure:

> All our principles were right, but our results were wrong. This is a diseased century. We diagnosed the disease and its causes with microscopic exactness, but wherever we applied the healing knife a new sore appeared. Our will was hard and pure, we should have been loved by the people. But they hate us. Why are we so odious and detested?
>
> We brought you truth, and in our mouth it sounded like a lie. We brought you freedom, and it looks in our hands like a whip. We brought you the living life, and where our voice is heard the trees wither and there is a rustling of dry leaves. We brought you the

> promise of the future, but our tongue stammered and
> barked . . . (*84*, p. 58)

Example 5: If we now compare this with the autobiographical
account of a schizophrenic (*15*), we notice that his dilemma is in-
trinsically the same as Rubashov's. The patient is placed by his
"voices" into an untenable situation and is then accused of deceit
or unwillingness when he finds himself unable to comply with
their paradoxical injunctions. What makes his narrative so extraordinary is that it was written almost 130 years ago, long before
the days of modern psychiatric theory:

> I was tormented by the commands of what I imagined
> was the Holy Spirit, to say other things, which as often
> as I attempted, I was fearfully rebuked for beginning
> in my own voice and not in a voice given to me. These
> contradictory commands were the cause, now as before,
> of the incoherency of my behavior, and these imagina-
> tions formed the chief causes of my ultimate total de-
> rangement. For I was commanded to speak, on pain of
> dreadful torments, of provoking the wrath of the Holy
> Spirit, and of incurring the guilt of the grossest in-
> gratitude; and at the same time whenever I attempted
> to speak, I was harshly and contumeliously rebuked for
> not using the utterance of a spirit sent to me; and
> when again I attempted, I still went wrong, and when
> I pleaded internally that I knew not what I was to do,
> I was accused of falsehood and deceit; and of being
> really unwilling to do what I was commanded. I then
> lost patience, and proceeded to say what I was desired
> pell-mell, determined to show that it was not fear or
> want of will that prevented me. But when I did this, I
> felt as formerly the pain in the nerves of my palate
> and throat on speaking, which convinced me that I was
> not only rebelling against God, but against nature;
> and I relapsed into an agonizing sense of hopeless-
> ness and of ingratitude. (*15*, pp. 32–3)

Example 6: When in about 1616 the Japanese authorities started a concerted persecution of converts to the Christian faith, they gave their victims a choice between a death sentence and an abnegation that was as elaborate as it was paradoxical. This abnegation was in the form of an oath which is reported by Sansom in a study of the interaction between European and Asian cultures. He writes:

> In denying the Christian faith each apostate had to repeat reasons for his disbelief in a prescribed formula. . . . The formula is an involuntary tribute to the power of the Christian faith, for the converts, having abjured their religion (generally under duress), were by a curious logic made to swear by the very powers that they had just denied: By the Father, the Son, and the Holy Ghost, Santa Maria and all the Angels . . . if I break this oath may I lose the grace of God forever and fall into the wretched state of Judas Iscariot. By an even further departure from logic all this was followed by an oath to Buddhist and Shinto deities. (*134,* p. 176)

The consequences of this paradox are worth analyzing in detail. The Japanese had set themselves the task of changing the belief of a whole group of people, a notoriously difficult endeavor in view of the fact that any belief is both powerful and intangible. They must have realized from the outset that methods of persuasion, coercion, or corruption were quite inadequate, for these methods can certainly enforce lip service but always leave the doubt that the ex-convert's mind is not "really" changed. And, of course, this doubt will linger on even in the face of the most profuse protestations by the apostate because not only those sincerely renouncing but anyone who wants to save his skin and yet preserve his faith in his heart of hearts will behave precisely in this way.

Faced with this problem of "really" bringing about a change in someone's mind, the Japanese resorted to the expedient of the

oath, and it was obviously clear to them that, as far as the converts
were concerned, such an oath would only be binding if sworn in
the name of the Christian as well as the Buddhist or Shinto deities.
But this "solution" led them straight into the undecidability of
self-reflexive statements. The formula prescribed for the oath of
abnegation was supposed to derive its binding power from an invocation of the very divinity that was to be abjured by it. In
other words, a statement was made *within* a clearly defined frame
of reference (the Christian faith) that asserted something *about*
this frame and, therefore, about itself, namely it denied the frame
of reference, and, with it, the oath itself. Now special attention
needs to be paid to the two emphasized words in the preceding
sentence, *within* and *about*. Let *C* be the class of all statements
that can be made *within* the framework of the Christian faith.
Then any statement about *C* can be called a metastatement, i.e., a
statement about a body of statements. It can now be seen that the
oath is both a member of *C*, since it invokes the Trinity, and at the
same time a metastatement denying *C*—therefore, about *C*. This,
however, creates the by now well-known logical impasse. No statement made within a given frame of reference can at the same time
step outside the frame, so to speak, and negate itself. This is the
dilemma of the dreamer caught in a nightmare: nothing he tries to
do in his dream will be of any avail.[9] He can escape his nightmare

[9] Cf. again Lewis Carroll in *Through the Looking Glass*, which (just as *Alice
in Wonderland*) is far more a primer of story problems in logic than a children's book. Tweedledum and Tweedledee are talking about the sleeping Red
King:

> . . . "He's dreaming now," said Tweedledee: "and what do you
> think he's dreaming about?"
> Alice said, "Nobody can guess that."
> "Why, about *you!*" Tweedledee exclaimed, clapping his hands
> triumphantly, "and if he left off dreaming about you, where do
> you suppose you'd be?"
> "Where I am now, of course," said Alice.
> "Not you!" Tweedledee retorted contemptuously. "You'd be
> nowhere. Why, you're only a sort of thing in his dream!"
> "If that there King was to wake," added Tweedledum, "you'd
> go out—bang!—just like a candle!"
> "I shouldn't!" Alice exclaimed indignantly. "Besides, if I'm

only by waking up, which is by stepping outside the dream. But waking is not part of the dream, it is a different frame altogether; it is nondream, as it were. Theoretically, the nightmare could go on forever, as some schizophrenic nightmares obviously do, for nothing inside the frame has the power to negate the frame. But this—mutatis mutandis—is precisely what the Japanese oath was meant to accomplish.

While to our knowledge no historical accounts exist about the effects of the oath on either the converts or the administering authorities, it is not difficult to speculate on these effects. For the converts who took the oath the dilemma is fairly evident. By abjuring, they stayed within the frame of the paradoxical formula and were thus caught in the paradox. Of course, their chances of stepping outside the frame must have been very slim. But having been forced to take the oath, the converts must have found themselves in a tremendous personal religious dilemma. Leaving aside the question of duress, was their oath valid or not? If they wanted to remain Christians, did not this very fact make the oath valid and excommunicate them? But if they sincerely wished to abjure Christianity, did not the oath by that faith now firmly bind them to it? In ultimate analysis the paradox here invades metaphysics; it is in the essence of an oath that it not only binds the juror but also the deity invoked. In the experience of the convert, was not God Himself then in an untenable situation and if so, where in the whole universe was there any hope left for a solution?

But the paradox must also have affected the persecutors themselves. It cannot possibly have escaped their awareness that the

---

only a sort of thing in his dream, what are *you,* I should like to know?"

"Ditto," said Tweedledum.

"Ditto, ditto!" cried Tweedledee.

He shouted this so loud that Alice could not help saying, "Hush! You'll be waking him, I'm afraid, if you make so much noise."

"Well, it's no use *your* talking about waking him," said Tweedledum, "when you're only one of the things in his dream. You know very well you're not real."

"I *am* real!" said Alice, and began to cry.

formula placed the Christian deity over their own gods. Thus, instead of purging "the Father, the Son, and the Holy Ghost, Santa Maria and all the Angels" from the souls of the converts, they enthroned them even in their own religion. Therefore, in the end they must have found themselves enmeshed in their own fabrication, which denied what it asserted and asserted what it denied.

At this point we can touch peripherally on the subject of brainwashing, which, after all, is based almost exclusively on pragmatic paradox. The history of mankind shows that by and large there are two kinds of mind benders: those who consider the physical destruction of their opponents a passable solution of the problem and could not care less about what their victims "really" think, and those who out of an eschatological concern worthy of a better cause care very much. It may be assumed that the latter are inclined to denounce a shocking lack of spirituality in the former, but this is neither here nor there. In any case, the second group's concern is primarily the changing of a man's mind, and only secondarily his elimination. O'Brien, the torturer in Orwell's *1984*, is an accomplished authority on the subject, which he explains to his victim:

> "For every heretic it [the Inquisition] burned at the stake, thousands of others rose up. Why was that? Because the Inquisition killed its enemies in the open, and killed while they were still unrepentant; in fact it killed them because they were unrepentant. Men were dying because they would not abandon their true beliefs . . . Later . . . there were the German Nazis and the Russian Communists . . . We do not make mistakes of that kind. We make them true . . . You will be annihilated in the past as well as in the future. You will never have existed."
>
> "Then why bother to torture me?" thought Winston.
>
> O'Brien smiled slightly. "You are a flaw in the pat-

tern, Winston, you are a stain that must be wiped out. Did I not tell you just now that we are different from the persecutors of the past? *We are not content with negative obedience, nor even with the most abject submission. When finally you surrender to us it must be of your own free will.* We do not destroy the heretic because he resists us; as long as he resists us we never destroy him. We convert him, we capture his inner mind, we reshape him. We burn all evil and all illusion out of him; we bring him over to our side, not in appearance, *but genuinely, heart and soul.* We make him one of ourselves before we kill him. It is intolerable to us that an erroneous thought should exist anywhere in the world, however secret and powerless it may be." (*113*, p. 258; italics ours)

Here, indeed, is the "be spontaneous" paradox in its starkest form. The reader, of course, is left in no doubt that O'Brien is mad, but while O'Brien is only a fictional character, his madness is that of a Hitler, Himmler, Heydrich, *et al.*

Example 7: A situation essentially similar to that of the Japanese converts and their persecutors arose between Sigmund Freud and the Nazi authorities in 1938, except that in this case the paradox was imposed by the victim on his persecutors and, moreover, in such a way as to enable him to leave the field. The Nazis had promised Freud an exit visa from Austria on condition that he sign a declaration purporting that he had been "treated by the German authorities and particularly by the Gestapo with all the respect and consideration due to my scientific reputation," etc. (*81*, p. 226). While in Freud's personal case this may have been true, in the wider context of the appalling persecution of the Viennese Jews, this document still amounted to a shameless pretense of fairness on the part of the authorities, obviously with the aim of using Freud's international fame for Nazi propaganda. Thus the Gestapo had an interest in having Freud sign it, and Freud on the other hand must have found himself faced with the dilemma of either signing it and thereby aiding the enemy at the expense of his integrity, or refusing to sign and suffering whatever consequences might ensue. In terms of experimental psychology he was faced with an avoidance-avoidance conflict (s. 6.434). He managed to turn the tables by trapping the Nazis in their own fabrication. When the Gestapo official brought the document for his signature, Freud asked if he would be allowed to add one more sentence. Obviously sure of his one-up position, the official agreed, and Freud wrote in his own handwriting, "I can heartily recommend the Gestapo to anyone." Now the shoe was on the other foot—for the Gestapo, having first compelled Freud to praise them, could not possibly object to further praise. But to anyone who was even dimly aware of what was going on in Vienna in those days (and the world was increasingly aware of it), this "praise" amounted to a devastating sarcasm that made the document worthless for propaganda purposes. In short, Freud had framed the document with a statement that was both part of the document and a negation, via sarcasm, of the entire document.

Example 8: In *Les Plaisirs et les Jours* Proust provides a beautiful example of a pragmatic paradox arising out of the frequent contradiction between socially approved behavior and individual emotion. Alexis is thirteen years old, and on his way to visit his uncle who is dying of an incurable disease. The following conversation takes place between him and his tutor.

> As he started to speak, he blushed deeply:
> "Monsieur Legrand, should my uncle think that I know he must die, or not?"
> "He should not, Alexis!"
> "But what if he talks to me about it?"
> "He won't talk to you about it."
> "He won't talk to me about it?" said Alexis with astonishment, for this was the only alternative which he had not anticipated; every time that he began to

imagine his visit to his uncle he heard him talk about
death with the sweetness of a priest.

"But, after all, what if he does talk to me about it?"

"You'll say that he is wrong."

"And if I cry?"

"You have already cried too much this morning,
you won't cry at your uncle's."

"I won't cry!" exclaimed Alexis in despair, "but
he'll think that I feel no grief, that I don't love him
. . . my little uncle!"

And he burst into tears. (*118*, pp. 19–20)

If Alexis, out of concern, hides his feelings of concern, then he may,
he feels, appear unconcerned and therefore unloving.

Example 9: A young man sensed that his parents did not ap-
prove of the girl he was going with and intended to marry. His
father was a wealthy, dynamic, handsome man who completely
ruled the three children and his wife. The mother lived in the
complementary one-down position. She was a withdrawn, quiet person who on several occasions had gone to a sanitarium "for a rest."
One day the father asked the young man into his study—a procedure reserved for very solemn pronouncements only—and told
him: "Louis, there is something you should know. We Alvarados
always marry women better than ourselves." This was said with
a perfectly straight face and left the boy puzzled because he could
not decide what the implications of this statement were. Which-
ever way he tried to interpret it, it led him into a bewildering
contradiction and thereby left him with a sense of insecurity as
to the wisdom of his decision to marry that particular girl.

The father's statement could be expanded into the following:
We Alvarados are superior people; among other things, we marry
upward. The latter evidence of this superiority is, however, not
only starkly contrary to the facts the son observes, but in itself
implies that Alvarado men are *inferior* to their wives. And this
negates the assertion that it was intended to support. If the state-

ment of superiority, including the definition of spouse and self, is true, then it is not true.

Example 10: In the course of a young man's psychotherapy, his psychiatrist asked him to invite his parents to come from a somewhat distant city so that they could have at least one conjoint therapy session. During this session it became apparent that the parents agreed with each other only when they were in coalition against their son, but that otherwise they disagreed on a great many topics. It was also revealed that the father had had a depression when the boy was small and had not worked for five years, during which time they lived on his wealthy wife's money. A little later in the course of the interview, the father sharply criticized the boy for not being more responsible, for not becoming independent and more successful. At this point the therapist intervened and cautiously pointed out that perhaps father and son had more in common than they realized . . . While this innuendo was lost on the two men, the mother quickly intervened and attacked the psychiatrist for being a troublemaker. She then looked at her son with love and admiration and stated, "After all, it's a simple matter. All we want in the world is for George to have as happy a marriage as we have." Defined in these terms, the only conclusion is that a marriage is happy when it is unhappy and, by implication, unhappy when it is happy.

As a side line it seems worth mentioning that the boy was depressed after this meeting, and when he came for his next individual session he was unable to trace the origin of his mood. When the paradox of his mother's wish was pointed out to him, he recalled it and looked as if an electric light had just been turned on. He said that she probably had been saying "things like that" for many years, but that he had never been able to pinpoint or identify them as he had just now. He used to have dreams of carrying something heavy, of fighting something, or of being dragged down by something, without ever being able to recognize this "something."

Example 11: A mother was talking to her schizophrenic daughter's psychiatrist on the telephone, complaining that the girl was getting sick again. By this the mother usually meant that the girl had been more independent and had been arguing with her. Recently, for instance, the daughter had moved into an apartment of her own, and the mother was somewhat bothered by this. The therapist asked for an example of her allegedly disturbed behavior, and the mother said, "Well, like today, I wanted her to come over to dinner, and we had this big discussion because she did not think she wanted to come." When the therapist then asked what finally happened, the mother stated with some anger, "Well, I talked her into coming, of course, because I knew she really wanted to anyway and she never has the nerve to tell me No." In the mother's view, when the girl says "no," it means that she really does want to come, because the mother knows better than she what goes on in the daughter's confused mind; but what if the girl says "yes"? A "yes" does not mean "yes," it only means the daughter never has the nerve to say "no." Both mother and daughter are thus bound by this paradoxical labeling of messages.

Example 12: A charming and hair-raising collection of paradoxical maternal communications has recently been published by Greenburg. Here is one of his pearls:

> Give your son Marvin two sport shirts as a present.
> The first time he wears one of them, look at him sadly
> and say in your Basic Tone of Voice:
> "The other one you didn't like?" (*58*, p. 16)

6.43—THE DOUBLE BIND THEORY

The effects of paradox in human interaction were first described by Bateson, Jackson, Haley, and Weakland in a paper entitled "Toward a Theory of Schizophrenia" (*18*), published in 1956. This research group approached the phenomenon of schizophrenic communication from a viewpoint that is radically different from those hypotheses that view schizophrenia as primarily an intrapsychic disturbance (a thinking disorder, weak ego function, swamping of consciousness by primary process material, or the like), which secondarily affects the patient's relationships with other people and eventually theirs with him. Bateson *et al.* instead took the converse approach and asked themselves what sequences of interpersonal experience would *induce* (rather than be caused by) behavior that would justify the diagnosis of schizophrenia. The schizophrenic, they hypothesized, *"must live in a universe where the sequences of events are such that his unconventional communicational habits will be in some sense appropriate."* (*18*, p. 253) This led them to postulate and identify certain essential characteristics of such interaction, for which they coined the term *double bind*. These characteristics are also the common denominator underlying the otherwise perhaps bewildering medley of examples in the preceding section of this chapter.

6.431

In a somewhat modified and expanded definition, the ingredients of a double bind can be described as follows:

(1) Two or more persons are involved in an intense relationship that has a high degree of physical and/or psychological survival value for one, several, or all of them. Situations in which such intense relationships typically exist include but are not limited to family life (especially parent-child interaction); infirmity; material dependence; captivity; friendship; love; loyalty to a creed, cause, or ideology; contexts influenced by social norms or tradition; and the psychotherapeutic situation.

(2) In such a context, a message is given which is so structured that (a) it asserts something, (b) it asserts something about its own assertion and (c) these two assertions are mutually exclusive. Thus, if the message is an injunction, it must be disobeyed to be obeyed; if it is a definition of self or the other, the person thereby defined is this kind of person only if he is not, and is not if he is. The meaning of the message is, therefore, undecidable in the sense described in s. 3.333.

(3) Finally, the recipient of the message is prevented from stepping outside the frame set by this message, either by metacommunicating (commenting) about it or by withdrawing. Therefore, even though the message is logically meaningless, it is a pragmatic reality: he cannot *not* react to it, but neither can he react to it

appropriately (nonparadoxically), for the message itself is paradoxical. This situation is frequently compounded by the more or less overt prohibition to show any awareness of the contradiction or the real issue involved. A person in a double bind situation is therefore likely to find himself punished (or at least made to feel guilty) for correct perceptions, and defined as "bad" or "mad" for even insinuating that there be a discrepancy between what he does see and what he "should" see.[10]

This is the essence of the double bind.

6.432

Since its formulation this concept has gained considerable attention in psychiatry [11] and the behavioral sciences in general (*156*) and it has even entered into political jargon (*97*). The question of the double bind's *pathogenicity* immediately became and has remained the most debated and misunderstood aspect of the theory. It therefore requires attention before we can proceed with our subject matter.

There can be no doubt that the world we live in is far from logical and that we all have been exposed to double binds, yet most of us manage to preserve our sanity. However, most of these experiences are isolated and spurious, even though at the time they may be of a traumatic nature. A very different situation arises when the exposure to double binds is long-lasting and gradually becomes a habitual expectation. This, of course, applies especially in child-

---

[10] This holds equally for one person's perceptions of another's moods or behavior. Cf. Johnson, *et al.*, from which the following is quoted:

> When these children perceived the anger and hostility of a parent, as they did on many occasions, immediately the parent would deny that he was angry and would insist that the child deny it too, so that the child was faced with the dilemma of whether to believe the parent or his own senses. If he believed his senses he maintained a firm grasp on reality; if he believed the parent, he maintained the needed relationship, but distorted his perception of reality. (*80*, p. 143)

For essentially the same pattern, Laing (*89*) has introduced the concept of mystification.

[11] Its authors received the 1961–62 Frieda Fromm-Reichmann Award of the Academy of Psychoanalysis for significant contribution to the understanding of schizophrenia.

hood, since all children are inclined to conclude that what happens to them, happens all over the world—is the law of the universe, so to speak. Here, then, there is no question of isolated trauma; rather we are faced with a definite pattern of interaction. The interactional quality of this pattern may become clearer if it is kept in mind that double-binding cannot, in the nature of human communication, be a unidirectional phenomenon. If, as we have seen under (3) above, a double bind produces paradoxical behavior, then this very behavior in turn double-binds the double-binder.[12] Once this pattern has sprung into operation it is virtually meaningless to ask *when, how,* and *why* it was established, for, as will be seen in the next chapter, pathological systems have a curiously self-perpetuating, vicious-circle quality. In view of this, we contend that the question of the double bind's pathogenicity cannot be answered in terms of a cause-effect relationship, taken from the medical model of, say, the connection between infection and inflammation; the double bind does not *cause* schizophrenia. All that can be said is that where double-binding has become the predominant pattern of communication, and where the diagnostic attention is limited to the *overtly* most disturbed individual,[13] the

[12] This mutuality exists even when all the power is apparently in the hands of one side and the other is totally helpless, e.g., in political persecution. For in the end, as Sartre (*135*) explains, the torturer is as debased as his victim. See also Weissberg's account (*163*) of his experiences as victim of the Great Purge in the USSR, and Meerloo's (*103*) concept of the "mysterious masochistic pact" between the brainwasher and his victim.

For a detailed study of the mutuality of double-binding in families see Weakland (*160*); see also Sluzki, *et al.* (*144*).

[13] It is not possible to discuss in this book all the aspects and ramifications of the double bind theory, but the question of the degree of disturbance does require a short digression. It has been our repeated experience that the parents of schizophrenics may first appear to be consistent, well-adjusted individuals, lending credence to the myth that these families would be a happy lot if it were not for the fact that their son or daughter is psychotic. But even when they are interviewed in the patient's absence, their extraordinary communicational inconsistencies may soon become apparent. Attention must again be drawn to the numerous examples presented by Laing and Esterson (*90*) and to an earlier, pioneering paper by Searles from which the following is quoted:

For example, one deeply schizophrenic young man's mother, a very intense person who talked with machine-gun rapidity, poured out to me in an uninterrupted rush of words the following sentences, which were so full of *non sequiturs,* as

behavior of this individual will be found to satisfy the diagnostic criteria of schizophrenia. Only in this sense can a double bind be considered causative and, therefore, pathogenic. This distinction may seem to be talmudic, but we consider it necessary if the conceptual step from "schizophrenia as a mysterious disease of the individual mind" to "schizophrenia as a specific pattern of communication" is to be achieved.

6.433

With this in mind we can now add two more criteria to the above-mentioned three essential characteristics (s. 6.431) of a double bind, in order to define its connection with schizophrenia. They are

(4) Where double-binding is of long-lasting, possibly chronic duration, it will turn into a habitual and autonomous expectation regarding the nature of human relationships and the world at large, an expectation that does not require further reinforcement.

(5) The paradoxical behavior imposed by double-binding (point (3) of s. 6.431) is in turn of a double-binding nature, and this leads to a self-perpetuating pattern of communication. The behavior of the most overtly disturbed communicant, if examined in isolation, satisfies the clinical criteria of schizophrenia.

6.434

From the above it will be seen that double binds are not simply *contradictory* injunctions, but true paradoxes. We have already considered the essential difference between a contradiction and a paradox when examining the antinomies, and have found that every antinomy is a logical contradiction, but not every logical contradiction is an antinomy. The same distinction holds for contradictory versus paradoxical injunctions (double binds), and it is

---

regards emotional tone, that they left me momentarily quite dazed: "He was very happy. I can't imagine this thing coming over him. He never was down, ever. He loved his radio repair work at Mr. Mitchell's shop in Lewiston. Mr. Mitchell is a very perfectionistic person. I don't think any of the men at his shop before Edward lasted more than a few months. But Edward got along with him beautifully. He used to come home and say (the mother imitates an exhausted sigh), 'I can't stand it another minute!' " (*142*, pp. 3–4)

a distinction of the highest importance, because the pragmatic effects of these two classes of injunctions are very different. (See illustrations facing page 225.)

Our thinking, the logical structure of language, and our perception of reality in general are so firmly based on the Aristotelian law that *A* cannot at the same time also be *not-A,* that this kind of contradiction is too obviously wrong to be taken seriously. Even the contradictions imposed by the daily business of living are not pathogenic. When faced with two mutually exclusive alternatives, one has to choose; one's choice may quickly turn out to have been wrong or one may vacillate too long and thereby fail. Such a dilemma may be anything from the mild regret that one cannot eat one's cake and have it too to the desperate predicament of a man caught on the sixth floor of a burning house and left only with the alternatives of dying either in the fire or by jumping out the window. Similarly, in the classical experiments in which an organism is exposed to a conflict situation (approach-avoidance, approach-approach, avoidance-avoidance), the conflict stems from what amounts to a contradiction between the alternatives offered or imposed. The behavioral effects of these experiments may be anything from indecision to a wrong choice to starvation as an escape from punishment, but never the peculiar pathology that can be observed when the dilemma is truly paradoxical.

However, this pathology is clearly present in the famous Pavlovian experiments in which a dog is first trained to discriminate between a circle and an ellipse and then is caused to be unable to discriminate when the ellipse is gradually expanded to look more and more like a circle. This, we contend, is a context containing all the ingredients of a double bind as set out above, and for its behavioral effects Pavlov coined the term "experimental neurosis." The crux of the matter is that in this type of experiment the experimenter first imposes on the animal the vital necessity of correct discrimination and then, within this frame makes discrimination impossible. The dog is thus cast into a world in which his survival depends on compliance with a law which violates itself: paradox raises its Gorgonian head. At this point the animal begins to exhibit typical behavior disorders; he may become comatose or viciously violent and in addition will display the physiological concomitants of severe anxiety.[14]

To summarize: The most important distinction between contradictory and paradoxical injunctions is that in the face of a contradictory injunction, one chooses one and loses, or suffers, the other alternative. The result is not a happy one—as already mentioned, one cannot eat one's cake and have it too, and the lesser evil is still an evil. But in the face of a contradictory injunction, choice is logically possible. The paradoxical injunction, on the other hand, *bankrupts choice itself,* nothing is possible, and a self-perpetuating oscillating series is set in motion.

As a side remark we should like to point to the interesting fact that the paralyzing effect of pragmatic paradox is by no means limited to primates or mammals in general; even organisms with a relatively rudimentary brain and nervous system are similarly vulnerable to the effects of paradox. This would imply that some fundamental law of existence is here involved.

6.435

But to return to the pragmatics of human communication, let us consider briefly what behavioral effects are likely to be produced by double binds. It was pointed out in s. 4.42 that in any communicational sequence every exchange of messages narrows down the number of possible next moves. In the case of double binds, the complexity of the pattern is particularly constraining and only a very few reactions are pragmatically possible. Following are some of the possible reactions.

Faced with the untenable absurdity of his situation, a person is likely to conclude that he must be overlooking vital clues either inherent in the situation or offered him by significant others. He would be strengthened in the latter assumption by the obvious fact that for the others the situation appears to be quite logical and consistent. That these vital clues may be deliberately withheld from

---

[14] Significantly, animals that have not been trained to discriminate in the first place do not show this kind of behavior in a context in which discrimination is impossible.

him by the others would merely be a variation of the theme. In either case—and this is the central issue—he will be obsessed with the need of finding these clues, of giving a meaning to what is going on in and around him, and he will eventually be forced to extend this scanning for clues and meaning to the most unlikely and unrelated phenomena. This shift away from the real issues becomes all the more plausible if it is remembered that an essential ingredient of a double bind situation is the prohibition to be aware of the contradiction involved.

On the other hand he may choose what recruits quickly find to be the best possible reaction to the bewildering logic, or lack of it, in army life: to comply with any and all injunctions with complete literalness and to abstain overtly from any independent thinking. Thus rather than engaging in an interminable search for hidden meanings, he will discard a priori the possibility that there is any other than the most literal, superficial aspect to human relationships or, furthermore, that one message should have any more meaning than another. As can be imagined, such behavior would strike any observer as foolish, for the inability to distinguish between the trivial and the important, the plausible and the implausible, is in the essence of foolishness.

The third possible reaction would be to withdraw from human involvement. This can be achieved by physically isolating oneself as much as possible and, moreover, by blocking input channels of communication where isolation alone is not possible to the desired extent. In regard to the blocking of inputs, reference must again be made to the phenomenon of "perceptual defense" which was briefly described in s. 3.234. A person defending himself in this fashion would strike an observer as withdrawn, unapproachable, autistic. Virtually the same result—escape from double-binding involvement—can conceivably be achieved by hyperactive behavior that is so intense and sustained that most incoming messages are thereby drowned out.

These three forms of behavior in the face of the undecidability of actual or habitually expected double binds are, as the authors of the theory point out in their original paper, suggestive of the clinical pictures of schizophrenia, that is, of the paranoid, the hebephrenic, and the (stuporous or agitated) catatonic subgroups respectively. They add:

> These three alternatives are not the only ones. The point is that a person cannot choose the one alternative which would help him to discover what people mean; he cannot, without considerable help, discuss the messages of others. Without being able to do that, the human being is like any self-correcting system which has lost its governor; it spirals into never-ending, but always systematic, distortions. (*18*, p. 256)

As pointed out several times earlier, schizophrenic communication is itself paradoxical and therefore imposes paradox on the other communicants, and this completes the vicious cycle.

6.44—PARADOXICAL PREDICTIONS [15]

In the early 1940's a new, particularly fascinating paradox made its appearance. Although its origin seems to be unknown, it quickly gained attention and has since been dealt with extensively in a variety of papers, no fewer than nine of which have appeared in the journal *Mind*.[16] As we shall see, this paradox has particular relevance to our study, because it derives its power and charm from the fact that it is only conceivable as an ongoing interaction between persons.

6.441

Of the several versions in which the essence of this paradox has been given, we have selected the following:

> A headmaster announces to his pupils that there will be an unexpected examination during the next week, i.e., on any day from Monday through Friday. The students—who seem to be an unusually sophisticated

---

[15] Parts of this section were first published in (*158*).

[16] For a review of some of the earlier articles and a comprehensive presentation of this paradox, see Nerlich (*111*); see also Gardner (*54*) for an excellent resumé comprising most of the different versions in which the paradox has been presented.

bunch—point out to him that, unless he violates the terms of his own announcement and does not intend to give an *unexpected* examination *some time* next week, there can be no such examination. For, they argue, if no examination has been held by Thursday evening, then it cannot be held unexpectedly on Friday, since Friday would be the only possible day left. But if Friday can thus be ruled out as a possible examination day, Thursday can be ruled out for the same reason. Obviously, on Wednesday evening there would be only two days left: Thursday and Friday. Friday, as already shown, can be ruled out. This leaves only Thursday, so that an examination held on Thursday would no longer be unexpected. By the same reasoning, of course, Wednesday, Tuesday, and eventually also Monday can be eliminated: there can be no *unexpected* examination. It may be assumed that the headmaster listens to their "proof" in silence and then on, say, Thursday morning holds the examination. From the very moment of his announcement *he* had planned to hold it on that morning. *They*, on the other hand, are now faced with a totally unexpected examination—unexpected for the very reason that they had convinced themselves that it could not be unexpected.

In the foregoing it is not too difficult to distinguish the by now familiar features of paradox. On the one hand, the students have engaged in what appears to be a rigorous logical deduction from the premises set by the headmaster's announcement and have concluded that there can be no unexpected examination the following week. He, on the other hand, obviously can hold the examination on any day of the week without violating in the least the terms of his announcement. The most surprising aspect of this paradox is the fact that upon closer investigation it will be seen that the examination can be held even on Friday and yet be unexpected. In fact, the essence of the story is the situation existing on Thursday evening, while the inclusion of the other days of the week only serves to embellish the story and complicate the problem secondarily. By Thursday evening, Friday is the only possible day left and this makes a Friday examination fully expectable. "It *must* be tomorrow, if there is to be an examination at all; it *cannot* be tomorrow, because it would not be unexpected"; this is how the students see it. Now, this very act of deducing that the examination is expected and therefore impossible, makes it possible for the headmaster to hold an unexpected examination on Friday or, for that matter, any other day of the week, in full conformity with the terms of his announcement. Even if the students realize that their conclusion that there can be no unexpected examination is the very reason it is possible to hold it unexpectedly, their discovery does not help them in the least. All it proves is that if on Thursday evening they expect the examination on Friday, thereby ruling out the possibility of its being given, according to the headmaster's own rules, then it *can* be held unexpectedly, which makes it fully expectable, which makes it totally unexpectable and so forth ad infinitum. It therefore cannot be predicted.

Here, then, is again a true paradox:

(1) the announcement contains a prediction in the *object* language ("there will be an examination");

(2) it contains a prediction in the *meta*language negating the predictability of (1), i.e., "the (predicted) examination will be unpredictable";

(3) the two predictions are mutually exclusive;

(4) the headmaster can successfully prevent the students from stepping outside the situation created by his announcement and from gaining additional information that could enable them to discover the examination date.

6.442

So much for the logical structure of the headmaster's prediction. When its pragmatic consequences are considered, two surprising conclusions emerge. The first is that to make good the prediction contained in his announcement, the headmaster *needs* the opposite conclusion to be reached by the students (that is, that an examination as announced is logically impossible), for only then does a situation exist in which his prediction of an unexpected examination can be borne out. But this is tantamount to saying that the dilemma can arise only thanks to the sophistication of the students. If their wits were duller, they would very probably miss the subtle complexity of the problem; they would probably expect the examination as unexpectable and thus lead the headmaster ad absurdum. For as soon as they—illogically—resign themselves to the fact that the unexpected must be expected, no examination at any time between Monday and Friday would be unexpected for them. Does it not look as if defective logic would make their outlook more realistic? For there is no reason why the examination cannot be held unexpectedly on any day of the week, and only the sophisticated students miss this undeniable fact.

In psychotherapeutic work with intelligent schizophrenics one again and again is tempted to conclude that they would be much better off, much more "normal," if they could only somehow blunt the acuity of their thinking and thus alleviate the paralyzing effect it has on their actions. In their own ways they all seem to be descendants from the troglodytic hero of Dostoevsky's *Notes from Underground*, who explains:

> I swear, gentlemen, that to be too conscious is an illness—a real thoroughgoing illness. (*38*, p. 132)

And later:

> . . . inertia overcame me. You know the direct, legitimate fruit of consciousness is inertia, that is, conscious sitting-with-the-hands-folded. I have referred to this already. I repeat, I repeat with emphasis: all "direct" persons and men of action are active just because they are stupid and limited. How explain that? I will tell you: in consequence of their limitation they take immediate and secondary causes for primary ones, and in

that way persuade themselves more quickly and easily than other people do that they have found an infallible foundation for their activity, and their minds are at ease and you know that is the chief thing. To begin to act, you know, you must first have your mind completely at ease and no trace of doubt left in it. Why, how am I, for example, to set my mind at rest? Where are the primary causes on which I am to build? Where are my foundations? Where am I to get them from? I exercise myself in reflection, and consequently with me every primary cause at once draws after itself another still more primary, and so on to infinity. That is just the essence of every sort of consciousness and reflection. (*38*, pp. 139–40)

Or compare *Hamlet* (IV/4):

> Now whether it be
> Beastly oblivion, or some craven scruple
> Of thinking too precisely on the event,—
> A thought which, quarter'd, hath but one part wisdom
> And ever three parts coward,—I do not know
> Why yet I live to say "this thing's to do,"
> Sith I have cause, and will, and strength, and means
> To do't.

If, as we have seen in s. 6.435, double-binding determines behavior that is suggestively similar to the paranoid, hebephrenic, and catatonic subgroups of schizophrenia respectively, it seems that paradoxical predictions are related to behavior suggestive of the typical inertia and abulia in simple schizophrenia.

6.443

But the second conclusion that imposes itself is perhaps even more disconcerting than this apparent apology for sloppy thinking. The dilemma would be equally impossible if the students did not trust the headmaster implicitly. Their entire deduction stands and falls on the assumption that the headmaster can and must be trusted. Any doubt of his trustworthiness would not dissolve the paradox logically, but would certainly dissolve it pragmatically. If he cannot be trusted, then there is no point in taking his announcement seriously, and the best the students can do under the circumstances is to expect an examination some time from Monday through Friday. (This means that they only accept that part of the announcement that is on the content—object language—level, i.e., "There will be an examination next week," and disregard the metacommunicational aspect dealing with its predictability.) So we reach the conclusion that not only logical thinking but also trust make one vulnerable to this kind of paradox.

6.444
It might seem that such a paradox occurs rarely, if ever, in actual life. This argument, however, cannot be sustained in the area of schizophrenic communication. A person carrying the diagnostic label "schizophrenic" can be thought of as playing both the students' and the headmaster's parts. Like the students he is caught in the dilemma of logic and trust, as set out above. But he is also very much in the headmaster's position, for like the latter he engages in communicating messages that are undecidable. Nerlich, obviously without realizing how much the concluding remarks of his paper are applicable to our subject, has beautifully summarized this state of affairs: "One way of saying nothing is to contradict yourself. And if you manage to contradict yourself by saying that you are saying nothing, then you do not, in the end, contradict yourself at all. You *can* eat your cake and have it, too" (*111*, p. 513).

If, as postulated in ss. 2.23 and 3.2, the schizophrenic is attempting *not* to communicate, then the "solution" to this dilemma is the use of undecidable messages which say of themselves that they are saying nothing.

6.445
But even outside the field of strictly schizophrenic communications, paradoxical predictions can be found to play their havoc in human relations. They occur, for instance, whenever person P is implicitly trusted by the other, O, and threatens to do something

"You sure write good!"

FIGURE 1

FIGURE 2

Contradiction and Paradox, Respectively, As Exemplified by Signs

The two injunctions in Figure 1 simply contradict each other. Therefore, only one can be obeyed. The sign in Figure 2 (a practical joke, we assume) creates a true paradox through its self-reflexivity: to obey the injunction of ignoring it, one first has to notice it. But this very act of noticing it is in disobedience of the injunction itself. Therefore, this sign can only be obeyed by disobeying it, and is disobeyed by obeying it. (See s. 6.434, on simple contradictions versus paradoxes.)

to O that would make him, P, untrustworthy. The following example may illustrate this interaction.

A married couple are seeking psychiatric held because of the wife's excessive jealousy, which makes life unbearable for both of them. It turns out that the husband is an extremely rigid, moralistic person who takes great pride in his ascetic style of life and in the fact that "I've never, in all my life, given anybody reason to distrust my word." The wife, who comes from a very different background, has accepted the complementary one-down position, except in one area: she is unwilling to forgo her predinner drink, a habit that to him, as a teetotaler, is disgusting and has been the theme of endless quarrels practically since the beginning of their marriage. About two years ago the husband, in a fit of anger, told her, *"If you don't stop your vice, I'll start one of my own,"* adding that he would have affairs with other women. This did not bring about any change in their relationship pattern, and a few months later the husband decided to let her have her drinks for the sake of domestic peace. At this precise point in time her jealousy flared up, the rationale of which was and is: He is absolutely trustworthy; therefore he must be carrying out his threat and be unfaithful, that is, untrustworthy. The husband, on the other hand, is just as helplessly caught in the web of his paradoxical prediction, as he cannot convincingly reassure her that his threat was impulsive and should not be taken seriously. They realize that they are caught in a self-made trap, but see no way out of it.

The structure of the husband's threat is identical with that of the headmaster's announcement. As she sees it, he is saying:

(1) I am absolutely trustworthy;
(2) I shall now punish you by being untrustworthy (unfaithful, deceitful);
(3) therefore, I am going to remain trustworthy to you by being untrustworthy, for if I now did not destroy your trust in my marital trustworthiness, I would not be trustworthy any more.

From a semantic point of view the paradox arises over the two different meanings of "trustworthy." In (1) the term is used in the metalanguage to denote the common property of *all* his actions, promises, and attitudes. In (2) it is used in the object language and refers to marital faithfulness. The same holds for the two uses of "expected" in the headmaster's announcement. *All* his predictions can be expected to take place with certainty. In other words, expectability is the common property determining the *class* of his predictions. Thus, if the expectability of one *member* of this class —that is, one specific prediction—is negated, it is expectability of a different—that is, lower—logical type than the one which is the property of the class, designated by the same term. From a pragmatic point of view, both the headmaster's and the husband's announcements create contexts that are untenable.

6.446 Trust—The Prisoners' Dilemma

In human relations, all prediction is connected in one way or another with the phenomenon of trust. If person *P* hands the other, *O,* a personal check, the question of whether this check is covered remains unknown to *O* on the strength of the information available to him at the time. In this sense, *P*'s and *O*'s positions are very different. *P* knows whether his check is good or not; *O* can only trust or distrust him,[17] for he will not know until he takes the check to the bank. At that moment his trust or distrust will be replaced by the same certainty that *P* had from the very start. There is in the nature of human communication no way of making another person a participant in information or perceptions available exclusively to oneself. The other can at best trust or distrust, but he can never *know*. On the other hand, human activity would virtually be paralyzed if people acted only on the strength of firsthand information or perceptions. The vast majority of all decisions is based on trust of one kind or another. Trust is thus always related to future outcomes and, more specifically, to their predictability.

So far interactions have been considered in which one person

---

[17] *O's* trust or distrust will, of course, be influenced by his past experiences, if any, with *P,* and the outcome of the present problem will influence *O's* amount of trust in *P* on future occasions. But for the present purposes this can be left aside.

has firsthand information and the other can only trust or distrust the communication of this information. The headmaster knows that he is going to give the examination on Thursday morning; the husband knows that he does not intend to betray his wife; the man who writes a check (usually) knows whether it is covered or not. Now, in any interaction of the "Prisoners' Dilemma" type, *neither* person has any firsthand information. They both have to rely on their trust in the other, on a tentative assessment of their own trustworthiness in the eyes of the other, and on their attempts at predicting the decision procedure of the other that they know depends largely on his predictions about theirs. These predictions, as shall now be shown, invariably become paradoxical.

The Prisoners' Dilemma [18] can be represented by a matrix such as the following:

	b_1	b_2
a_1	5, 5	−5, 8
a_2	8, −5	−3, −3

in which two players, *A* and *B*, have two alternative moves each. That is, *A* can choose either a_1 or a_2, and *B* can choose either b_1 or b_2. Both are fully aware of the gains or losses defined by the matrix. Thus *A* knows that if he chooses a_1 and *B* chooses b_1, they will win five points each; but if *B* chooses alternative b_2 instead, *A* will lose five points and *B* will win eight points. *B* is faced with a similar situation vis-à-vis *A*. Their dilemma consists of the fact that each does not know what alternative the other will choose, since they must choose simultaneously but cannot communicate about their decision.

It is usually assumed that no matter whether the game is played just once or a hundred times in succession, decision a_2, b_2 is the

[18] As will be remembered, the Prisoners' Dilemma is a nonzero-sum game. So the goal for each player is his own absolute gain, irrespective of the other's gain or loss. Thus, co-operation is not only not ruled out (as it is in the zero-sum game), but may even be the optimal strategy. Nor is randomization of moves (in the case of successive plays) an automatically desirable strategy.

safest one, even though it entails a loss of three points for both player A and player B.[19] A more reasonable solution would, of course, be a_1, b_1, for it insures both players a gain of five points. But this decision can be reached only under conditions of mutual trust. For if, say, player A played the game only from the point of view of maximizing his gains and minimizing his losses, *and* if player A has sufficient reason to believe that player B trusts him and will therefore choose b_1, then player A has every reason to choose a_2, since joint decision a_2, b_1, gives player A a maximum gain. But if A is a sufficiently clear thinker, he cannot fail to predict that B will follow the analogous line of reasoning and will therefore play b_2 rather than b_1, especially if B also thinks that he is trusted enough by A and has himself enough trust in A for A to play a_1. Consequently, the melancholy conclusion imposes itself that joint decision a_2, b_2, with a loss for both players, is the only feasible one.

This outcome is by no means a theoretical one. It is perhaps the most elegant abstract representation of a problem encountered over and over again in marriage psychotherapy. Spouses who live lives of quiet desperation, deriving minimum gratification from their joint experiences, have been known to psychiatrists for a long time. Traditionally, however, the reason for their misery is sought in the assumed *individual* pathology of one or both of them. They may be diagnosed as depressive, passive-aggressive, self-punishing, sadomasochistic, and so on. But these diagnoses obviously fail to grasp the *interdependent* nature of their dilemma, which may exist quite apart from their personality structure and may reside exclusively in the nature of their relationship "game." It is as if they were saying, "Trust would make me vulnerable; therefore I have to play it safe," and the inherent prediction thus is, "The other *will* take advantage of me."

This is the point where most spouses (or, for that matter, nations) stop in the evaluation and definition of their relationship. But those who are sharper thinkers cannot stop there, and this is where

---

[19] See the detailed discussions in Rapoport (*122*) and Schelling (*140*).

the paradox of the Prisoners' Dilemma becomes most patent. Solution a_2, b_2 becomes unreasonable as soon as A realizes that this solution is only a lesser evil, but still an evil, and that B cannot fail to see it in these identical terms—that is, as an evil. B then must have as little reason as A to want this outcome, a conclusion that is certainly accessible to A's predictive thinking. Once both A and B have arrived at this insight, then solution a_2, b_2 is no longer the most reasonable decision, but rather the cooperative decision a_1, b_1. But with a_1, b_1 the whole cycle starts all over again. No matter how they look at it, as soon as the "most reasonable" decision is deduced, a "more most reasonable" decision always emerges. Thus the dilemma is identical to that of the students for whom the examination is predictable only when it is unpredictable.

6.5

Summary

A paradox is a logical contradiction following consistent deductions from correct premises. Of the three types of paradox—logico-mathematical, semantical, and pragmatic—the latter is of interest here because of its behavioral implications. Pragmatic paradoxes are distinguished from simple contradiction especially in that choice is a solution in the latter but not even possible in the former. The two kinds of pragmatic paradoxes are *paradoxical injunctions* (double binds) and *paradoxical predictions*.

Chapter 7

Paradox in Psychotherapy

7.1

The Illusion of Alternatives

7.11

In *The Wife of Bath's Tale,* Chaucer presents the story of one of King Arthur's knights who "lustily riding home one day from hawking" comes upon a maiden in his path and rapes her. This crime, "at which the outcry was so keen," nearly costs him his life, except for the fact that the queen and her ladies want him spared, as Arthur leaves the decision of the knight's fate to the queen. The queen tells the knight she will grant him his life if he can find the answer to the question "What is the thing that most of all women desire?" She gives him a year and a day to return to the castle, and, faced with a death sentence as the only alternative, the knight accepts the task. As can be imagined, the year passes, the last day comes, and the knight is on his way back to the castle, not having found the answer. This time he chances upon an old woman ("as ugly a witch as fancy could devise"), sitting in a meadow, who addresses him with the rather prophetic words: "Sir knight, here runs no thoroughfare." Upon hearing his predicament, she tells him that she knows the answer and that she will reveal it to him if he swears that "whatsoever I next ask of you, you'll do if it lies within your might." Faced again with a choice between two alternatives (beheading or the witch's wish, whatever it might be), he of course chooses the latter and is told the secret ("Most of all women desire to have the sovereignty and sit in rule and government above their husbands and to have their way in love"). This answer fully satisfies the ladies of the court, but now the witch, having fulfilled her part of the bargain, demands that the knight marry her. The wedding night comes, and there the knight lies in despair by her side, unable to overcome his revulsion at her ugliness. At last the witch again offers him two alternatives from which he may choose: either he accept her ugly as she is, and she will be a true and humble wife to him all her life, or she will turn herself into a young and beautiful maiden, but will never be faithful to him. For a long time the knight ponders the two alternatives and eventually *chooses neither of them, but rejects choice itself.* This climax of the Tale is contained in the one single line: "I do no fors the whether of the two" (I do not choose either of the two). At this moment the witch not only turns into a beautiful maiden but into a most faithful, obedient wife as well.

To the knight, woman appears as innocent maiden, queen, witch, and whore, but her power over him remains the same under all these guises until he no longer feels compelled to choose and be led into further predicament, but eventually questions the need for choice itself.[1] *The Wife of Bath's Tale* is also a beautiful piece of female psychology and as such has received a most interesting analysis by Stein (*148*). In our conceptual framework we would say that as long as this kind of woman is capable of double-binding the male by means of a never-ending illusion of alternatives (and, of course, as long as the male cannot extricate himself from it), she cannot be free either, and remains caught in an illusion of alternatives involving ugliness or promiscuity as the only choices.

7.12

The term *illusion of alternatives* was first used by Weakland and Jackson (*161*) in a report on the interpersonal circumstances of a schizophrenic episode. They observed that in trying to make the

---

[1] Compare with this a famous Zen *koan* (a paradoxical meditation) imposed by Tai-hui with a bamboo stick: "If you call this a stick, you affirm; if you call it not a stick, you negate. Beyond affirmation and negation, what would you call it?"

right choice between two alternatives, schizophrenic patients encounter a typical dilemma: they cannot, in the nature of the communicational situation, make a *right* decision, because both alternatives are part and parcel of a double bind and the patient is, therefore, "damned if he does and damned if he doesn't." There are no actual alternatives of which the "right" one "should" be chosen—the whole assumption that choice is possible and should be made is an illusion.[2] But to realize the absence of choice would be tantamount to recognizing not only the overt "alternatives" offered, but the actual nature of the double bind. In fact, as has been shown in s. 6.431, the blocking of any escape from the double-binding situation and the resulting impossibility of looking at it from the outside are an essential ingredient of the double bind. People in these situations are as caught as the defendant who is asked, "Have you stopped beating your wife? Answer 'yes' or 'no' " and is threatened with a charge of contempt of court if he tries to reject both alternatives as inapplicable because he has never beaten her. But while the interrogator in this example knows that he is using a nasty trick, this knowledge and intent are usually absent in real life situations. Paradoxical communications, as we have already observed, invariably bind all concerned: the Witch is as much caught as the Knight, the husband of the example in s. 6.445 as much as his wife, etc. What all these patterns have in common is that no change can be generated from *within* and that any change can only come from stepping *outside* the pattern. This problem of successful intervention, of bringing about change in such a system, will now be examined.

7.2

The "Game Without End"

To begin with a highly theoretical example, imagine the following. Two persons decide to play a game consisting of the substitution of negation for affirmation and vice versa in everything they com-

---

[2] This is, of course, the basic difference between a double bind and a simple contradiction (see s. 6.434).

municate to each other. Thus "yes" becomes "no," "I don't want" means "I want," and so forth. It can be seen that this coding of their messages is a semantic convention and similar to the myriad other conventions used by two people sharing a common language. It is not immediately evident, however, that once this game is under way the players cannot easily revert to their former "normal" mode of communication. In keeping with the rule of inversion of meaning, the message "Let's stop playing" means "Let's continue." To stop the game it would be necessary to step outside the game and communicate about it. Such a message would clearly have to be constructed as a metamessage, but whatever qualifier were tried for this purpose would itself be subject to the rule of inversion of meaning and would therefore be useless. The message "Let's stop playing" is undecidable, for (1) it is meaningful both at the object level (as part of the game) and on the metalevel (as a message *about* the game); (2) the two meanings are contradictory; and (3) the peculiar nature of the game does not provide for a procedure that would enable the players to decide on the one or the other meaning. This undecidability makes it impossible for them to stop the game once it is under way. Such situations we label *games without end*.

It may be argued that the dilemma could be avoided and the game terminated at will by simply using the opposite message, "Let's continue playing." But closer examination reveals that this is not the case from the strictly logical viewpoint. For, as we have now seen repeatedly, no statement made within a given frame (here the game of inversion of meaning) can at the same time be a valid assertion about the frame. Even if the message "Let's continue playing" were given by one player and, by the rule of inversion, understood by the other to signify "Let's stop playing," he would still be faced with an undecidable message, provided that he remained strictly logical about it. For the rules of the game simply do not make allowance for metamessages and a message proposing the end of the game is of necessity a metamessage. By the rules of the game every message is part of the game, no message is exempt from it.

We have presented this example at some length because it is paradigmatic not only of such dramatic examples as described in s. 5.43, but of countless relationship dilemmas in real life. It highlights an important aspect of the kind of system we are now examining: once the original agreement regarding the inversion of meaning is reached, it can no longer be altered by the two players, for to alter it they would have to communicate and their communications are the very substance of the game. This means that in such a system *no change can be generated from within.*

7.21

What could the players have done to prevent their dilemma? Three possibilities offer themselves.

(1) The players, anticipating the possible need for communications about the game once the game has started, could have agreed that they would play it in English but would use French for their metacommunications. Any statement in French, such as the proposal to stop playing, would therefore clearly remain outside the body of those messages that are subject to the rule of inversion of meaning, that is, outside the game itself. This would constitute a perfectly effective decision procedure for this game. In actual human communication, however, it would be inapplicable, since there does not exist a metalanguage that is used only for communications about communication. Indeed, behavior and, more narrowly, natural language are used for communications both at the object and at the metalanguage level, and this results in some of the problems we are describing (s. 1.5).

(2) The players could have agreed beforehand on a time limit after which they would revert to their normal mode of communicating. It is noteworthy that this solution, although impracticable in actual human communication, entails recourse to an outside factor—time—which is not caught up in their game.

(3) This leads to the third possibility, which seems to be the only generally effective procedure and has the additional advantage that it can be resorted to after the game has started: the players could take their dilemma to a third person with whom they

have both maintained their normal mode of communication and have him rule that the game is over.

The therapeutic quality of the mediator's intervention may become clearer by comparison with another example of a game without end in which, by the nature of the situation, there exists no mediator whose intervention could be invoked.

The constitution of an imaginary country guarantees the right of unlimited parliamentary debate. This rule is quickly found to be impractical, for any party can prevent any decision from being reached by simply engaging in endless speeches. An amendment of the constitution is obviously necessary, but the adoption of the amendment itself is subject to the same right of unlimited debate that it is supposed to amend, and can, therefore, be delayed indefinitely by unlimited debate. This country's government machinery is consequently paralyzed and unable to produce a change of its own rules, for it is caught in a game without end.

In this case there obviously exists no mediator who would stand outside the rules of the game embodied in the constitution. The only change that can conceivably be brought about is a violent one, a revolution through which one party gains power over the others and imposes a new constitution. The equivalent of such a violent change in the area of relationships between individuals caught in a game without end would be separation, suicide, or homicide. As we have seen in Chapter 5, a less violent variation of this theme is George's "killing" of the imaginary son, which destroys the old rules of his and Martha's marriage game.

7.22

In our view this third possibility (of outside intervention) *is a paradigm of psychotherapeutic intervention.* In other words, the therapist as outsider is capable of supplying what the system itself cannot generate: a change of its own rules. For instance, in the example presented in s. 6.445 the couple were caught in a game without end, the basic rule of which was set by the husband's claim of absolute trustworthiness and the wife's absolute acceptance of this self-definition. In this relationship game an irreversible paradox arose the moment the husband promised to be untrustworthy (unfaithful). The irreversibility of the situation lies in the fact that, like any other game without end, this one was governed by rules but lacked metarules for the change of its rules. One could say that the essence of psychotherapeutic intervention in such a case consists of the formation of a new, enlarged system (husband, wife, and therapist), in which it is not only possible to look at the old system (the marital dyad) from the outside, but for the therapist to use the power of paradox for amelioration; the therapist can impose on this new relationship game such rules as are appropriate for his therapeutic purposes.[3]

7.3

Prescribing the Symptom

7.31

Therapeutic communication, then, must necessarily transcend such counsel as is customarily but ineffectually given by the protagonists themselves, as well as their friends and relatives. Prescriptions such as "Be nice to each other," "Don't get in trouble with the police," and the like can hardly qualify as therapeutic, although they naïvely define the desired change. These messages are based on the assumption that "with a little will power" things could be changed and that it is, therefore, up to the person or persons concerned to choose between health and misery. Yet this assumption is nothing but an illusion of alternatives, at least in-

---

[3] However, it is our experience and that of many others working in this field that successful therapeutic intervention is subject to an important time factor. It seems to be in the nature of human relationships that the therapist has a rather limited period of grace in which to accomplish his goal. Relatively soon the new system itself consolidates to the point where the therapist is almost inextricably caught in it and from then on is much less able to produce change than at the very start of the treatment. This is especially true of families containing a schizophrenic member; their power of "absorption" of anything threatening their rigid stability (the chaotic surface manifestations notwithstanding) is truly impressive. Typically, and quite appropriately, a therapist consults another therapist whenever he feels he has been caught up in the game with his patient or patients. Only by taking this problem to another therapist is he able to step outside the frame in which he is caught.

sofar as the patient can at all times reject it by the unassailable retort: "I can't help it." Bona fide patients—by which we simply mean persons who are not deliberately simulating—usually have tried and failed in all kinds of self-discipline and exercises in will power long before they revealed their distress to others and were told to "pull themselves together." It is in the essence of a symptom that it is something unwilled and therefore autonomous. But this is simply another way of saying that a symptom is a piece of spontaneous behavior, so spontaneous indeed that even the patient himself experiences it as something uncontrollable. It is this oscillation between spontaneity and coercion that makes the symptom paradoxical, both in the patient's experience and in its effect on others.

If one person wants to influence another person's behavior, there are basically only two ways of doing it. The first consists of trying to make the other behave differently. This approach, as we have just seen, fails with symptoms because the patient has no deliberate control over this behavior. The other approach (examples of which are given in s. 7.5) consists in making him behave as he is already behaving. In the light of the foregoing, this amounts to a "be spontaneous" paradox. If someone is asked to engage in a specific type of behavior which is seen as spontaneous, then he cannot be spontaneous any more, because the demand makes spontaneity impossible.[4] By the same token, if a therapist instructs a patient to perform his symptom, he is demanding spontaneous behavior and by this paradoxical injunction imposes on his patient a behavioral change. The symptomatic behavior is no longer spontaneous; by subjecting himself to the therapist's injunction the patient has stepped outside the frame of his symptomatic game without end, which up to that moment had no metarules for the

---

[4] The inescapable effect of this kind of communication can easily be tested. If P remarks to O: "The way you sit there in that chair looks extremely relaxed" and keeps looking at O, he has not even prescribed but merely described O's behavior, yet O will probably feel immediately uneasy and cramped, and will have to shift from the posture described to regain a feeling of comfort and relaxation. And there is the fable of the cockroach who asked the centipede how he managed to move his hundred legs with such elegant ease and perfect co-ordination. From that moment on, the centipede could not walk any more.

change of its own rules. Something done "because I can't help it" and the same behavior engaged in "because my therapist told me to" could not be more different.

7.32

The technique of *prescribing the symptom* (as a double-binding technique for its removal) seems to stand in sharp contradiction to those tenets of psychoanalytically oriented psychotherapy that proscribe direct interference with symptoms. However, in recent years much evidence has been accumulated in support of the proposition that if only the symptom is removed, no dire consequences will follow—depending, of course, on how the symptomatic behavior is approached.[5] While there can be no doubt that, for instance, an anorexia patient who is forcibly fed may become depressive and suicidal, this is not the kind of therapeutic intervention we are describing here. Moreover, it should be borne in mind that one's expectations about the outcome of an intervention depend on one's philosophy of therapy. The so-called behavior therapists (Wolpe, Eysenck, Lazarus, *et al.*), for instance, apply learning rather than psychoanalytic theory to emotional disturbances and therefore worry very little about possible ill effects of purely symptomatic treatment. Their claim that symptom removal does not produce new and worse symptoms and that their patients do not turn suicidal must by now be taken seriously. Likewise, if a patient is instructed to perform his symptom and in the process of doing so finds that he can get rid of it, this, in our opinion, is virtually equivalent to the result of "insight" in classical psychoanalysis, although no insight whatsoever seems to be gained. But even in real life, the ever-present phenomenon of change is rarely accompanied by "insight"; more often than not one changes and knows not why. We would even go so far as to suggest that, from a communicational viewpoint, probably most traditional forms of psychotherapy are far more symptom-oriented than would appear on the surface. The therapist who consistently, deliberately disregards the

---

[5] One way not to approach symptomatic behavior would be to bring about change in only *one* person involved in a close relationship (see s. 7.33).

patient's complaints about his symptom is signaling, in a more or less overt way, that for the time being it is all right to have the symptom and all that matters is what is "behind" it. This permissive attitude vis-à-vis the symptom is probably given far too little attention as a curative factor.

7·33

There is, however, one important issue that our system-oriented, interactional perspective of psychopathology forces us to take up with the behavior therapists and that, in a wider sense, corroborates the psychodynamic caveat against purely symptomatic relief. While we are convinced of the effectiveness of behavior (deconditioning) therapy as far as the patient as a monad is concerned, we miss both in the theory as well as in the reported case histories any reference to the interactional effect of the patient's often very drastic improvement. In our experience (s. 4.44; 4.443) such a change is more often than not accompanied by the appearance of a new problem or the exacerbation of an existing condition in another family member. From the behavior therapy literature one gets the impression that the therapist (concerned as he is only with his individual patient) would not see any reciprocal connection between these two phenomena and would, if called upon, consider the new problem again in monadic isolation.

7·34

The technique of prescribing the symptom has probably been used by intuitive psychiatrists for a long time. To the best of our knowledge it was introduced into the literature by Dunlap (39, 40) in 1925 in a passage dealing with negative suggestion. Although he describes it only briefly, his method consists of telling a patient that he (the patient) could *not* do something in order to motivate him to do it. Frankl (46, 47) refers to this intervention as "paradoxical intention," but gives no rationale for its effectiveness. In the psychotherapy of schizophrenia, the same technique is an important tactic of Rosen's *direct analysis* (129). He refers to it as "reductio ad absurdum" or "re-enacting the psychosis"; a detailed description of his technique can be found in Scheflen's extensive evaluation (*137*). The term "prescribing the symptom" was first introduced in the work of the Bateson "Family Therapy in Schizophrenia" project. This group explicitly clarified the paradoxical, double-binding nature of this technique. For instance, Haley (*60*, pp. 20–59) has shown that this kind of paradoxical injunctions plays an essential role in virtually all techniques of trance induction, and gives many examples of its use in hypnotherapy from both his observation of Milton Erickson's technique and his own experiences with it. Jackson has written on the application of this method especially with paranoid patients (*71, 72, 77*), and this work will be described in greater detail later in this chapter. In an earlier paper, Jackson and Weakland (*75*) discuss such techniques in family therapy.

7.4
Therapeutic Double Binds

Prescribing the symptom is only one form of many different paradoxical interventions that can be subsumed under the term therapeutic double binds; they in turn are of course only one class of therapeutic communications, and there are many other approaches that have traditionally been used in psychotherapy. If in this chapter we concentrate on paradoxical communications as curative factors, it is because from a communication point of view they are the most complex and powerful interventions known to us and because it is difficult to imagine that symptomatic double binds can be broken by anything other than counter double binds, or games without end terminated by anything of less complexity than a countergame (*155*). *Similia similibus curantur*—in other words, what has been found to drive people crazy must ultimately be useful in driving them sane. This does not deny the overwhelming importance of the therapist's human attitude toward his patients or that firmness, understanding, sincerity, warmth, and compassion have no place in this context, nor does it imply that all that matters are ploys, games, and tactics. Psychotherapy would be unthinkable without these qualities in the therapist, and it will be seen in subsequent examples that more traditional techniques of explanation and understanding often work hand in hand with double-binding interventions. What is being suggested, however, is that these qualities alone are not enough to deal with the paradoxical complexities of disturbed interaction.

Structurally, a therapeutic double bind is the mirror image of a pathogenic one (cf. s. 6.431).

(1) It presupposes an intense relationship, in this case, the psychotherapeutic situation, which has a high degree of survival value and of expectation for the patient.

(2) In this context, an injunction is given which is so structured that it (a) reinforces the behavior the patient expects to be changed, (b) implies that this reinforcement is the vehicle of change, and (c) thereby creates paradox because the patient is told to change by remaining unchanged. He is put into an untenable situation with regard to his pathology. If he complies, he no longer "can't help it"; he does "it," and this, as we have tried to show, makes "it" impossible, which is the purpose of therapy. If he resists the injunction, he can do so only by *not* behaving symptomatically, which is the purpose of therapy. If in a pathogenic double bind the patient is "damned if he does and damned if he doesn't," in a therapeutic double bind he is "changed if he does and changed if he doesn't."

(3) The therapeutic situation prevents the patient from withdrawing or otherwise dissolving the paradox by commenting on it.[6] Therefore, even though the injunction is logically absurd, it is a pragmatic reality: the patient cannot *not* react to it, but neither can he react to it in his usual, symptomatic way.

The following examples are aimed at showing how a therapeutic double bind always forces the patient to step outside the frame set by his dilemma. This is the step which he cannot make by himself, but which becomes possible when the original system is ex-

[6] This may not seem very convincing, but in actual fact it is extraordinarily rare to find a patient who would not accept even the most absurd injunctions (e.g., "I want you to increase your pain") without much questioning.

panded—either from an individual and his symptom, or from two or more persons and their game without end (but most frequently a combination of both)—into a larger system that now includes an expert outsider. This not only makes it possible for everyone concerned to look at the old system from the outside, but also permits the introduction of metarules that the old system was unable to generate from within itself.

So much for the theoretical aspects of therapeutic double binds. Their practical application is a much more thorny subject. May it suffice to say here that the choice of the appropriate paradoxical injunction is extremely difficult and that, if the slightest loophole is left, the patient will usually have little difficulty in spotting it and thereby escaping the supposedly untenable situation planned by the therapist.

7.5

Examples of Therapeutic Double Binds

The following collection of examples is not claimed to be especially representative, nor more illustrative than those which can be found in the references cited in s. 7.34. They should, however, show some of the possible applications of this therapeutic technique, drawing the instances from both individual and conjoint treatments and involving a variety of diagnostic entities.

Example 1: In the discussion of the double bind theory it has already been suggested that the paranoid patient will often extend his scanning for meaning to totally peripheral and unrelated phenomena, since correct perception of, and commenting upon, the central issue (the paradox) has been made impossible for him. Indeed, what is so striking about paranoid behavior is extreme suspiciousness, coupled with virtual inability to put these suspicions to a definitive test that would resolve them one way or the other. Thus while the patient appears aloof and all-knowing, he suffers from huge gaps in living experience, and the ever-present injunction against correct perception has a twofold effect: it prevents him from filling these gaps with the appropriate information, and it strengthens his suspicions. Basing himself on the concept of paradoxical communications, Jackson (72, 77) has described a specific technique for interacting with paranoid patients, referred to simply as *teaching the patient to be more suspicious.* Two of the examples given are the following.

(a) A patient expressed his fear that somebody had installed a hidden microphone in the therapist's office. Rather than trying to interpret this suspicion, the therapist became "appropriately" concerned and put the patient into a therapeutic double bind by suggesting that together they make a thorough search of the office before proceeding with the session. This left the patient with an illusion of alternatives: he could accept the search or dismiss the paranoid idea. He chose the former alternative, and as the search painstakingly got under way, he became increasingly unsure and embarrassed about his suspicion; but the therapist would not let the matter rest until every nook and cranny of the office had been explored by them together. The patient then plunged into a meaningful description of his marriage, and it turned out that in *this* area he had good reasons to be suspicious. However, by focusing on a suspicion that was unrelated to the real problem, he had rendered himself unable to do anything useful about his concerns and doubts. If, on the other hand, the patient had rejected the therapist's suggestions to search the office, he would himself have implicitly disqualified his suspicion, or labeled it as an idea that was not worth taking seriously. In either case the therapeutic function of doubt could shift to the appropriate context.

(b) A clinical demonstration to psychiatric residents was to show techniques of establishing rapport with withdrawn schizophrenics. One of the patients was a tall, bearded young man who considered himself to be God and who kept completely aloof from other patients and the staff. Upon entering the lecture room, he deliberately placed his chair some twenty feet from the therapist and ignored any questions or remarks. The therapist then told him that this idea of being God was a dangerous one, for the patient could easily be lulled by it into a false sense of omniscience and omnipotence and therefore would neglect to be on his guard and constantly check what was going on around him. He made clear that if the patient wanted to take this kind of chance, this would be exclusively his problem, and if he wanted to be treated as if he were God, the therapist would go along with this. During this structuring of the double bind the patient became increasingly nervous and at the same time interested in what was going on. The interviewer then took the ward key from his pocket, knelt in front of the patient and offered the key to him, stating that since the patient was God, he did not need the key, but if he were God, he would be more deserving of the key than the doctor. No sooner had the interviewer returned to his desk than the patient grabbed up his chair and pulled it to within two feet of the interviewer. Leaning forward, he said earnestly and with genuine concern, "Man, one of the two of us is certainly crazy."

Example 2: Not only the psychoanalytic but more generally most psychotherapeutic settings are rich in implicit double binds. The paradoxical nature of psychoanalysis was realized by one of Freud's earliest collaborators, Hans Sachs, who is credited with saying that an *analysis terminates when the patient realizes that it could go on forever,* a statement strangely reminiscent of the Zen Buddhist tenet that enlightenment comes when the pupil realizes that there is no secret, no ultimate answer, and therefore no point in continuing to ask questions. For an extensive treatment of this subject, the reader is referred to Jackson and Haley (76), whose study will be summarized here very briefly.

Traditionally, it is assumed that in the transference situation the patient "regresses" to earlier, "inappropriate" patterns of behavior. Jackson and Haley again took the converse approach and asked themselves: what would be appropriate behavior in the psychoanalytic situation? In this view, it seems that the only mature reaction to the whole ritual of couch, free associations, imposed spontaneity, fees, strict time schedule, etc., would be to reject the entire situation. But this is exactly what the patient, who is in need of help, cannot do. The stage is thus set for a very peculiar communicational context. Some of the more outstanding paradoxes involved in it are the following.

(a) The patient expects the analyst to be an expert who will, of course, tell him what to do. The analyst responds by putting the patient in charge, making him responsible for the course of the treatment, demanding spontaneity at the same time he sets rules that completely circumscribe the patient's behavior. The patient is in effect told "Be spontaneous."

(b) No matter what the patient does in this situation, he will be faced with a paradoxical response. If he points out that he is not improving, he is told that this is due to his resistance, but that it is good because it affords a better opportunity to understand his problem. If he states that he believes he is improving, he is tóld that he is again resisting treatment by trying to escape into health before his real problem has been analyzed.

(c) The patient is in a situation where he cannot behave in an adult way, yet when he does not, the analyst interprets his child-like behavior as a carryover from childhood and therefore inappropriate.

(d) A further paradox resides in the very tricky question of whether the analytic relationship is a compulsory or a voluntary one. On the one hand the patient is constantly told that his relationship is a voluntary and, therefore, *symmetrical* one. Yet if the patient is late, or misses a session, or otherwise violates any of the rules, it becomes obvious that the relationship is a compulsory, *complementary* one, with the analyst in the one-up position.

(e) The analyst's one-up position becomes especially obvious whenever the concept of the unconscious is invoked. If the patient rejects an interpretation the analyst can always explain that he is pointing to something that the patient must by definition be unaware of, because it is unconscious. If, on the other hand, the patient tries to claim unconsciousness for something, the analyst can reject this by saying that if it were unconscious the patient could not refer to it.[7]

From the above it will be seen that regardless what else the analyst does to bring about change, the situation itself is virtually

[7] To point out its interpersonal implications is not to deny the existence of the unconscious, nor the usefulness of the concept (cf. s. 1.62).

one complex therapeutic double bind in which the patient is "changed if he does and changed if he doesn't." It will also be seen that this is not only true of the strictly psychoanalytic treatment situation, but of psychotherapy in the wider sense.

Example 3: Doctors are supposed to cure. From an interactional point of view this places them in a very curious position: they occupy the complementary one-up position in the doctor-patient relationship as long as their treatment is successful. On the other hand, when their efforts fail the positions are reversed; the nature of the doctor-patient relationship is then dominated by the intractability of the patient's condition, and the physician finds himself in the one-down position. He is then likely to be double-bound by those patients who for often very recondite reasons cannot accept a change for the better or for whom it is more important to be one-up on any partner in a relationship, including the physician, regardless of the pain and discomfort this may produce for themselves. In either case it is as if these patients communicated through their symptoms: "Help me, but I will not let you."

Such a patient, a middle-aged woman, was referred to a psychiatrist because of persistent, incapacitating headaches. The pains had started shortly after she sustained an occipital injury in an accident. This injury had cleared up without complications, and exhaustive medical examinations had failed to reveal anything that could account for her headaches. The patient had been adequately compensated by an insurance company, and no court action or further claims were pending. Prior to her referral to the psychiatrist, she had been examined and treated by a number of specialists in a large clinic. In the course of these consultations she had accumulated an impressively voluminous file and had become a source of considerable professional frustration to these doctors.

Upon studying her case, the psychiatrist realized that with this history of medical "failures" any implication that psychotherapy might *help* would doom such treatment from the very start. He therefore began by informing the patient that from the results of all the previous examinations and in view of the fact that no treatment had given her the slightest relief, there could be no doubt that her condition was irreversible. As a result of this regrettable fact, the only thing that he could do for her was to help her to learn how to live with her pain. The patient seemed more angry than upset about this explanation and inquired rather pointedly if this was all psychiatry had to offer. The psychiatrist countered this by waving her weighty case history in the air, and repeated that in the face of this evidence there simply was no hope for any improvement and that she would have to learn to resign herself to this fact. When the patient returned for her second interview a week later, she announced that in the meantime she had suffered much less from her headaches. At this the psychiatrist showed great concern; he criticized himself for not having warned her beforehand of the possibility of such a temporary, purely subjective lessening of the pain, and expressed his fear that the pain would now unavoidably return in its old intensity, and she would be even more miserable for having placed an unrealistic hope in a merely temporary lessening of her pain perception. He again produced her case history, pointed to its exhaustiveness and repeated that the sooner she abandoned any hope of improvement, the sooner she would learn to live with her condition. From this point on her psychotherapy took a rather stormy turn, with the psychiatrist becoming more and more skeptical about his usefulness to her because she would not accept the "irreversibility of her condition," and the patient angrily and impatiently claiming constant improvement. Large portions of the interview time between these rounds of the game, however, could be used for an exploration of other significant aspects of this woman's interpersonal relations, and she eventually left treatment, greatly improved, on her own decision, having obviously realized that her game with the psychiatrist could go on forever.

Example 4: Psychogenic pain cases like the above are usually particularly amenable to brief psychotherapy based on paradoxical communication. The imposition of a therapeutic double bind can often begin with the very first contact, often even the telephone request by a new patient for an appointment. If the therapist can be reasonably certain of the psychogenicity of the complaint (as he may be, for instance, from prior discussion with the referring physician), he may warn the caller that not infrequently people feel a marked improvement before they report for their first interview, but that this improvement is purely momentary and that no hope should be placed in it. If the patient does not feel any improvement by the time he comes for his first appointment, no harm is done, and the patient will appreciate the therapist's concern and foresight. But if he does feel better, the stage is set for further structuring of the therapeutic double bind. The next step to be taken may be the explanation that psychotherapy cannot alleviate the pain, but that the patient himself can usually "shift the pain in time" and "telescope its intensity." The patient is, for instance, asked to name a two-hour period every day during which it would be least inconvenient for him to feel *more* pain. He is then told to increase his pain during these two hours, the silent implication being that he would feel better during the rest of the day. The extraordinary thing about this is that patients usually manage to feel worse at the time selected, as suggested, and by going through this experience they cannot fail to realize that somehow they have control over their pain. At no time, of course, does the therapist suggest that they should try to feel better; rather, he maintains the same skeptical attitude toward improvement as explained in Example 3. For numerous further examples of this paradoxical technique, involving insomnia, bed-wetting, tics, and a variety of other conditions, cf. Haley (*60*, pp. 41–59).

Example 5: A young college student was in danger of flunking because she was unable to get out of bed in time to attend her eight o'clock classes. No matter how she tried, she found it impossible to be in class before ten. The therapist told her that this problem could be taken care of in a fairly simple though unpleasant fashion, and that he was sure that she would not cooperate in this. This prompted the girl (who was quite worried about her immediate future and had developed a reasonable amount of trust in the therapist during the preceding interviews) to promise that she would go along with anything he told her to do. She was then told to set her alarm clock for seven o'clock. The following morning, when the alarm went off, she would find herself faced with two alternatives: she could either get up, have breakfast, and be in class by eight, in which case nothing further was to be done about the whole matter; or she could stay in bed, as usual. In the latter case, however, she would not be allowed to get up shortly before ten, as she used to, but she would have to reset the alarm to *eleven* A.M. and stay in bed on this and on the following morning until it went off. For these two mornings, she would not be allowed to read, write, listen to the radio or do anything else except to sleep or just lie in bed; after eleven she could do whatever she wanted. On the evening of the second day she was to set the alarm again for seven A.M., and if she was again unable to get up when it rang, she would again have to stay in bed until eleven on that and the following morning, and so on. Finally, he completed the double bind by telling her that if she did not live up to the terms of this agreement, which she had accepted of her own free will, he would no longer be of any use to her as her therapist and would, therefore, have to discontinue the treatment. The girl was delighted with this apparently pleasant instruction. When she came back for her next session three days later, she reported that she had as usual been unable to get up in time the first morning, that she had stayed in bed until eleven as instructed, but that this enforced bed rest (and especially the time from ten to eleven) had been almost unbearably boring. The second morning had been been even worse, and she was totally unable to sleep a minute longer than seven even though the alarm did not, of course, go off until eleven. From then on she attended her morning classes, and only then was it possible to enter into an exploration of the reasons that seemingly made it compulsory for her to fail in college.

Example 6: The conjoint psychotherapy of a family, composed of the parents and two daughters (ages seventeen and fifteen), had progressed to the point where a long-standing relationship problem of the parents began to emerge. At this point there was a marked change in the behavior of the older girl. She began to argue and to sidetrack the discussions in every conceivable manner. Any attempts by the father to control her remained ineffectual, and the girl eventually told the therapist that she would not cooperate in therapy any more in any way. The therapist countered this by telling her that her anxiety was understandable and that he *wanted* her to be as disruptive and unco-operative as possible. By this simple injunction he put her into an untenable situation: if she continued to disrupt the course of the therapy, she was cooperating and this she was determined not to do; but if she wanted to disobey the injunction she could do so only by *not* being disruptive and unco-operative, and this would make it possible to continue the therapy undisturbed. She could, of course, have refused to continue coming to the sessions, but the therapist had blocked this escape by implying that she would then be the sole subject of the family discussion, a prospect which he knew she simply could not face.

Example 7: The drinking husband or wife usually maintains a rather stereotyped communication pattern with the other spouse. For the sake of simplicity we will in the following assume that the husband is the drinker, but the roles could be reversed without significant change in the over-all pattern.

The primary difficulty is often a discrepancy in the punctuation of the sequence of events. The husband, for instance, may state that his wife is very controlling and that he feels a little more like a man only after a few drinks. The wife quickly counters this by stating that she would gladly relinquish command if he would only show a little more responsibility, but since he gets drunk every evening she is forced into taking care of him. She may go on to say that if it were not for her, the husband could on numerous occasions have set the house on fire by falling asleep in bed with a burning cigarette; he probably then retorts that he would never dream of taking this risk if he were still a bachelor. Perhaps he may add that this is a good example of her emasculating influence on him. In any case, after a few rounds of this, their game without end becomes quite obvious to the uninvolved outsider. Behind their façade of discontent, frustrations and accusations, they are confirming each other by means of a *quid pro quo* (73): he by enabling her to be sober, reasonable, and protective, and she by making it possible for him to be irresponsible, childish, and, generally, a misunderstood failure.

One of the possible therapeutic double binds that could be imposed on such a couple would consist of instructing them to drink together, but with the added condition that the wife is always to be one drink ahead of her husband. The introduction of this new rule into their interaction virtually wrecks the old pattern. First of all, drinking is now a task and no longer something that he "cannot help doing." Second, they both have to watch the number of their drinks constantly. Third, the wife who is usually a very moderate drinker if she drinks at all, quickly reaches a degree of intoxication which requires *him* to take care of *her*. This is not only a total reversal of their habitual roles, but it places him in an untenable position with regard to his drinking: if he lives up to the terms of the therapist's instruction, he must now stop drinking or force more drinks on her, at the risk of making her sick, more helpless, etc. If, when his wife can drink no more, he wants to break the rule (that she must remain one drink ahead of him) by continuing to drink alone, he is faced with the unfamiliar situation of being deprived of his guardian angel, and even being responsible for both himself and her. (We are, of course, not implying that it is a simple matter to get a couple to co-operate with such a prescription, nor that this intervention is by itself a "cure" for alcoholism.)

Example 8: A couple seeks help because they feel they are arguing too much. Rather than concentrating his attention on an analysis of their conflicts, the therapist, redefines their quarrels by telling them that they are really in love, and the more they argue the more they are in love because they care enough to be at each other and because fighting the way they fight presupposes a deep emotional involvement. No matter how ridiculous the couple may consider this interpretation—or precisely *because* it is so ridiculous to them—they will set about to prove to the therapist how wrong he is. This can best be done by stopping their arguing, just to show that they are *not* in love. But the moment they stop arguing, they find that they are getting along much better.

Example 9: That the therapeutic effect of paradoxical communication is by no means a recent discovery is shown by the following Zen story that contains all the ingredients of a therapeutic double bind:

> A young wife fell sick and was about to die. "I love you so much," she told her husband. "I do not want to leave you. Do not go from me to any other woman. If you do, I will return as a ghost and cause you endless trouble."
>
> Soon the wife passed away. The husband respected her last wish for the first three months, but then he met another woman and fell in love with her. They became engaged to be married.
>
> Immediately after the engagement, a ghost appeared every night to the man, blaming him for not keeping his promise. The ghost was clever, too. She told him exactly what had transpired between himself and his new sweetheart. Whenever he gave his fiancée a present, the ghost would describe it in detail. She would even repeat conversations, and it so annoyed the man that he could not sleep. Someone advised him to take his problem to a Zen master who lived close to the village. At length, in despair, the poor man went to him for help.
>
> "Your former wife became a ghost and knows everything you do," commented the master. "Whatever you do or say, whatever you give your beloved, she knows. She must be a very wise ghost. Really, you should admire such a ghost. The next time she appears, bargain with her. Tell her she knows so much you can hide nothing from her, and that if she will answer you one question, you promise to break your engagement and remain single."

"What is the question I must ask her?" inquired the man.

The master replied, "Take a large handful of soy beans and ask her exactly how many beans you hold in your hand. If she cannot tell you, you will know she is only a figment of your imagination and will trouble you no longer."

The next night when the ghost appeared, the man flattered her and told her that she knew everything.

"Indeed," replied the ghost, "and I know you went to see that Zen master today."

"And since you know so much," demanded the man, "tell me how many beans I hold in this hand."

There was no longer any ghost to answer the question. (*131*, p. 82)

7.6

Paradox in Play, Humor, and Creativity

Why organisms, from the invertebrates to humans, should be so susceptible to the effects of paradox is still mostly unclear, but it is evident that these effects go far beyond merely cultural or species-specific factors. As this chapter has attempted to show, additional complexity occurs at the human level because of the fact that paradox can be therapeutic and not only pathogenic. But this by no means exhausts the positive aspects of paradox, for it can be seen that many of the noblest pursuits and achievements of the human mind are intimately linked with man's ability to experience paradox. Fantasy, play, humor, love, symbolism, religious experience in the widest sense (from ritual to mysticism), and above all *creativity,* in both the arts and the sciences, appear to be essentially paradoxical.

However, these areas are so vast and extend so far beyond the scope of this book that only the barest hints and references will here be given. The outline of a theory of *play* and *fantasy* based on the theory of logical types (and paradoxes thereof) was offered by

Bateson in 1954. Reporting on observations at the Fleishacker Zoo in San Francisco, he mentions that he

> saw two young monkeys *playing,* i.e., engaged in an interactive sequence of which the unit actions or signals were similar to but not the same as those of combat. It was evident, even to the human observer, that the sequence as a whole was not combat, and evident to the human observer that to the participant monkeys this was "not combat."
>
> Now, this phenomenon, play, could only occur if the participant organisms were capable of some degree of meta-communication, i.e., of exchanging signals which would carry the message "this is play."
>
> The next step was the examination of the message "this is play," and the realization that this message contains those elements which necessarily generate a paradox of the Russellian or Epimenides type—a negative statement containing an implicit negative meta-statement. Expanded, the statement "this is play" looks something like this: "These actions in which we now engage do not denote what those actions *for which they stand* would denote." (*8,* p. 41)

Fry, one of Bateson's associates, applied this perspective to the phenomenon of *humor* and in an extensive study of many forms of jokes, summarizes his findings as follows:

> During the unfolding of humor, one is suddenly confronted by an explicit-implicit reversal when the punch line is delivered. The reversal helps distinguish humor from play, dreams, etc. Sudden reversals such as characterize the punch line moment in humor are disruptive and foreign to play, etc. (Only in psychotherapy is this sort of reversal operation compatible with the general structure of the experience.) But the reversal also has the unique effect of forcing upon the humor participants an internal redefining of re-

ality. Inescapably, the punch line combines communication and metacommunication. One receives the explicit communication of the punch line. Also, on a higher level of abstraction, the punch line carries an implicit metacommunication about itself and about reality as exemplified by the joke. . . . this implicit-now-explicit punch-line material becomes a metacommunicative message regarding the joke content in general (as a sample of communication). In this reversal of content, what seems to be reality can be presented in terms of what seems to be unreality. Content communicates the message "This is unreal," and in so doing makes reference to the whole of which it is a part. We are thus again confronted with the paradox of the negative part defining the whole. Real is unreal, and unreal is real. The punch line precipitates internal paradox *specific to the joke content,* and stimulates a reverberation of the paradox generated by the surrounding play frame. (*53,* pp. 153–4)

Creativity, finally, has been the subject of many significant studies of which one of the most recent is *The Act of Creation* by Koestler. In this monumental work it is proposed that humor and scientific discovery as well as artistic creation are the result of a mental process termed *bisociation.* Bisociation is defined as "the perceiving of a situation or idea . . . in two self-consistent but habitually incompatible frames of reference . . ." (*87,* p. 35). The author makes a distinction

between the routine skills of thinking on a single "plane," as it were, and the creative act, which . . . always operates on more than one plane. The former may be called single-minded, the latter a double-minded, transitory state of unstable equilibrium where the balance of both emotion and thought is disturbed. (*87,* pp. 35–6)

Although nowhere in his book does the author consider the possibility that bisociation may have the structure of paradox (that is, that the "two self-consistent, but habitually incompatible frames of reference" may stand to each other in a relation of level and meta-level), his view of creativity has many affinities to the hypotheses reported or set forth by us in the area of pathology and therapy. Compare, for instance, a partial summary offered by Koestler in one of his concluding chapters.

> One of the main contentions of this book is that organic life, in all its manifestations, from morphogenesis to symbolic thought, is governed by "rules of the game" which lend it coherence, order, and unity-in-variety; and that these rules (or functions in the mathematical sense), whether innate or acquired, are represented in coded form on various levels, from the chromosomes to the structure in the nervous system responsible for symbolic thought. . . . The rules are fixed, but there are endless variations to each game, their variability increasing in ascending order. . . . There is also an overall-rule of the game, which says that no rule is absolutely final; that under certain circumstances they may be altered and combined into a more sophisticated game, which provides a higher form of unity and yet increased variety; this is called the subject's creative potential. (*87*, p. 631)

Bearing in mind the encyclopedic sweep of the author's investigation, one can only regret but not criticize the fact that he did not extend it beyond the limits of the individual as a monad.

Epilogue

Existentialism and the Theory of Human

Communication: An Outlook

> It is not the things themselves
> which trouble us, but the opinions
> which we have about these things.
> —Epictetus (1st century A.D.)

8.1

We have in the foregoing considered individuals in their social nexus—in their interaction with other human beings—and we have seen that the vehicle of this interaction is communication. This may or may not be the extent to which a theory of human communication should be applied. In any case, it seems obvious to us that to view man only as a "social animal" would fail to account for man in his *existential* nexus, of which his social involvement is only one, although a very important, aspect.

The question then arises whether any of the principles of our theory of the pragmatics of human communication can be of any use when the focus is shifted from the interpersonal to the existential, and if so, in what way. This question is not answered herein; perhaps it cannot be answered finally, since in pursuing the issue we must leave the domain of science and become avowedly subjective. Since man's existence is not observable in the same sense as are his social relations, we are forced to abandon the

257

objective, "outside" position we have tried to maintain throughout the preceding seven chapters of this book. For at this point of our inquiry, there is no "outside" any more. Man cannot go beyond the limits set by his own mind; subject and object are ultimately identical, the mind studies itself, and any statement made about man in his existential nexus is likely to run into the same phenomena of self-reflexiveness, which, as we have seen, generate paradox.

In a sense, then, this chapter is a statement of faith: the belief that man exists in a broad, complex, and private relation to life. We wish to speculate on the possibility that some of our concepts might be of use in exploring this area which is too often neglected in purely psychological theories of man.

8.2

In modern biology it would be unthinkable to study even the most primitive organism in artificial isolation from its environment. As postulated particularly by General System Theory (s. 4.2.ff), organisms are open systems that maintain their steady state (stability) and even evolve toward states of higher complexity by means of a constant exchange of both energy and information with their environment. If we realize that in order to survive any organism must gain not only the substances necessary for its metabolism but adequate information about the world around it, we see that communication and existence are inseparable concepts. The environment, then, is subjectively experienced as a set of instructions about the organism's existence, and in this sense the environmental effects are similar to a computer program; Norbert Wiener once said about the world that it "may be viewed as a myriad of To Whom It May Concern messages." There is, however, the important difference that while the computer program is presented in a language that the machine completely "understands," the impact of the environment on an organism comprises a set of instructions whose meaning is by no means self-evident but rather is left up to the organism to decode as best it can. If to this consideration we add the obvious fact that the organism's reactions in turn affect the environment, it becomes apparent that even on the very primitive levels of life, complex and continuous interactions take place that are nonrandom and are, therefore, governed by a program or, to use an existentialist term, by *meaning*.

Seen in this light, then, existence is a *function* (as defined in s. 1.2) of the relationship between the organism and its environment. At the human level this interaction between organism and environment reaches its highest degree of complexity. Although in modern societies problems of biological survival have receded far into the background and the environment, in the ecological sense of the term, is largely controlled by man, the vital messages from the environment that must be correctly decoded have merely undergone a shift from the biological to the more psychological realm.

8.3

Man has an apparently very deep-seated propensity to hypostatize reality, to make of it a friend or an antagonist with whom he has to come to terms. A highly relevant thought can be found in Zilboorg's classic study on suicide:

> It appears that originally man accepted life on his own terms: a sickness, any sort of discomfort, any strong affective tension, made him feel that *life had violated its contract with him,* so to speak, and he then would leave his unfaithful partner. . . . Evidently [the idea of] Paradise was thus created by mankind not through the birth of Adam and Eve but through the acceptance of death by primitive man *who preferred voluntary death rather than relinquish his ideal of what life should be.* (*170*, pp. 1364–6; italics ours)

Life—or reality, fate, God, nature, existence, or whatever name one prefers to give it—is a partner whom we accept or reject, and by whom we feel ourselves accepted or rejected, supported or betrayed. To this existential partner, perhaps even as much as to a human partner, man proposes his definition of self and then finds it confirmed or disconfirmed; and from this partner man endeavors to receive clues about the "real" nature of their relationship.

8.4

But what, then, can we say about those vital messages that man must decode as best he can to ensure his survival as a human being? Let us return briefly to Pavlov's dog (s. 6.434), and then attempt from there the step into the realm of specifically human experience. We know first that there are two kinds of knowledge: knowledge *of* things and knowledge *about* things. The former is that awareness of objects which our senses convey; it is what Bertrand Russell has called "knowledge by acquaintance," or Langer "a most direct and sensuous knowledge." It is the kind of knowledge Pavlov's dog has upon perceiving the circle or the ellipse, a knowledge which knows nothing *about* the perceived. But in the experimental situation the dog quickly also learns something about these two geometrical figures, namely that they are somehow indicative of pleasure and pain respectively and that they therefore have a meaning for his survival. Thus, if sensuous awareness can be called first-order knowledge, this latter knowledge (knowledge about an object) is knowledge of a second order; it is knowledge about first-order knowledge, and therefore metaknowledge. (This is the same distinction we already proposed in s. 1.4, when we remarked that to know a language and to know something about a language are two very different orders of knowledge.) [1] Once the dog has understood the meaning of the circle and the

[1] Throughout this book we have had occasion to point to the fact that a hierarchy of levels seems to pervade the world we live in and our experience of selves and others, and that valid statements about one level can only be made from the next higher one. This hierarchy became apparent in

  (1) The relation between mathematics and metamathematics (s. 1.5) as well as between communication and metacommunication (s. 1.5 and 2.3)
  (2) The content and relationship aspects of communication (s. 2.3 and 3.3)
  (3) The definitions of self and others (s. 3.33)
  (4) The logico-mathematical paradoxes and the theory of logical types (s. 6.2)
  (5) The theory of levels of languages (s. 6.3)
  (6) The pragmatic paradoxes, double binds and paradoxical predictions (s. 6.4)
  (7) The illusion of alternatives (s. 7.1)
  (8) The game without end (s. 7.2)
  (9) Therapeutic double binds (s. 7.4)

ellipse in relation to his survival, he will behave as if he had concluded "This is a world in which I am safe as long as I discriminate between the circle and the ellipse." This conclusion, however, would no longer be of the second order; it would be knowledge gained about second-order knowledge and would, therefore,
be third-order knowledge. With man this process of acquisition
of knowledge, of attributing levels of meaning to his environment,
to reality, is essentially the same.

In an adult human, first-order knowledge alone is probably a
very rare thing. It would be tantamount to a perception for which
neither past experience nor the present context provides an explanation, and its inexplicability and unpredictability would probably
make this perception very anxiety-producing. Man never ceases
to seek knowledge about the objects of his experience, to understand their meaning for his existence and to react to them according to his understanding. Finally, out of the sum total of the
meanings that he has deduced from his contacts with numerous
single objects of his environment there grows a unified view of
the world into which he finds himself "thrown" (to use an existentialist term again), and this view is of the third order. There
is strong reason to believe that it is really quite irrelevant what
this third-order view of the world consists of, as long as it offers a
meaningful premise for one's existence. The delusionary system of
a paranoiac seems to fulfill its function as an explanatory principle
for the patient's universe just as well as a "normal" view of the
world for somebody else.[2] What is important, however, is that

[2] To this it may be objected that the latter view is better adapted to reality
than the former. But the much-invoked criterion of reality should be treated
with great caution. The usual fallacy involved here is the tacit assumption that
there is such a thing as an "objective reality" and that sane people are more
aware of it than lunatics. On the whole, this assumption is too uncomfort-
ably reminiscent of a similar premise regarding Euclidian geometry. For two
thousand years the assumption that Euclid's axioms correctly and fully em-
braced the reality of space remained unquestioned, until it was realized that
Euclid's was only one of any number of possible geometries that could not
only be different from, but even incompatible with one another. To quote
Nagel and Newman:

> The traditional belief that the axioms of geometry (or, for that
> matter, *the axioms of any discipline*) can be established by their
> apparent self-evidence was thus radically undermined. Moreover,

man operates with a set of premises about the phenomena he perceives and that his interaction with reality in the widest sense (that is, not only with other human beings) will be determined by these premises. As far as we can speculate, these premises themselves are the outcome of the whole enormous gamut of an individual's experiences, and their genesis is therefore virtually beyond exploration. But there can be no doubt that man not only punctuates the sequences of events in an interpersonal relation but that the same punctuation process is at work in the constantly necessary process of evaluating and sorting the ten thousand sensory impressions that man receives every second from his inner and outer environment. To repeat a speculation of s. 3.42: reality is very largely what we make it to be. Existential philosophers propose a very similar relationship between man and his reality: they conceive of man as thrown into an opaque, formless, meaningless world out of which man himself creates his situation. His specific way of "being-in-the-world," therefore, is the outcome of his choice, is the meaning *he* gives to what is presumably beyond objective human understanding.

8.41

Concepts equivalent or analogous to third-order premises have been defined by other workers in the behavioral sciences. In learning theory, levels of learning corresponding to the levels of knowledge postulated in the foregoing, were independently identified and investigated by Hull, *et al.* (*66*) in 1940, by Bateson (*7, 13*) in 1942 and again in 1960, and by Harlow (*63*) in 1949, to mention just the more important studies. Briefly, this branch of learning theory postulates that together with the acquisition of knowledge or of a skill there also takes place a process that makes the acquisition itself progressively easier. In other words, one not only learns, but *learns to learn*. For this higher-order type of learning,

---

it gradually became clear that the proper business of the pure mathematician is to *derive theorems from postulated assumptions*, and that it is not his concern as a mathematician to decide whether the axioms he assumes are actually true. (*108*, p. 11; italics ours)

Bateson coined the term *deutero-learning* and described it as follows:

> In semi-gestalt or semi-anthropomorphic phraseology, we might say that the subject is learning to orient himself to certain types of contexts, or is acquiring "insight" into the contexts of problem-solving. . . . We may say that the subject has acquired a habit of looking for contexts and sequences of one type rather than another, a habit of "punctuating" the stream of events to give repetitions of a certain type of meaningful sequence. (7, p. 88)

A similar concept is at the basis of Kelly's monumental *Psychology of Personal Constructs* (*83*), although this author does not consider the question of levels and presents his theory almost exclusively in terms of intrapsychic, not interactional, psychology. Miller, Galanter, and Pribram, in their *Plans and the Structure of Behavior* (*104*), have proposed that purposive behavior is guided by a plan, very much as a computer is guided by a program. Their concept of *plan* is highly relevant to the ideas put forward in this chapter and, without exaggeration, their study can be considered one of the most important recent breakthroughs in the understanding of behavior. Related to this latter work are some of the very elegant *noncontingent reward experiments* carried out at Stanford University under the supervision of Dr. Bavelas, even though their declared purpose is outside the matters considered in this chapter. One of these experiments in particular deserves mention (*169*): The experimental device consists of an array of push buttons. The subject is told that certain of these buttons must be pushed in a certain order and that it is his task to discover this order in a number of trial runs. He is further told that correct performance will be signaled by a buzzer. However, in actual fact the push buttons are not connected to anything and the buzzer is rung quite independently of the subject's performance, and with increasing frequency, that is, relatively rarely at the beginning and more and more often toward the end of the experiment. Invariably, a person undergoing this experiment quickly forms what we have termed third-order premises, and is extraordinarily reluctant to abandon them even if afterward it is shown to him that his performance had no connection whatsoever with the ringing of the buzzer. In a certain way, then, this experimental device is a micromodel of the universe in which we have all developed our specific third-order premises, our ways of being-in-the-world.

8.5

A striking difference comes to light when one compares man's ability to accept or tolerate change on the second and the third levels respectively. Man has an almost unbelievable ability to adapt to changes at the second level, as anybody will agree who has had occasion to watch human endurance under the most excruciating circumstances. But it appears that this endurance is only possible as long as his third-order premises about his existence, and the meaning of the world he lives in, remain inviolate.[3] This must be what Nietzsche had in mind when he postulated that he who has a *why* of living will endure almost any *how*. But man, perhaps much more than Pavlov's dog, seems singularly ill equipped to deal with inconsistencies which threaten his third-order premises. Man cannot survive psychologically in a universe for which his third-order premises fail to account, a universe which is for him senseless. Double-binding, as we have seen, has this disastrous result; but the same outcome is equally possible through circumstances or developments beyond human control or intent. Existential writers, from Dostoevsky to Camus, have dealt extensively with this theme, which is at least as old as the Book of Job. Kirillov, for

---

[3] This difference is, for instance, reflected in letters (e.g., 57) written by prisoners condemned by the Nazis for political crimes of varying degrees. Those who felt that their actions had served some purpose in defeating the regime were able to face death with a certain serenity. The really tragic, desperate outcries, on the other hand, came from those who had been sentenced to death for such meaningless offenses as listening to Allied radio stations or making a hostile remark about Hitler. Their deaths were apparently a violation of a significant third-order premise: that one's death should be meaningful and not petty.

example, a character in Dostoevsky's *Possessed,* has decided that "God does not exist" and therefore sees no sense in living any longer.

> . . . Listen." Kirillov stood still, gazing before him with fixed and ecstatic look. "Listen to a great idea: there was a day on earth and in the midst of the earth there stood three crosses. One on the cross had such faith that he said to another, 'To-day thou shalt be with me in Paradise.' The day ended; both died and passed away and found neither Paradise nor resurrection. His words did not come true. Listen: that Man was the loftiest of all on earth, He was that who gave meaning to life. The whole planet, with everything on it, is mere madness without that man. There has never been any like Him before or since, never, up to a miracle. For that is the miracle, that there never was or never will be another like Him. And if that is so, if the laws of nature did not even spare Him, have not even spared their miracle and made Him live in a lie and die for a lie, then all the planet is a lie and rests on a lie and mockery. So then, the very laws of the planet are a lie and a vaudeville of devils. What is there to live for? Answer, if you are a man."

And Dostoevsky lets the man of whom this question is asked give the striking answer: "That's a different matter. It seems to me you have mixed up two different causes and that's a very unsafe thing to do . . ." (37, pp. 581–2).

It is our contention that whenever this theme arises, the question of *meaning* is involved, and "meaning" here is not to be taken in its semantic but in its existential connotation. The absence of meaning is the horror of existential Nothingness. It is that subjective state in which reality has receded or disappeared altogether, and with it any awareness of self and others. For Gabriel Marcel "Life is a fight against Nothingness." And over a hundred years ago Kierkegaard wrote: "I want to go to a madhouse and see whether the profundity of madness will not solve the riddle of life for me."

In this sense, man's position vis-à-vis his mysterious partner is not essentially different from that of Pavlov's dog. The dog quickly learns the *meaning* of the circle and the ellipse, and his world is shattered when the experimenter suddenly destroys this meaning. If we search our subjective experience in comparable situations, we find that we are likely to assume the actions of a secret "experimenter" behind the vicissitudes of our lives. The loss or the absence of a meaning in life is perhaps the most common denominator of all forms of emotional distress; it is especially the much-commented-on "modern" illness. Pain, disease, loss, failure, despair, disappointment, the fear of death, or merely boredom—all lead to the feeling that life is meaningless. It seems to us that in its most basic definition, existential despair is the painful discrepancy between what *is* and what *should be,* between one's perceptions and one's third-order premises.

8.6

There is no reason to postulate only three levels of abstraction in the human experience of reality. At least theoretically, these levels rise one above the other in infinite regress. Thus, if man wants to change his third-order premises, which to us seems an essential function of psychotherapy, *he can do so only from a fourth level.* But we doubt that the human mind is equipped to deal with higher levels of abstraction without the aid of mathematical symbolism or computers. It seems significant that only glimpses of understanding are possible at the fourth level, and articulation becomes extremely difficult if not impossible. The reader may remember how difficult it was already to grasp the meaning of the "class of classes which are not members of themselves" (s. 6.2), which in terms of its complexity is the equivalent of a third-order premise. Or, likewise, while it is still possible to understand the meaning of "This is how I see you seeing me seeing you" (s. 3.34), the next higher (fourth) level ("This is how I see you seeing me seeing you seeing me") is virtually beyond understanding.

Let us repeat this essential point: to communicate or even think *about* third-order premises is only possible at the fourth level. The fourth level, however, seems to be very close to the limits of the human mind and awareness at this level is rarely, if at all, present. It seems to us that this is the area of intuition and empathy, of the "aha"—experience, perhaps of the immediate awareness provided by LSD or similar drugs, and, certainly, it is the area where therapeutic change takes place, change of which, after successful therapy, one is unable to say how and why it came about and what it actually consists of. For psychotherapy is concerned with third-order premises and with bringing about change at this level. But to change one's third-order premises, to become aware of the patterning of sequences of one's own behavior and of that of the environment, is only possible from the vantage point of the next higher, the fourth, level. Only from this level can it be seen that reality is not something objective, unalterable, "out there," with a benign or sinister meaning for our survival, but that for all intents and purposes our subjective experience of existence is reality—reality is our patterning of something that most probably is totally beyond objective human verification.

8.61

Hierarchies such as those with which we are now concerned have been most thoroughly explored in a branch of modern mathematics with which our study has great affinity, save for the fact that mathematics is of incomparably greater consistency and rigor than we can ever hope to attain. The branch in question is proof theory, or metamathematics. As the latter term clearly implies, this area of mathematics deals with itself, that is, with the laws inherent in mathematics and with the problem of whether or not mathematics is consistent. It is, therefore, not surprising that essentially the same paradoxical consequences of self-reflexiveness should have been encountered and worked through by metamathematicians long before analysts of human communication were even aware of their existence. In fact, work in this area reaches back to Schröder (1895), Löwenheim (1915), and especially Hilbert (1918). Proof theory, or metamathematics, was then the highly abstract concern of a brilliant though small group of mathematicians standing, as it were, outside the mainstream of mathematical endeavors. Two events, it appears, subsequently brought proof theory very much into the focus of attention. One was the publication, in 1931, of Gödel's epochal paper on formally undecidable propositions (56), a paper described by the faculty of Harvard University as the most important advance in mathematical logic in a quarter century (108). The other is the almost explosive emergence of the computer since the end of World War II. These machines were quickly developed from rigidly programmed automata into enormously versatile artificial organisms that began to pose fundamental proof-theoretical problems as soon as their structural complexity had progressed to the point where they could be made to decide for themselves on one optimal computational procedure among several. In other words, the question arose whether computers could be designed that would not only carry out a program, but would at the same time be able to effect changes in their program.

In proof theory, the term *decision procedure* refers to methods of finding proofs for the truth or falsity of a statement, or a whole class of statements, made within a given formalized system. The related term *decision problem* refers to the question of whether or not there exists a procedure of the kind just described. Therefore, a decision problem has a positive solution if a decision procedure can be found for solving it, while a negative solution consists in proving that no such decision procedure exists. Accordingly, decision problems are referred to as either computable or unsolvable.

However, there exists a third possibility. Definite (positive or negative) solutions of a decision problem are only possible where the problem in question lies *within the domain* (the area of applicability) of the particular decision procedure. If this decision procedure is applied to a problem *outside* its domain, the computation will go on indefinitely without ever proving that no solution (positive or negative) will be forthcoming.[4] It is at this point that we encounter again the concept of *undecidability*.

8.62

This concept is the central issue of Gödel's above-mentioned paper, which deals with formally undecidable propositions. The formalized system chosen by him for his theorem is *Principia Mathematica*, the monumental work by Whitehead and Russell exploring the foundations of mathematics. Gödel was able to show that in this or an equivalent system it is possible to construct a sentence, *G*, which (1) is provable from the premises and axioms of the system, but which (2) proclaims of itself to be unprovable. This means that if *G* be provable in the system, its unprovability (which is what it says of itself) would also be provable. But if both provability and unprovability can be derived from the axioms of the system, and the axioms themselves are consistent (which is part of Gödel's proof), then *G* is *undecidable in terms of the system*, just as the paradoxical prediction presented in s. 6.441 is undecidable in terms of its "system," which is the information contained in the headmaster's announcement and the context in which it is made.[5] Gödel's proof has consequences that go far beyond the field of mathematical logic; indeed, it proves once and for all that any formal system (mathematical, symbolic, etc.) is necessarily incomplete in the sense set out above, and that, furthermore, the consistency of such a system can only be proved by recourse to methods of proof that are more general than those the system itself can generate.

[4] This is the so-called *halting problem* in decision procedures; it provides a suggestive analogy to our concept of the game without end in human communication (s. 7.2).

[5] The interested reader is referred to Nagel and Newman's excellent nonmathematical presentation of Gödel's proof (*108*). To the best of our knowledge the similarity between Gödel's theorem and paradoxical predictions was first pointed out by Nerlich (*111*), and we believe that this paradox is probably the most elegant nonmathematical analogy of the theorem, preferable even to Findlay's nonnumerical approach (*44*).

8.63

If we have dwelled on Gödel's work at some length, it is because we see in it the mathematical analogy of what we would call the ultimate paradox of man's existence. Man is ultimately subject and object of his quest. While the question whether his mind can be considered to be anything like a formalized system, as defined in the preceding paragraph, is probably unanswerable, his quest for an understanding of the meaning of his existence *is an attempt at formalization.* In this and only this sense we feel that certain results of proof theory (especially in the areas of self-reflexiveness and undecidability) are pertinent. This is by no means our discovery; in fact, ten years before Gödel presented his brilliant theorem, another great mind of our century had already formulated this paradox in philosophical terms, namely Ludwig Wittgenstein in his *Tractatus Logico-Philosophicus (168)*. Probably nowhere has this existential paradox been defined more lucidly nor has the *mystical* been accorded a more dignified position as the ultimate step transcending this paradox.

Wittgenstein shows that we could only know something about the world in its totality if we could step outside it; but if this were possible, this world would no longer be the *whole* world. However, our logic knows of nothing outside it:

> Logic fills the world: the limits of the world are also its limits.
>
> We cannot therefore say in logic: This and this there is in the world, that there is not.
>
> For that would apparently presuppose that we exclude certain possibilities, and this cannot be the case since otherwise logic must get outside the limits of the world: that is, if it could consider these limits from the other side also.
>
> What we cannot think, we cannot think: we cannot therefore say what we cannot think. (*168*, pp. 149–51)

The world, then, is finite and at the same time limitless, limitless precisely because there is nothing outside that together with the inside could form a boundary. But if this be so, then it follows that "The world and life are one. I am my world" (p. 151). Subject and world are thus no longer entities whose relational function is in some way governed by the auxiliary verb *to have* (that one *has* the other, contains it or belongs to it), but by the existenial *to be:* "The subject does not *belong* to the world, but it *is* a limit of the world" (p. 151; italics ours).

Within this limit meaningful questions can be asked and answered: "If a question can be put at all, then it *can* also be answered" (p. 187). But "the solution to the riddle of life in space and time lies *outside* space and time" (p. 185). For, as it should be by now abundantly clear, nothing *inside* a frame can state, or even *ask*, anything *about* that frame. The solution, then, is not the finding of answer to the riddle of existence, but the realization that there is no riddle. This is the essence of the beautiful, almost Zen Buddhist closing sentences of the *Tractatus:*

> For an answer which cannot be expressed the question too cannot be expressed. *The riddle* does not exist. . . .
> We feel that even if *all possible* scientific questions be answered, the problems of life have still not been touched at all. Of course there is then no question left, and just this is the answer.
> The solution of the problem of life is seen in the vanishing of this problem. (Is not this the reason why men to whom after long doubting the sense of life became clear, could not then say wherein this sense consisted?)
> There is indeed the inexpressible. This *shows* itself; it is the mystical. . . .
> Whereof one cannot speak, thereof one must be silent. (pp. 187–9)

References

1. Albee, Edward, *Who's Afraid of Virginia Woolf?* New York: Atheneum Publishers, 1962.

2. Apter, Julia T., "Models and Mathematics. Tools of the Mathematical Biologist." *Journal of the American Medical Association,* 194:269–72, 1965.

3. Artiss, Kenneth L., ed., *The Symptom as Communication in Schizophrenia.* New York: Grune & Stratton, Inc., 1959.

4. Ashby, W. Ross, *Design for a Brain.* New York: John Wiley & Sons, Inc., 1954.

5. Ashby, W. Ross, *An Introduction to Cybernetics.* London: Chapman & Hall, Ltd., 1956.

6. Bateson, Gregory, "Culture Contact and Schismogenesis." *Man,* 35:178–83, 1935.

7. Bateson, Gregory, "Social Planning and the Concept of 'Deutero-Learning' in Relation to the Democratic Way of Life." *Science, Philosophy and Religion, Second Symposium,* New York: Harper & Brothers, 1942, pp. 81–97.

8. Bateson, Gregory, "A Theory of Play and Fantasy." *Psychiatric Research Reports,* 2:39–51, 1955.

9. Bateson, Gregory, "The Message 'This is Play.'" In *Transactions of the Second Conference on Group Processes.* New York: Josiah Macy, Jr., Foundation, 1956, pp. 145–242.

10. Bateson, Gregory, *Naven,* 2nd ed. Stanford: Stanford University Press, 1958.

11. Bateson, Gregory, "The New Conceptual Frames for Behavioral Research." Proceedings of the Sixth Annual Psychiatric Institute. Princeton: The New Jersey Neuro-Psychiatric Institute, 1958, pp. 54–71.

12. Bateson, Gregory, "The Group Dynamics of Schizophrenia." In Lawrence Appleby, Jordan M. Scher, and John Cumming, eds., *Chronic Schizophrenia. Exploration in Theory and Treatment*. Glencoe, Illinois: The Free Press, 1960, pp. 90–105.

13. Bateson, Gregory, "Minimal Requirements for a Theory of Schizophrenia." *Archives of General Psychiatry*, 2:477–91, 1960.

14. Bateson, Gregory, "The Biosocial Integration of the Schizophrenic Family." In Nathan W. Ackerman, Frances L. Beatman, and Sanford N. Sherman, eds., *Exploring the Base for Family Therapy*. New York: Family Service Association, 1961, pp. 116–22.

15. Bateson, Gregory, ed., *Perceval's Narrative, A Patient's Account of his Psychosis, 1830–1832*. Stanford: Stanford University Press, 1961.

16. Bateson, Gregory, "Exchange of Information about Patterns of Human Behavior." Paper read at Symposium on Information Storage and Neural Control, Houston, Texas, 1962.

17. Bateson, Gregory, personal communication.

18. Bateson, Gregory; Jackson, Don D.; Haley, Jay; and Weakland, John, "Toward a Theory of Schizophrenia." *Behavioral Science*, 1:251–64, 1956.

19. Bateson, Gregory, and Jackson, Don D., "Some Varieties of Pathogenic Organization." In David McK. Rioch, ed., *Disorders of Communication*, Volume 42, Research Publications. Association for Research in Nervous and Mental Disease, 1964, pp. 270–83.

20. Bavelas, Alex, personal communication.

21. Benedict, Ruth, *Patterns of Culture*. Boston: Houghton-Mifflin Company, 1934.

22. Berdyaev, Nicholas, *Dostoevsky*. New York: Meridian Books, 1957.

23. Berne, Eric, *Transactional Analysis in Psychotherapy*. New York: Grove Press, Inc., 1961.

24. Berne, Eric, *Games People Play*. New York: Grove Press, Inc., 1944.

25. Bertalanffy, Ludwig von, "An Outline of General System Theory." *British Journal of the Philosophy of Science*, 1: 134–65, 1950.

26. Bertalanffy, Ludwig von, "General System Theory." *General Systems Yearbook*, 1:1–10. 1956.

27. Bertalanffy, Ludwig von, "General System Theory—A Critical Review." *General Systems Yearbook*, 7:1–20, 1962.

28. Birdwhistell, Ray L., "Contribution of Linguistic-Kinesic Studies to the Understanding of Schizophrenia." In Alfred Auerback, ed., *Schizophenia. An Integrated Approach.* New York: The Ronald Press Company, 1959, pp. 99–123.

29. Bochénski, I. M., *A History of Formal Logic.* Notre Dame, Indiana: University of Notre Dame Press, 1961.

30. Bolzano, Bernard, *Paradoxien des Unendlichen* [Paradoxes of the Infinite], 2nd ed., Fr. Přihonsky, ed., Berlin: Mayer und Müller, 1889.

31. Boole, George, *Mathematical Analysis of Logic; Being an Essay towards a Calculus of Deductive Reasoning.* Cambridge: Macmillan, Barclay, & Macmillan, 1847.

32. Buber, Martin, "Distance and Relation." *Psychiatry*, 20:97–104, 1957.

33. Carnap, Rudolph, *Introduction to Semantics.* Cambridge: Harvard University Press, 1942.

34. Cherry, Colin, *On Human Communication.* New York: Science Editions, 1961.

35. Cumming, John, "Communication: an approach to chronic schizophenia." In Lawrence Appleby, Jordan M. Scher, and John Cumming, eds., *Chronic Schizophrenia. Exploration in Theory and Treatment.* Glencoe, Illinois: The Free Press, 1960, pp. 106–19.

36. Davis, R. C., "The Domain of Homeostasis." *Psychological Review*, 65:8–13, 1958.

37. Dostoevsky, Fedor M., *The Possessed.* New York: The Macmillan Company, 1931.

38. Dostoevsky, Fedor M., "Notes from Underground." In *The Short Novels of Dostoevsky.* New York: The Dial Press, Inc., 1945, pp. 127–342.

39. Dunlap, Knight, "A Revision of the Fundamental Law of Habit Formation." *Science*, 67:360–2, 1928.

40. Dunlap, Knight, "Repetition in the Breaking of Habits." *Scientific Monthly*, 30:66–70, 1930.

41. Durrell, Lawrence, *Clea*. New York: E. P. Dutton & Co., Inc., 1960.

42. Ferreira, Antonio J., "Family Myth and Homeostasis." *Archives of General Psychiatry*, 9:457–63, 1963.

43. Ferreira, Antonio J., "Psychosis and Family Myth." Unpublished manuscript.

44. Findlay, J., "Goedelian Sentences: a non-numerical approach." *Mind*, 51:259–65, 1942.

45. Frank, Lawrence K., "The Prospects of Genetic Psychology." *American Journal of Orthopsychiatry*, 21:506–22, 1951.

46. Frankl, Victor E., *The Doctor and the Soul*. New York: Alfred A. Knopf, Inc., 1957.

47. Frankl, Victor E., "Paradoxical Intention." *American Journal of Psychotherapy*, 14:520–35, 1960.

48. Frege, Gottlob, *Grundgesetze der Arithmetik begriffsschriftlich abgeleitet* [Basic Laws of Arithmetic], Volume 1. Jena; Verlag Hermann Pohle, 1893.

49. Freud, Sigmund, *New Introductory Lectures on Psychoanalysis*. New York: W. W. Norton & Company, Inc., 1933.

50. Freud, Sigmund, "The Interpretation of Dreams." In *The Basic Writings of Sigmund Freud*. New York: The Modern Library, Inc., 1938.

51. Fromm-Reichmann, Frieda, "A Preliminary Note on the Emotional Significance of Stereotypies in Schizophrenics." *Bulletin of the Forest Sanitarium*, 1:17–21, 1942.

52. Fry, William F., Jr., "The Marital Context of the Anxiety Syndrome." *Family Process*, 1:245–52, 1962.

53. Fry, William F., Jr., *Sweet Madness: A Study of Humor*. Palo Alto: Pacific Books, 1963.

54. Gardner, Martin, "A New Paradox, and Variations on it, about a Man Condemned to be Hanged." In section "Mathematical Games," *Scientific American*, 208:144–54, 1963.

55. George, F. H., *The Brain as a Computer*. Oxford: Pergamon Press, Ltd., 1962.

56. Gödel, Kurt, "Ueber formal unentscheidbare Sätze der Principia Mathematica und verwandter Systeme I." *Monatshefte für Mathematik und Physik*, 38:173–98, 1931. [English translation: "On Formally Undecidable Propositions of Principia

Mathematica and Related Systems I." Edinburgh and London: Oliver and Boyd, 1962.]

57. Gollwitzer, Helmut, et al., eds., Dying We Live. The Final Messages and Records of the Resistance. New York: Pantheon Books, Inc., 1956.

58. Greenburg, Dan, How to be a Jewish Mother. Los Angeles: Price/Stern/Sloan, 1964.

59. Haley, Jay, "Family Experiments: A New Type of Experimentation." Family Process, 1:265–93, 1962.

60. Haley, Jay, Strategies of Psychotherapy. New York: Grune & Stratton, Inc., 1963.

61. Haley, Jay, "Research on Family Patterns: An Instrument Measurement." Family Process, 3:41–65, 1964.

62. Hall, A. D., and Fagen, R. E., "Definition of System." General Systems Yearbook, 1:18–28, 1956.

63. Harlow, H. F., "The Formation of Learning Sets." Psychlogical Review, 56:51–65, 1949.

64. Hilbert, David, and Bernays, Paul, Grundlagen der Mathematik [Foundations of Mathematics], 2 volumes. Berlin: J. Springer Verlag, 1934–39.

65. Hora, Thomas, "Tao, Zen, and Existential Psychotherapy." Psychologia. 2:236–42, 1959.

66. Hull, C. L., Hovland, C. L., Ross, R. T., et al., Mathematico-Deductive Theory of Rote Learning: A Study in Scientific Methodology. New Haven: Yale University Press, 1940.

67. Jackson, Don D., "Some Factors Influencing the Oedipus Complex." Psychoanalytic Quarterly, 23:566–81, 1954.

68. Jackson, Don D., "A Note on the Importance of Trauma in the Genesis of Schizophrenia." Psychiatry, 20: 181–4, 1957.

69. Jackson, Don D., "The Question of Family Homeostasis." Psychiatric Quarterly Supplement, 31:79–90, part 1, 1957.

70. Jackson, Don D., "Family Interaction, Family Homeostasis, and Some Implications for Conjoint Family Psychotherapy." In Jules Masserman, ed., Individual and Familial Dynamics. New York: Grune & Stratton, Inc., 1959, pp. 122–41.

71. Jackson, Don D., "Interactional Psychotherapy." In Morris I. Stein, ed., Contemporary Psychotherapies. Glencoe, Illinois: The Free Press, 1962, pp. 256–71.

72. Jackson, Don D., "A Suggestion for the Technical Handling of Paranoid Patients." *Psychiatry*, 26:306–7, 1963.

73. Jackson, Don D., "Family Rules: The Marital *Quid Pro Quo*." *Archives of General Psychiatry*, 12:589–94, 1965.

74. Jackson, Don D., "The Study of the Family." *Family Process*, 4:1–20, 1965.

75. Jackson, Don D., and Weakland, John H., "Conjoint Family Therapy. Some Considerations on Theory, Technique, and Results." *Psychiatry*, 24:30–45, supplement to No. 2, 1961.

76. Jackson, Don D., and Haley, Jay, "Transference Revisited." *Journal of Nervous and Mental Disease*, 137:363–71, 1963.

77. Jackson, Don D., and Watzlawick, Paul, "The Acute Psychosis as a Manifestation of Growth Experience." *Psychiatric Research Reports*, 16:83–94, 1963.

78. Jackson, Don D., and Yalom, Irvin, "Conjoint Family Therapy as an Aid to Intensive Psychotherapy." In Arthur Burton, ed., *Modern Psychotherapeutic Practice. Innovations in Technique*. Palo Alto: Science and Behavior Books, 1965, pp. 81–97.

79. Joad, C. E. M., *Why War?* Harmondsworth: Penguin Special, 1939.

80. Johnson, Adelaide M.; Giffin, Mary E.; Watson, E. Jane; and Beckett, Peter G. S., "Studies in Schizophrenia at the Mayo Clinic. II. Observations on Ego Functions in Schizophrenia." *Psychiatry*, 19:143–8, 1956.

81. Jones, Ernest, *The Life and Work of Sigmund Freud*, Volume 3. New York: Basic Books, Inc., 1957.

82. Kant, O., "The Problem of Psychogenic Precipitation in Schizophrenia." *Psychiatric Quarterly*, 16:341–50, 1942.

83. Kelly, George A., *The Psychology of Personal Constructs*, 2 volumes. New York: W. W. Norton & Company, Inc., 1955.

84. Koestler, Arthur, *Darkness at Noon*. New York: The Modern Library, Inc., 1941.

85. Koestler, Arthur, *Arrival and Departure*. New York: The Macmillan Company, 1943.

86. Koestler, Arthur, *The Invisible Writing*. New York: The Macmillan Company, 1954.

87. Koestler, Arthur, *The Act of Creation*. New York: The Macmillan Company, 1964.

88. Laing, Ronald D., *The Self and Others, Further Studies in Sanity and Madness*. London: Tavistock Publications, Ltd., 1961.

89. Laing, Ronald D., "Mystification, Confusion, and Conflict." In I. Boszormenyi-Nagy and J. L. Framo, eds., *Intensive Family Therapy: Theoretical and Practical Aspects*. New York: Harper & Row, 1965, pp. 343–63.

90. Laing, Ronald D., and Esterson, A., *Sanity, Madness, and the Family*. Volume 1, *Families of Schizophrenics*. London: Tavistock Publications, Ltd., 1964.

91. Langer, S. K., *Philosophy in a New Key*. Cambridge: Harvard University Press, 1942.

92. Lasègue, Ch., and Falret, J., "La folie à deux, ou folie communiquée." *Annales Médico-Psychologiques*, t. 18, novembre 1877. [English translation by Richard Michaud, *American Journal of Psychiatry*, supplement to Volume 121, No. 4, pp. 2–18, 1964.]

93. Lee, A. Russell, "Levels of Imperviousness in Schizophrenic Families." Paper read at the Western Division Meeting of the American Psychiatric Association, San Francisco, September 1963.

94. Lennard, Henry L., and Bernstein, Arnold, with Hendin, Helen C., and Palmore, Erdman B., *The Anatomy of Psychotherapy*. New York: Columbia University Press, 1960.

95. Lidz, T.; Cornelison, A. R.; Fleck, S.; and Terry, D., "The Intrafamilial Environment of Schizophrenic Patients. II. Marital Schism and Marital Skew." *American Journal of Psychiatry*, 114:241–8, 1957.

96. Lorenz, Konrad Z., *King Solomon's Ring*. London: Methuen, 1952.

97. Luce, Clare Boothe, "Cuba and the Unfaced Truth: Our Global Double Bind." *Life*, 53:53–6, 1962.

98. Luft, Joseph, "On Non-verbal Interaction." Paper presented at the Western Psychological Association Convention, San Francisco, April 1962.

99. Mach, Ernst, *The Science of Mechanics*. La Salle, Ill.: The Open Court Publishing Co., 1919.

100. Maruyama, Magoroh, "The Multilateral Mutual Causal Relationships among the Modes of Communication, Sociometric Pattern and the Intellectual Orientation in the Danish Culture." *Phylon*, 22:41–58, 1961.

101. McCulloch, Warren S., and Pitts, Walter, "A Logical Calculus of the Ideas Immanent in Nervous Activity." *Bulletin of Mathematical Biophysics*, 5:115–33, 1943.

102. McGinnies, Elliott, "Emotionality and Perceptual Defense." *Psychological Review*, 56:244–51, 1949.

103. Meerloo, Joost A. M., *The Rape of the Mind: The Psychology of Thought Control, Menticide and Brainwashing*. Cleveland: The World Publishing Company, 1956.

104. Miller, George A.; Galanter, Eugene; and Pribram, Karl H., *Plans and the Structure of Behavior*. New York: Henry Holt and Company, Inc., 1960.

105. Miller, James G., "Living Systems: Basic Concepts; Structure and Process; Cross-Level Hypotheses." *Behavioral Science*, 10:193–237, 337–411, 1965.

106. Morris, Charles W., "Foundations of the Theory of Signs." In Otto Neurath, Rudolf Carnap, and Charles W. Morris, eds., *International Encyclopedia of Unified Science*, Volume 1, No. 2. Chicago: University of Chicago Press, 1938, pp. 77–137.

107. Muggeridge, Malcolm, "Books." *Esquire*, Volume 63, No. 4, April 1965, pp. 58–60.

108. Nagel, Ernst, and Newman, James R., *Gödel's Proof*. New York: New York University Press, 1958.

109. Nagels, Ivan, in *Spectaculum, Moderne Theaterstücke*, Volume 7. Frankfurt/M., Suhrkamp Verlag, 1964.

110. Nash, Ogden, "Don't Wait, Hit Me Now!" In *Marriage Lines*. Boston: Little, Brown and Company, 1964, pp. 99–101.

111. Nerlich, G. C., "Unexpected Examinations and Unprovable Statements." *Mind*, 70:503–13, 1961.

112. Northrop, Eugene P., *Riddles in Mathematics*. New York: D. Van Nostrand Co., Inc., 1944.

113. Orwell, George, *1984*. New York: Harcourt, Brace & Co., 1949.

114. Oster, Gerald, and Nishijima, Yasunori, "Moiré Patterns." *Scientific American*, 208:54–63, 1963.

115. Parkinson, C. Northcote, *Parkinson's Law and Other Studies in Administration*. Boston: Houghton Mifflin Company, 1957.

116. Potter, Stephen, *One-upmanship*. Harmondsworth: Penguin Books, 1947.

117. Pribram, Karl H., "Reinforcement Revisited: A Structural View." In M. Jones, ed., *Nebraska Symposium on Motivation, 1963*. Lincoln: University of Nebraska Press, 1963, pp. 113–59.

118. Proust, Marcel, *Les plaisirs et les jours*, 13th ed. Paris: Gallimard, 1924.

119. Quine, Willard van Orman, *Methods of Logic*. New York: Henry Holt and Company, Inc., 1960.

120. Quine, Willard van Orman, "Paradox." *Scientific American*, 206:84–95, 1962.

121. Ramsey, Frank Plumpton, *The Foundations of Mathematics and Other Logical Essays*. New York: Harcourt, Brace & Co., 1931.

122. Rapoport, Anatol, and Chammah, Albert M., with the collaboration of Carol J. Orwant, *Prisoner's Dilemma; a study in conflict and cooperation*. Ann Arbor: University of Michigan Press, 1965.

123. Reichenbach, Hans, *Elements of Symbolic Logic*. New York: The Macmillan Company, 1947.

124. Renaud, Harold, and Estess, Floyd, "Life History Interviews with One Hundred Normal American Males: 'Pathogenicity' of Childhood." *American Journal of Orthopsychiatry*, 31: 786–802, 1961.

125. Richardson, Lewis Fry, "Mathematics of War and Foreign Politics." In James R. Newman, ed., *The World of Mathematics*, Volume 2. New York: Simon and Schuster, Inc., 1956, pp. 1240–53.

126. Rilke, Rainer Maria, *Duino Elegies*, trans. by J. B. Leishman and Stephen Spender. New York: W. W. Norton & Company, Inc., 1939.

127. Rioch, David McK., "The Sense and the Noise." *Psychiatry*, 24:7–18, 1961.

128. Rioch, David McK., "Communication in the Laboratory and Communication in the Clinic." *Psychiatry*, 26:209–21, 1963.

129. Rosen, John N., *Direct Analysis*. New York: Grune & Stratton, Inc., 1953.

130. Rosenthal, Robert, "The Effect of the Experimenter on the Results of Psychological Research." In B. A. Mahr, ed., *Progress in Experimental Personality Research*, Volume 1. New York: Academic Press Inc., 1964, pp. 79–114.

131. Ross, Nancy Wilson, ed., "The Subjugation of a Ghost," in *The World of Zen*. New York: Random House, Inc., 1960.

132. Ruesch, Jurgen, and Bateson, Gregory, *Communication: The Social Matrix of Psychiatry*. New York: W. W. Norton & Company, Inc., 1951.

133. Russell, Bertrand, Introduction to Ludwig Wittgenstein, *Tractatus Logico-Philosophicus*. New York: Humanities Press, 1951.

134. Sansom, G. B., *The Western World and Japan, A Study in the Interaction of European and Asiatic Cultures*. New York: Alfred A. Knopf, Inc., 1950.

135. Sartre, Jean-Paul, Introduction to Henry Alleg, *The Question*. New York: George Braziller, Inc., 1958.

136. Scheflen, Albert E., "Regressive One-to-One Relationships." *Psychiatric Quarterly*, 23:692–709, 1960.

137. Scheflen, Albert E., *A Psychotherapy of Schizophrenia: Direct Analysis*. Springfield, Illinois: Charles C. Thomas, Publisher, 1961.

138. Scheflen, Albert E., "Quasi-Courtship Behavior in Psychotherapy." *Psychiatry*, 28:245–57, 1965.

139. Scheflen, Albert E., *Stream and Structure of Communicational Behavior. Context Analysis of a Psychotherapy Session*. Behavioral Studies Monograph No. 1. Philadelphia: Eastern Pennsylvania Psychiatric Institute, 1965.

140. Schelling, Thomas C., *The Strategy of Conflict*. Cambridge: Harvard University Press, 1960.

141. Schimel, John L., "Love and Games." *Contemporary Psychoanalysis*, 1:99–109, 1965.

142. Searles, Harold F., "The Effort to Drive the Other Person Crazy–An Element in the Aetiology and Psychotherapy of Schizophrenia." *British Journal of Medical Psychology*, 32: 1–18, Part 1, 1959.

143. Sluzki, Carlos E., and Beavin, Janet, "Simetría y complementaridad: una definición operacional y una tipología de parejas" [Symmetry and Complementarity: An Operational Definition and a Typology of Dyads]. *Acta psiquiátrica y psicológica de América latina*, 11:321–30, 1965.

144. Sluzki, Carlos E.; Beavin, Janet; Tarnopolsky, Alejandro; and Verón, Eliseo, "Transactional Disqualification." To be published in *Archives of General Psychiatry*, 1967.

145. Smith, Michael, in *The Village Voice*, Volume 7, No. 52 (October 18, 1962).

146. Spengler, Oswald, *The Decline of the West, Form and Actuality*, Volume 1. New York: Alfred A. Knopf, Inc., 1926.

147. Stegmüller, Wolfgang, *Das Wahrheitsproblem und die Idee der Semantik* [The Truth Problem in Semantics]. Vienna: Springer-Verlag, 1957.

148. Stein, L., "Loathsome Women." *Journal of Analytical Psychology*, 1:59–77, 1955–56.

149. Stern, David J., "The National Debt and the Peril Point." *The Atlantic*, 213:35–8, 1964.

150. Styron, William, *Lie Down in Darkness*. New York: The Viking Press, 1951.

151. Szasz, Thomas S., *The Myth of Mental Illness, Foundations of a Theory of Personal Conduct*. New York: Hoeber-Harper, 1961.

152. Taubman, Howard, in *The New York Times*, Volume 112, No. 38, 250 (October 15, 1962), p. 33.

153. Tinbergen, Nicolaas, *Social Behavior in Animals with Special Reference to Vertebrates*. London: Methuen, 1953.

154. Toch, H. H., and Hastorf, A. H., "Homeostasis in Psychology." *Psychiatry*, 18:81–91, 1955.

155. Watts, Alan Wilson, "The Counter Game," in *Psychotherapy, East and West*. New York: Pantheon Books, Inc., 1961, pp. 127–67.

156. Watzlawick, Paul, "A Review of the Double Bind Theory." *Family Process*, 2:132–53, 1963.

157. Watzlawick, Paul, *An Anthology of Human Communication; Text and Tape*. Palo Alto: Science and Behavior Books, 1964.

158. Watzlawick, Paul: "Paradoxical Predictions." *Psychiatry,* 28: 368–74, 1965.

159. Watzlawick, Paul, "A Structured Family Interview." *Family Process,* 5:256–71, 1966.

160. Weakland, John H., "The 'Double-Bind' Hypothesis of Schizophrenia and Three-Party Interaction." In Don D. Jackson, ed., *The Etiology of Schizophrenia,* New York: Basic Books, Inc., 1960.

161. Weakland, John H., and Jackson, Don D., "Patient and Therapist Observations on the Circumstances of a Schizophrenic Episode." *Archives of Neurology and Psychiatry,* 79:554–74, 1958.

162. Weiss, Paul, "Cell Interactions." In *Proceedings Fifth Canadian Cancer Conference,* New York: Academic Press,, Inc., 1963, pp. 241–76.

163. Weissberg, A., *The Accused.* New York: Simon and Schuster, Inc., 1951.

164. Whitehead, Alfred North, and Russell, Bertrand, *Principia Mathematica,* 3 volumes. Cambridge: Cambridge University Press, 1910–13.

165. Whorf, Benjamin Lee, "Science and Linguistics." In John B. Carroll, ed., *Language, Thought, and Reality. Selected Writings of Benjamin Lee Whorf.* New York: John Wiley & Sons, Inc., 1956, pp. 207–19.

166. Wiener, Norbert, "Time, Communication, and the Nervous System." In R. W. Miner, ed., *Teleological Mechanisms.* Annals of the New York Academy of Sciences, Volume 50, Article 4, pp. 197–219, 1947.

167. Wieser, Wolfgang, *Organismen, Strukturen, Maschinen* [Organisms, Structures, Machines]. Frankfurt/M., Fischer Bücherei, 1959.

168. Wittgenstein, Ludwig, *Tractatus Logico-Philosophicus.* New York: Humanities Press, 1951.

169. Wright, John C., *Problem Solving and Search Behavior under Non-Contingent Rewards.* Unpublished doctoral thesis, Stanford University, 1960.

170. Zilboorg, Gregory, "Suicide Among Civilized and Primitive Races." *American Journal of Psychiatry,* 92:1347–69, 1935–36.

Glossary

This glossary contains only such terms as are not defined in the text or are not part of everyday language. The sources, where cited, are *Dorland's Medical Dictionary* (DMD) and Hinsie and Shatzky's *Psychiatric Dictionary* (H&S).

abulia. Loss or deficiency of will power. (DMD)

acting-out. The expression of emotional tension through direct behavior in a situation which may have nothing to do with the origin of the tension; usually applied to impulsive, aggressive, or, generally, antisocial behavior. (Adapted from H&S)

anorexia. Lack or loss of the appetite for food. Specifically, a nervous condition exhibited by a patient who loses his appetite and eats so little food that he becomes emaciated. (Adapted from DMD)

autism (adj. *autistic*). The condition of being dominated by subjective, self-centered trends of thought or behavior. (DMD)

behavior therapy. A form of psychotherapy based on learning theory; behavior, including symptomatic behavior, is considered the result of a learning process and therefore amenable to "unlearning" (deconditioning).

compulsion (*-ive*). An irresistible impulse to perform some act contrary to one's better judgment or will. (DMD)

conjoint psychotherapy. The psychotherapy of couples or entire families whose members are treated together in joint sessions involving all individuals at the same time. (Cf. ref. *75*)

couple therapy → conjoint psychotherapy.

depersonalization. The process of being dissolved, of losing the identity, personality, the "I." A mental phenomenon characterized by loss of the sense of the reality of oneself. It often carries with it loss of the sense of the reality of others and of the environment. (H&S)

depression. A complex feeling, ranging from unhappiness to deep dejection and hopelessness; often accompanied by more or less absurd feelings of guilt, failure, and unworthiness, as well as by self-destructive tendencies. Its physical concomitants are usually disturbances of sleep and appetite and a general slowing-down of many physiological processes.

dyad. An ultimate unit referring to *the relation between* two entities, as contrasted to → monad; similarly "triad" for a three-element unit.

entelechy. The assumed innate or potential property of a living being to develop toward a specific end stage.

ethology. The study of animal behavior. (DMD)

folie à deux. French for "double insanity." A term applied when two persons closely associated with one another suffer a psychosis simultaneously, and when one member of the pair appears to have influenced the other. The condition is not of course confined to two persons, and may involve three and even more (*folie à trois*, etc.). (H&S)

games, theory of. A mathematical tool for the analysis of man's social relations; introduced by von Neumann in 1928 and originally applied to decision-making strategies in economic behavior, it is now extended to many sorts of interpersonal behaviors.
(1) *zero-sum games:* Situations in which the gain of one player and the loss of his opponent always sum to zero, i.e., there is pure competition, since the loss of one player is the gain of the other.
(2) *nonzero-sum games:* Situations in which gain and loss are not inversely fixed and thus do not necessarily sum to zero; they may be directly fixed (pure collaboration) or only partly fixed (mixed motive).

gestalt (pl. *gestalten*). Form, pattern, structure, or configuration.

gestalt psychology. The study of mental process and behavior as gestalten, rather than as isolated or fragmented units.

hysteria. A neurotic condition characterized by the conversion of emotional conflicts into physical manifestations—e.g., pain, anesthesia, paralysis, tonic spasms—without actual physical impairment of the afflicted organ or organs.

identified patient. That member of a family who carries a label of psychiatric diagnosis or of delinquency.

kinesics. (1) Nonverbal communication (body language, etc.); (2) the study thereof.

marital therapy → conjoint psychotherapy.

meta-. A prefix meaning "changed in position," "beyond," "higher," "transcending," etc. Used here generally as referring to the body of knowledge *about* a body of knowledge or field of study, e.g., metamathematics, metacommunication.

monad, (adj. *monadic*). An ultimate unit of *one,* considered in isolation. Used here mainly to denote the individual out of his communicational nexus, as contrasted to → dyad or triad.

nonzero-sum game → games, theory of.

Oedipus conflict. Oedipus Tyrannus, a character in Greek mythology who, raised by a foster parent, killed his actual father in a quarrel and subsequently married his mother. Later, when he discovered the true relationship, he blinded himself. (DMD) This myth was introduced into psychiatry by Freud as a paradigm for the attraction between the child and the parent of the opposite sex, for the specific intrafamilial conflicts stemming from this attraction and its wider implications for a person's psychosexual development.

paresis, general. (General paralysis of the insane, dementia paralytica, Bayle's disease.) A psychiatric condition characterized by mental and physical symptoms, due to syphilis of the central nervous system. (H&S)

pathogenicity. The quality of producing or the ability to produce pathological changes or disease. (DMD)

phenomenological. Pertaining to a specific approach (phenomenology) to the data of reality which investigates them without making any attempt to explain them.

phobia (-ic). A morbid fear associated either with a specific object or a specific situation.

psychogenic (psychogenicity). Of intrapsychic origin; having an emotional or psychologic origin (in reference to a symptom), as opposed to an organic basis. (DMD)

psychoneurotic. Pertaining to an emotional disorder, characterized by its → psychogenic nature and its functional (rather than organic) symptoms (e.g., → phobia, → hysteria).

286

psychopathology. (1) A generic term denoting emotional and/or mental illnesses or disturbances; (2) The branch of medicine dealing with these conditions.

psychosomatic. Pertaining to the mind-body relationship; having bodily symptoms of a psychic, emotional, or mental origin. (DMD)

psychotic. Pertaining to the psychoses, i.e., psychiatric conditions of either organic or functional (→ psychogenic) nature of such a degree that the patient's individual, intellectual, professional, social, etc. functioning is severely impaired, while in the → psychoneurotic patient this impairment is only partial and limited to certain areas of his life.

runaway. The loss of stability in a system due to uncontrolled deviation amplification.

sadomasochism (sadomasochistic symbiosis). A form of human relationship characterized by the infliction of physical and/or moral suffering by one partner upon the other.

schizophrenia. A psychiatric condition accounting for about half the patients in mental hospitals and about one quarter of all hospital patients in the United States. The term was coined by the Swiss psychiatrist E. Bleuler and denotes a psychosis marked by fundamental disturbances in the patient's perceptions of reality, concept formations, affects, and, consequently, his behavior in general. Depending on the specific symptomatology, schizophrenia is usually divided into various subgroups, e.g., the paranoid, hebephrenic, catatonic, and simple forms.

secondary gain. A psychoanalytic term referring to the indirect, interpersonal advantages which the neurotic derives from his condition, e.g., compassion, increased attention, freedom from everyday responsibilities, and the like.

transference. In psychoanalysis the reproduction of the forgotten and repressed experiences of early childhood. The reproduction or re-enactment generally takes the form of dreams or reactions occurring during psychoanalytic treatment. (H&S)

trauma, emotional. An emotional shock that makes a lasting impression on the mind. (DMD)

triad → dyad

zero-sum game → games, theory of.

Author and Subject Index

(Page numbers in bold type refer to definitions)